ADVERTISING
CAREER DIRECTORY

INSIDE

Visible Ink Press proudly presents the fifth edition of the acclaimed *Advertising Career Directory*, first published by the Career Press. The hallmark of this volume, part of VIP's Career Advisor Series, remains the essays by active professionals. Here, industry insiders describe opportunities and challenges in all segments of advertising, including:

- Art
- Graphic design
- Copywriting
- Account management
- Specialty advertising
- Sales promotion
- International advertising
- Media production
- Outdoor advertising
- Opportunities outside New York

In fully up-to-date articles, they describe:

- What to expect on the job
- Typical career paths
- What they look for in an applicant
- How their specialty is unique

New Edition Provides Greatly Enhanced Job Hunting Resources

Once this "Advice from the Pro's" has given you a feel for advertising careers, the *Directory* offers more help than ever before with your job search strategy:

- **The Job Search Process** includes essays on determining career objectives, resume preparation, networking, writing effective cover letters, and interviewing. With worksheets and sample resumes and letters. **NEW:** Resumes are now targeted to the realities of advertising.

- **Job Opportunities Databank** provides details on hundreds of agencies that hire at entry-level. **NEW:** More agencies are listed, and information on internships that they offer is now included.

- **Career Resources** identifies sources of help-wanted ads, professional associations, employment agencies and search firms, career guides, professional and trade periodicals, and basic reference guides. **NEW:** Resource listings are greatly expanded, and now include detailed descriptions to help you select the publications and organizations that will best meet your needs.

New Master Index Puts Information at Your Fingertips

This edition is more thoroughly indexed, with access to essays and directory sections both by subject and by organization name, publication title, or service name.

ADVERTISING CAREER DIRECTORY

A Practical, One-Stop Guide to Getting a Job in Advertising

5TH EDITION

Bradley J. Morgan

with Joseph M. Palmisano

VISIBLE INK PRESS

DETROIT • WASHINGTON, D.C. • LONDON

CAREER ADVISOR SERIES

ADVERTISING
CAREER DIRECTORY

Fifth Edition

A Practical, One-Stop Guide to Getting a Job in Advertising

Published by **Visible Ink Press** ™
a division of Gale Research Inc.
835 Penobscot Building
Detroit, MI 48226-4094

This publication is a creative work fully protected by all applicable copyright laws, as well as by misappropriation, trade secret, unfair competition, and other applicable laws.

Visible Ink Press™ will vigorously defend all of its rights in this publication.

Copyright © 1993 by **Visible Ink Press** ™

Some data was included from *Ward's Business Directory*, copyrighted by Information Access Company.

No part of this book may be reproduced in any form without permission in writing from the publisher, except by a reviewer who wishes to quote brief passages in connection with a review written for inclusion in a magazine or newspaper.

ISBN 0-8103-9429-4

Art Director: Cynthia Baldwin
Cover and Interior Design: Mary Krzewinski
Career Advisor Logo Designs: Kyle Raetz

Printed in the United States of America

All rights reserved

10 9 8 7 6 5 4 3 2 1

Contents

ACKNOWLEDGMENTS **x** INTRODUCTION **xi**
HOW TO USE THE JOB OPPORTUNITIES DATABANK **xv** HOW TO LOCATE CAREER RESOURCES **xvii**

PART ONE

Advice from the Pro's

1 Quo Vadis, World?

Norman Vale, Director-General, International Advertising Association
Changes in the international business climate will open up new career opportunities in international advertising. **1**

2 Advertising from Both Sides of the Brain

Ronald Scharbo, Former President and Chairman, Burton-Campbell, Inc.
Learning to develop your left-brain and right-brain skills will make getting the job you want that much easier. **7**

3 How to Make Sure You Never Become Disillusioned with Advertising

John V. Chervokas, Executive Vice-President/Chief Creative Officer, Sudler & Hennessey
Doing pro bono work can keep your portfolio fresh and teach you how important advertising can be. **13**

4 Getting Started as a Copywriter

Ron Bacsa, Chief Executive Officer, Creative Director, and Executive Art Director and Kaye Brinker, Copywriter, Ronald Bacsa Advertising, Inc.
Good grades and a good resume might help you land that first job, but not without a great portfolio of your writing samples. Learn the essentials in this essay. **15**

CONTENTS

5 Freelancing, the Kindest or Unkindest Cut of All (Depending on What Day It Is)

Marilyn Bagel

With many agencies cutting back on in-house staff, getting started as a freelance copywriter may be your best career bet. **19**

6 What Your Art School Won't Teach You

Walter Kaprielian, Chairman and Creative Director, Kaprielian/O'Leary Advertising

No college in the world can prepare you for your first art directing job, but this essay can give you the inside information you need to succeed. **25**

7 Working at a Graphics Design Agency

Mary Bode Byrd, President, Mary Byrd Productions, Inc.

Working at a small graphics design firm may be the best (and most rewarding!) way to break into the design business. **31**

8 How to Prepare Your Portfolio

Shinichiro Tora, Art Director, *Popular Photography*; Promotion Art Director, *American Photo* and *Popular Photography*, Hachette Magazines, Inc.

Assembling your first art portfolio can be difficult, but not if you follow the detailed instructions included in this essay. **35**

9 Great Is Better than Good

Sander A. Flaum, President and Chief Executive Officer, Robert A. Becker, Inc.

Being a good account manager is easy; this essay teaches you what you need to know to be a great one. **41**

10 Measuring Up to a Career in Media

Frank P. McDonald, President, R.J. Palmer, Inc.

Explains what a media department does, why working there is such an interesting career, and how to get an entry-level position. **47**

11 A Career in Outdoor Advertising Sales: The Billion-Dollar Industry You May Have Overlooked!

Robert J. Smith, President, General Outdoor Advertising

Often misunderstood and misused, outdoor advertising presents a constantly changing, always challenging career option. **55**

12 The Not-So-Invisible Promotional Product Industry

Cate Brennan Lisak, Manager of External Communications, Specialty Advertising Association International

Imprinted promotional products are popular business gifts—and a growing career field for advertising students. **61**

CONTENTS

13 Sales Promotion: America's Game

Chris Sutherland, Executive Director, Promotion Marketing Association of America

Sales promotion represents the largest single portion of the American marketing budget, which means career opportunities abound in this $130 billion business. **65**

14 Think about a Career in Sales Promotion

Kerry B. Didday, President/Creative Director, Daymark Inc. Sales Promotion+Marketing

A detailed look at the entry-level positions available in sales promotion. **71**

15 Advertising in the Motor City

Jim Dale, Chairman of the Board & Chief Executive Officer, W.B. Donor & Company Advertising

Diversity in the workplace and quality of life outside it are what makes working for a Detroit ad agency so attractive. **75**

16 Ad Makin' Town: The Advertising Scene in Chicago

Hall "Cap" Adams, Jr., Retired Chairman & Chief Executive Officer, Leo Burnett Company, Inc.

Job opportunities and excitement are plentiful in the Windy City, which is the third-largest advertising center in the world. **79**

17 Boston: A City of Tradition in Transition

George J. Hill III, Chairman/Worldwide Creative Director, Hill, Holliday, Connors, Cosmopulos, Inc.

Cultural attractions and career opportunities await the job-seeker who starts his or her search in Boston. **83**

18 Go West, Young Person!

Phillip Joanou, Chairman and Chief Executive, Dailey & Associates Advertising

New York may be the center of the advertising world, but the West Coast offers the same opportunities and challenges. **87**

CONTENTS

PART TWO

The Job Search Process

19 **Getting Started: Self-Evaluation and Career Objectives**
Defines what a "job search process" is and explains how to evaluate your own strengths and weaknesses. **95**

20 **Targeting Prospective Employers and Networking for Success**
Covers how to begin your job search, how to identify companies you would like to work for, what networking is and how to do it, informational interviews, and six good reasons to network. **105**

21 **Preparing Your Resume**
Provides an overview of resume preparation, reviews the records you will need, explains how to create your first resume, and provides tips on what to avoid. Also includes resume worksheets and examples of the three primary resume types. **117**

22 **Writing Better Letters**
Explains the importance of a good cover letter and provides information on other letters you will need to successfully complete your job search. Includes examples of letters for every job search situation. **145**

23 **Questions for You, Questions for Them**
Reveals the intricacies of the interview process and explains how you should prepare for any job interview. Provides sample questions and answers, including information on illegal interview questions. **161**

PART THREE

Job Opportunities Databank

24 **Job Opportunities Databank**
Entry-Level Job and Internship Listings **177**
Additional Companies **207**

PART FOUR

Career Resources

25 Career Resources
Sources of Help-Wanted Ads **211**
Professional Associations **218**
Employment Agencies and Search Firms **222**
Career Guides **225**
Professional and Trade Periodicals **238**
Basic Reference Guides **239**

PART FIVE

Master Index

26 Master Index 247

Acknowledgments

The editor would like to thank all the "pro's" who took the time out of their busy schedules to share their first-hand knowledge and enthusiasm with the next generation of job-seekers. A special thanks to Kathy Daniels, Assistant Director of the Career Planning and Placement office at the University of Detroit–Mercy, who provided much needed–help with the job search section on short notice.

Thanks are also owed to the human resources personnel at the companies listed in this volume, and to the public relations staffs of the associations who provided excellent suggestions for new essays. Hilary Lavine of Women in Marketing and Advertising and John Alliots of the Council of Sales Promotion Agencies deserve special mention.

Introduction

A recent *New York Times* article reported that 1992 college graduates were facing the toughest job market the United States has seen in twenty years. An ongoing series by the *Detroit Free Press* tracked the progress of six recent University of Michigan graduates; despite beginning their job search months before graduation day, only one of the six had landed that elusive first job one month after graduation.

Clearly, job-hunting in the 1990s is a challenging and demanding proposition, one that benefits from assistance at each step. The *Advertising Career Directory*, formerly published by the Career Press, was developed to provide job-seekers with all the help they need to break into the competitive world of advertising. It provides a comprehensive, one-stop resource for carrying out a successful job search, including:

- Essays by industry professionals that offer practical advice not found in any other career resource
- Job-search guidance designed to help you get in the door in advertising
- Job and internship listings from leading advertising agencies in the United States and Canada
- Information on additional career resources to further the job hunt
- A **Master Index** to facilitate easy access to the *Directory*

> Sidebars located throughout the *Directory* are intended to amplify the text or provide a counterpoint to information presented on the page. They'll help you build a context for your career and job-search efforts by bringing you discussions of trends in the advertising field and the business world, labor statistics, job-hunting techniques, and predictions about our future worklife. These and other tips and tidbits were gleaned from a wide range of sources—sources you can continue to draw upon for a broader understanding of your chosen field and of the job-search process.

The *Directory* is organized into four parts that correspond to the steps of a typical job search—identifying your area of interest, refining your presentation, targeting agencies, and researching your prospects.

Advice from the Pro's: An Invaluable Tool

Instead of offering "one-size-fits-all" advice or government statistics on what the working world is like, the *Advertising Career Directory* goes into the field for first-hand reports from experienced professionals working in all segments of advertising. This **"Advice from** the Pro's" is offered by people who know what it's like to land that first job and turn it into a rich and rewarding career. Learn about:

- working at a small graphics design agency from Mary Bode Byrd, President of Mary Byrd Productions, Inc.
- working as a freelance copywriter from award-winning freelancer Marilyn Bagel
- careers in sales promotion from Kerry B. Didday, President/Creative Director, Daymark, Inc. Sales Promotion+Marketing
- and 15 other areas of specialization, including:

Art	International advertising
Copywriting	Media department
Account management	Outdoor advertising
Specialty advertising	Opportunities outside New York

The essays cover the most important things a job applicant needs to know, including:

- Which college courses and other background experiences offer the best preparation
- Specific skills that are needed
- What agencies look for in an applicant
- Typical career paths
- How to put together a portfolio
- Salary information

The Job Search Process: Making Sense of It All

What is the first thing a new job-hunter should do?

What are the different types of resumes and what should they look like?

Which questions are off limits in an interview?

These important questions are among the dozens that go through every person's mind when he or she begins to look for a job. Part Two of the *Advertising Career Directory*, **The Job Search Process**, answers these questions and more. It is divided into five chapters that cover all the basics of how to aggressively pursue a job:

- **Getting Started: Self-Evaluation and Career Objectives.** How to evaluate personal strengths and weaknesses and set goals.
- **Targeting Prospective Employers and Networking for Success.** How to identify the companies you would like to work for and how to build a network of contacts.
- **Preparing Your Resume.** What to include, what not to include, and which style to use. Includes samples of the three basic resume types and worksheets to help you organize your information.
- **Writing Better Letters.** Which letters should be written throughout the search process and how to make them more effective. Includes samples.
- **Questions for You, Questions for Them.** How to handle an interview and get the job.

Job Opportunities Databank: Finding the Job You Want

Once you're ready to start sending out those first resumes, how do you know where to start? **The Job Opportunities Databank**, Part Three of the *Directory*, includes listings for more than 220 agencies in the United States and Canada that offer entry-level jobs in advertising. These listings provide detailed contact information and data on the agencies' business activities, hiring practices, benefits, and application procedures—everything you need to know to approach potential employers. And since internships play an increasingly important role in the career research and employment process, information on the internship opportunities offered by the agencies listed is also included.

For further information on the arrangement and content of the **Job Opportunities Databank**, consult "How to Use the Job Opportunities Databank" immediately following this introduction.

Career Resources: A Guide to Organizations and Publications in the Field

Need to do more research on the specialty you've chosen or the agencies you'll be interviewing with? Part Four of the *Advertising Career Directory*, **Career Resources**, includes information on the following:

- Sources of help–wanted ads
- Professional associations
- Employment agencies and search firms
- Career guides
- Professional and trade periodicals
- Basic reference guides

Listings now contain contact information and descriptions of each publication's content and each organization's membership, purposes, and activities, helping you to pinpoint the resources you need for your own specific job search.

For additional information on the arrangement and content of **Career Resources**, consult "How to Locate Career Resources" following this introduction.

New Master Index Speeds Access to Resources

A **Master Index** leads you to the information contained in all four sections of the *Advertising Career Directory* by citing all subjects, organizations, publications, and services listed throughout in a single alphabetic sequence. The index also includes inversions on significant words appearing in cited organization, publication, and service names. For example, the "Council of Sales Promotion Agencies" would also be listed in the index under "Sales Promotion Agencies; Council of." Citations in the index refer to page numbers.

New Information Keeps Pace with the Changing Job Market

This new edition of the *Advertising Career Directory* has been completely revised and updated. New essays in the **Advice from the Pro's** section were contributed by leading professionals in the advertising industry on subjects of particular interest to today's job seekers. The best essays from the previous edition were reviewed and completely updated as needed by the original authors. All employers listed in the **Job Opportunities Databank** were contacted by telephone or facsimile to obtain current information, and **Career Resources** listings were greatly expanded through the addition of selected material from databases compiled by Gale Research Inc.

INTRODUCTION

Special Thanks

Thanks to the many people at Visible Ink Press and Gale Research Inc. who helped to shape this book: Katherine Gruber and Linda Hubbard, whose guidance and skill made my job easy; Karen Hill, who kept the big picture in sight; Jennifer Arnold Mast and her staff; Barb Eschner for her invaluable advice on the world of advertising; and the staff of the Sourcebooks team for their superior skill and assistance.

Comments and Suggestions Welcome

The staff of the *Advertising Career Directory* appreciates learning of any corrections or additions that will make this book as complete and useful as possible. Comments or suggestions for future essay topics or other improvements are also welcome, as are suggestions for careers that could be covered in new volumes of the Career Advisor Series. Please contact:

Career Advisor Series
Visible Ink Press
835 Penobscot Bldg.
Detroit, MI 48226-4094
Phone: 800-347-4253
Fax: (313) 961-6815

Bradley J. Morgan

How to Use the Job Opportunities Databank

The Job Opportunities Databank comprises two sections:

Entry-Level Job and Internship Listings

Additional Companies

Entry-Level Job and Internship Listings

The first section provides listings for 33 of the 50 largest advertising agencies in the United States (as ranked by revenue) and nearly 200 selected other agencies in the U.S. and Canada. Entries for the remaining top 50 agencies are included in the following section. Entries in the **Job Opportunities Databank** are arranged alphabetically by agency name. When available, entries include:

- **Agency name.**
- **Address and telephone number.** A mailing address and telephone number are provided in every entry.
- **Fax and toll-free telephone number.** These are provided when known.
- **Business description.** Outlines the agency's business activities. The geographical scope of the agency's operations may also be provided.
- **Corporate officers.** Lists the names of executive officers, with titles.
- **Number of employees.** Includes the most recently provided figure for total number of employees. Other employee-specific information may be provided as well.
- **Average entry-level hiring.** Includes the number of entry-level employees the agency typically hires in an average year. Many agencies have listed "Unknown" or "0" for their average number of entry-level jobs. Because of current economic conditions, many firms could not estimate their projected entry-level hires for the coming years. However, because these firms have offered entry-level positions in the past and because their needs may change, we have continued to list them in this edition.
- **Opportunities.** Describes the entry-level positions that the agency typically offers, as well as the education and other requirements needed for those positions.
- **Benefits.** Lists the insurance, time off, retirement and financial plans, activities, and programs provided by the agency, if known.

USING THE DATABANK

- **Human resources contacts.** Lists the names of personnel-related staff, with titles.
- **Application procedure.** Describes specific application instructions, when provided by the agency.

Many entries also include information on available internship programs. Internship information provided includes:

- **Contact name.** Lists the names of officers or personnel-related contacts who are responsible for the internship program.
- **Type.** Indicates the type of internship, including time period and whether it is paid or unpaid. Also indicates if an agency does not offer internships.
- **Number available.** Number of internships that the agency typically offers.
- **Number of applications received.** Total number of applications received in a typical year.
- **Application procedures and deadline.** Describes specific application instructions and the deadline for submitting applications.
- **Decision date.** Final date when internship placement decisions are made.
- **Duties.** Lists the typical duties that an intern can expect to perform at the agency.
- **Qualifications.** Lists the criteria a prospective applicant must meet to be considered for an internship with the agency.

Additional Companies

Covers those companies that elected to provide only their name, address, and telephone number for inclusion in the *Advertising Career Directory*. Entries are arranged alphabetically by agency name.

How to Locate Career Resources

The **Career Resources** chapter contains six categories of information sources, each of which is arranged alphabetically by resource or organization name. The categories include:

▼ Sources of Help-Wanted Ads

- **Covers:** Professional journals, industry periodicals, association newsletters, placement bulletins, and online services that include employment ads or business opportunities. Includes sources that focus specifically on advertising, as well as general periodical sources such as the *National Business Employment Weekly*.
- **Entries include:** The resource's title; name, address, and telephone number of its publisher; frequency; subscription rate; description of contents; toll-free and additional telephone numbers; and facsimile numbers.

▼ Professional Associations

- **Covers:** Trade and professional associations that offer career-related information and services.
- **Entries include:** Association name, address, and telephone number; membership; purpose and objectives; publications; toll-free or additional telephone numbers; and facsimile numbers. In some cases, the publications mentioned in these entries are described in greater detail as separate entries cited in the Sources of Help–Wanted Ads, Career Guides, Professional and Trade Periodicals, and Basic Reference Guides categories.

▼ Employment Agencies and Search Firms

- **Covers:** Firms used by companies to recruit candidates for positions and, at times, by individuals to pursue openings. Employment agencies are generally geared towards filling openings at entry- to mid-level in the local job market, while executive search firms are paid by the hiring organization to recruit professional and managerial candidates, usually for higher-level openings. Also covers temporary employment agencies because they can be a method of identifying and obtaining regular employment.

LOCATING THE RESOURCES

Includes sources that focus specifically on advertising, as well as some larger general firms.

- **Entries include:** The firm's name, address, and telephone number; whether it's an employment agency, executive search firm, or temporary agency; descriptive information, as appropriate; toll-free and additional telephone numbers; and facsimile number.

▼ **Career Guides**

- **Covers:** Books, kits, pamphlets, brochures, videocassettes, films, and other materials that describe the job-hunting process in general or that provide guidance and insight into the job-hunting process in advertising.
- **Entries include:** The resource's title; name, address, and telephone number of its publisher or distributor; name of the editor or author; publication date or frequency; description of contents; arrangement; indexes; toll-free or additional telephone numbers; and facsimile numbers.

▼ **Professional and Trade Periodicals**

- **Covers:** Newsletters, magazines, newspapers, trade journals, and other serials that offer information to advertising professionals.
- **Entries include:** The resource's title; the name, address, and telephone number of the publisher; the editor's name; frequency; description of contents; toll-free and additional telephone numbers; and facsimile numbers.

▼ **Basic Reference Guides**

- **Covers:** Manuals, directories, dictionaries, encyclopedias, films and videocassettes, and other published reference material used by professionals working in advertising.
- **Entries include:** The resource's title; name, address, and telephone number of the publisher or distributor; the editor's or author's name; publication date or frequency; description of contents; toll-free and additional telephone numbers; and facsimile numbers.

Advice from the Pro's

CHAPTER ONE

Quo Vadis, World?

Norman Vale, Director-General
International Advertising Association

Quo vadis, indeed. Where in the world the world is going is a question the international business community has always concerned itself with, but never more so than right now. Global dynamics are shifting dramatically as walls tumble, borders open, dictators "retire." Combine those truly incredible and unexpected events with the impending unification of the European Common Market and the increasing impact of the Pacific Rim countries, and you have a business climate that is fascinating, to say the least.

The dramatic changes in international commerce will have direct and substantial effects on international advertising. Here's a brief look at how international advertising evolved, where it's headed, and what you can do to prepare yourself for participation in what promises to be an exciting, challenging, and rewarding field.

The Marketplace Takes Shape

To better understand what's ahead, a look at how business responded to political and economic changes in the past is helpful.

1950s: Post-War Recovery

As the world got back on its feet following World War II, European and Asian countries had to start virtually from scratch to rebuild their infrastructure destroyed by the war and, consequently, lived through a long period of deprivation. In the United States, rather than rebuild what *had been,* we were fortunate enough to be able to build upon what we still *had.* Our post-war boom fueled the U.S. economy and made the U.S. an important consumer market.

1960s: U.S. International Expansion

With such a head start, U.S. companies found openings in which to establish new markets and profit opportunities in the free world. At about the same time, the "brand revolution" began, as corporations began to extend their marketing opportunities by placing importance on individual brand-name products over corporate names. This was the beginning of U.S.-based companies' successful foray into the international arena.

1970s: Focus Shifts to Foreign Companies

The free world became more common, commercial brain power was no longer a U.S. monopoly, businesses matured, and, for the most part, technology began a decade of egalitarianism. Large foreign-based corporations looked outside their countries and saw niche opportunities, wholesale benefits, and openings where competition yielded profitable investments. The non-U.S. marketers began their international move, and their advertising agencies began to follow.

1980s: Enter Globalization

Contrary to what scientists were saying about the universe expanding, the world got smaller. Thanks in part to the accessibility of worldwide media, international borders in the free world became insignificant, as major corporations crossed from one country to another with products and services that met the world's increasingly homogeneous needs and wants. "Global" replaced international, transnational, or multinational as the word to describe how corporations should approach their worldwide business.

1990s: Centers of Economic Clout

There are three critical centers of influence that will take us through the next decade.

- **North America,** as a result of the 1989 trade agreement between the U.S. and Canada;
- The **European Community's** 12 member countries that form the Common Market and, as of January 1, 1993, will become the largest consumer market in the world;
- **Japan and Korea,** through a combination of industrial output and strong financial reserves to support increased products and services and overseas developments.

And, years of "reality" following the previous decade of greed.

Developments in Advertising

Let's look at developments that took place in the advertising business during these same decades:

1950s: Export Advertising

U.S. companies created advertising in this country and sent it abroad without too much consideration of its final destination. The international or global mindset was not fully evolved, and neither were most companies international capabilities.

1960s: International Overtures

Marketers began to perceive commonalities in overseas markets that created possibilities for international advertising—which, at that time, meant buying space in papers or magazines that reached consumers in two or more countries.

1970s: Multinational Takes Off

U.S.- and foreign-based companies were operating in so many markets around the world that the techniques of common strategy and execution became more cost efficient and, therefore, more attractive. Multinational advertising—advertising in 4-5 countries or more—hit its stride in this decade.

1980s: The Era of Globalization

Megatrends author John Naisbitt and Harvard Business School Professor Ted Levitt began the decade championing the concept that the successful corporation could do and sell the same things in the same way everywhere it operated. The advent of satellites allowed advertisers to think about reaching consumers all over the world at the same time with the same message. In 1985, "Live Aid," for example, simultaneously reached an estimated 1.5 billion people in more than 100 countries. Events such as World Cup Soccer regularly achieve almost the same global reach.

The Growth of Advertising

The following chart illustrates the scope and growth of advertising volumes in the United States and the balance of the free world. It also graphically demonstrates why global opportunities may be in your future:

Worldwide Advertising Trends
(in billions of U.S. dollars)

(Year)	1960	1970	1980	1990	2000
Worldwide Ad Expenditures	18	36	110	313	780
Non-U.S. Ad Expenditures	6	16	55	163	460
U.S. Ad Expenditures	12	20	55	150	320

As you can see, in the '60s and '70s, advertising outside the United States was developing its own momentum, but still did not come close to the level of advertising dollars invested in the U.S. During the '80s, all media expenditures approached the fifty-fifty mark.

ADVICE FROM THE PRO'S

What Will the '90s Bring?

For the '90s, we can expect international advertising expenditures to surpass U.S. volume. Reasons for this include:

- **New media** available, following full satellite deployment.
- **New markets,** such as China and its one billion people.
- **Increased confidence** in doing business away from home countries, achieved through four decades of experience.
- **Rapid technological improvements,** including continuing growth of computer interfacing, electronic mail (which will make it easier to do what we do), and high-definition TV (which will make what we do more attractive to consumers).
- **Strengthened gross national products** in so many countries.
- **Elimination of trade barriers** within the European community, in or about January 1, 1993, and, new nations applying for membership in the community.
- **Competition-driven increase in production** from Western Europe and the Pacific Rim, as those countries continue to generate products and services that will be supported by advertising and promotion funds.
- **Evolving events in Central Europe.**

All of us who have dedicated our lives to international business applaud the changes as we continue to interpret how they will affect our economic, political, commercial, and financial strategies. Following the initial chaos, we should expect order and opportunity to arise, creating a far better commercial climate for people considering an international future.

Preliminary forecasts indicate that worldwide expenditures will be nearing one *trillion,* dollars by the year 2000. And of that, close to 60 percent will be invested outside the U.S. So should you consider an international career in advertising? Quo vadis...world!

How to Get Ready

Should you decide to invest yourself in the global advertising arena, here are six important steps that you can take to prepare yourself for a career in a foreign country:

1. Acquire solid agency experience in either a large U.S. agency or its counterpart in another country, and plan to stay there for 3 to 5 years—less time may not sufficiently prepare you for that next international step.

2. Attempt to work your way into a multinational account, particularly if it's a feeder operation. Many positions are available within agencies where products and services are similarly introduced and available in foreign markets.

Creating Your International Career

It's clear that the opportunities for well-trained advertising professionals on both the agency and client sides will increase until the end of the decade. There are several substantive reasons for choosing to "go international."

- Inevitably, the world will be one large market. The best-prepared people for management positions will have a combination of U.S. and international experience.
- The relatively small scale of operations for agencies outside the U.S. necessarily increases your exposure to all facets of the business.
- Working within a small management group provides an accelerated advancement track; the chance to be involved in the decision-making process comes more quickly in comparison to a parallel course in the U.S.
- The challenge of working and living in a foreign culture is professionally and personally enriching.

3. Make your management aware of your interest, be diligent in your pursuit, and find an appropriate mentor within your organization.
4. Be open-minded and flexible about the country assignment offered. There is a world beyond London and Paris; besides, the talent pool in both England and France is sufficiently large. You may find similar challenges and satisfaction along with greater opportunity for advancement in other countries.
5. Don't view a career in international advertising as a free ticket to travel. It's hard work, and any other perception will not be appreciated by prospective employers.
6. Above all, have patience, patience, and even more patience.

Witnessing world developments in the coming decade will be fascinating. The prospect of participating in them is even more so. Good luck to those of you who choose a career path that leads you to the international arena.

▼

NORMAN VALE spent 30 years in agency management, lived and worked in three countries, and was a senior officer for Grey International—a $4.4 billion global advertising and communication agency—for 16 years. In April 1990, he was named the first director-general of the International Advertising Association.

Mr. Vale has been an occasional lecturer on international advertising and marketing at St. John's University, Wharton, NYU Graduate School of Business, World Trade Institute and at seminars and congresses on five continents. While those have been delivered principally in English, he also speaks Spanish, some Portuguese, and German. He was also the chairman of the 4A's International Committee.

CHAPTER TWO

Advertising from Both Sides of the Brain

**Ronald Scharbo, Former President and Chairman
Burton-Campbell, Inc.**

As you venture into the agency business, let me issue a daring challenge: How you think may be just as important to the enjoyment and success of your first job as what you know.

It's an intriguing phenomenon that, as we get well into our advertising careers, most of us fall into one of two categories: the left-brain types or the right-brain types.

But which type are you?

Left-brainers are the disciplined, logical thinkers...the number crunchers. If you are a left brain type, you will likely shine in account service, research, or media. Right-brainers—the creative visionaries—usually star as copywriters and art directors.

The amazing thing about the agency business is that these two very different types must somehow come together to produce one successful campaign.

If both sides *don't* come together, agencies are dominated by one or the other—and the resulting ads quickly show which side won out. Left-brain agencies turn out ads that are smart, but dull—strategy statements in print. It's advertising likely to go unnoticed.

On the other hand, right-brain agencies turn out ads that are arresting to look at, but don't seem to really say anything. You probably recall seeing what you thought was a great commercial—but been unable to remember what was advertised even a few hours later.

The Fears that Set the Two Sides at Odds

In other words, if either side is given complete control, it will probably produce advertising that neither side wants. Nevertheless, each type may well vie for complete control.

Left-Brainers Fear the Creative Thought Process

Left-brainers usually write the creative strategy and the creative work plans—the "blueprints" of advertising. As account people, they often have most of the votes on the creative review boards and can veto anything they don't understand. They also control the research that brings in the most powerful voting bloc of all—the consumer test groups, who can usually be counted on to vote against anything that's "too far out."

Why do many left-brainers try to seize so much control that they end up strangling the work? Because they're scared, and because the right-brainers—the creative people—let them.

Left-brainers are scared because they fear the creative thought process, one that is totally alien to their own "logical" pattern. They steer for the safe middle ground and avoid risks. After all, if a print ad or TV spot bombs, it's the left-brained account executive who has to take the heat from the irate client. So they adhere strictly to the numbers and avoid being different....and, in the process, avoid the freshness and excitement that's essential for superior advertising.

Right-Brainers Fear Their Creativity Will Be Stifled

Right-brainers, on the other hand, may shoot strictly for awards and not seemingly not care about results. They want something pretty for their portfolios. Something exciting and new. Unfortunately, it might not sell anything.

Why do they do this? Because they, too, are scared.

The right-brainers are afraid that their best ideas will be stifled by those unimaginative, left-brained bean-counters. So the right-brained copywriters and art directors vow to die before allowing the unsuspecting account executives to even *think* of changing a comma, let alone a word or picture.

Good Agencies Forge a Consensus

Though I've painted such a seemingly bleak picture, there *is* light at the end of the tunnel—in fact, the same light at the end of *both* tunnels. There don't *have* to be battles between the two sides...and in the good agencies, there aren't.

Let me strike a blow for future harmony and give you some tips on how to work with the "other side" by recognizing and managing an important process that takes place at any good agency.

For starters, every professional in every agency should agree that there's really only one common purpose: to create effective advertising. And that to *be* effective, advertising must stand out. Break through the clutter. Have impact.

Clients *like* impact. It's cost-efficient. It does the job with fewer magazine insertions or TV rating points. But to get impact you have to be different, and that involves risk. Risk demands going beyond reference sources, case studies, and the hard data—into that no man's land where being wrong can be very expensive. Clients hate risk, especially if it may cost them a lot of money if they (and their agency) are wrong.

Here is where the left- and right-brainers oftentimes come into head-to-head conflict. But it's also the same point at which, working together, they can rise above the ordinary and arrive at the real goal: advertising that works.

Finding the Good Agencies

How do you find an agency where the left-brain and right-brain people are willing to work together to create the best possible campaigns? Here are ten characteristics to look for:

1. A Healthy Mix of Good People and the Right Attitude

Bad account people can cancel out good creative people, and vice versa. The best agencies have account executives who possess the same excitement and passion for the product as the creative people. Try to find out how the AEs are involved in the creative product.

2. Management's Commitment to Always Doing Better Work

The agencies most likely to grow and prosper are those that get everyone asking, "Is this my best?" all the way down the line.

3. The Courage to Take Risks…

…and the ability to go easy if one fails. We all know that if you fear the consequence of failure, you won't try. Certainly in an agency, if your ideas are always met with, "You must be crazy. The client will never buy that!" you will stop trying and shoot for the easy sell. So look for management's permission to take risks.

4. A Planning Process Open to Both Sides…

…and open to overhaul when necessary. An agency's research and planning process should tell both the account people and the creative side about the product, its best buying prospects, what's important to them, and how the competition is communicating to those same potential buyers. It should then stop.

The best research tells you only *what* to say, not *how* to say it. Its goal should be to isolate the one most important message—not to generate a laundry list of 27 product benefits you could never state in one ad anyway.

5. Limited Decision Authority

In our agency, only two of us can say "no." The account people cannot kill work—they can only critique it. The creative side is expected to listen and respond appropriately. We want both an active dialogue and a protected environment for new ideas.

6. Involvement of the Creative People in the Research Mechanism

Yes, research can help you, but only if you avoid the pitfalls.

Consider qualitative research in its most common form—focus groups. Nothing is more harmful than a misdirected focus group. They should be used to probe or explore, but never as a means of ranking or "approving" different campaign executions. The right-brained creative people should be encouraged to attend and learn firsthand what makes the prospect—that potential buyer his or her ad is supposed to be reaching—really tick.

In quantitative research, agencies can go overboard sampling people so they have the security of big numbers on their side. Such research may be unnecessary in the face of already-good judgment and strong rationale. But some clients don't like good judgement and rationale—they want the raw data to back up every decision. The challenge here is to win without sacrificing the product. The solution is to keep creative people directly involved in the interpretation of the results.

But above all, remember that a lot of what really works on the air and in print got there without testing.

7. AEs Who Are Teammates, Not Adversaries

A healthy agency will bring its good AEs in at the rough concept stage and see what they think—for input, *not* for approval. This gives everyone a shared sense of authorship and helps the AE sell harder later.

8. The Desire and Ability to Sell Their Work, Not Just Show It

Virtually every advertising pro I know has been in a presentation where someone holds up a layout and says, "So, this is the ad...what do you think?"

For starters, the agency must be excited about its work, or no one else will be. Work must be presented with enthusiasm and conviction to gain a client's confidence, because—remember—risk is scary.

So look for an agency that uses aids and props to communicate its ideas, shows actual photographs to demonstrate the intended style, and plays music to set the mood. All of these things help to sell—and mean the agency's committed to selling.

Finally, a good agency will press hard when it truly believes that it is right. While it's not necessary to fall on your sword over everything, you should defend your work from unnecessary changes and expect your colleagues to do the same.

9. Client Involvement—Before, During and After the Fact

No matter what ad execution an agency hopes to do, it can't be done unless the client supports the effort. Most clients are left-brain types, just like account people, so they have trouble relating to the intangible. The agency has to sell them.

So look for an agency that creates the magic. The fact is that some clients willingly give you the freedom to do just that. After all, they hired their agency to do something they know they can't do. Also, be aware of those who try too hard to manage the process and prevent "problems with the client"—and end up strangling the work.

10. Appreciation of the People Who Make Things Happen

Management should know who the champions are, not just in creative, but throughout the entire agency.

Ask how they acknowledge good work—in person, in memos, in public, etc. Make sure there are financially fair salaries and perks. A nice touch is a spot bonus given for performance "above and beyond."

You are the young talents of tomorrow's agencies. If you absorb your educational training, if you can learn to work well with those other brain-types, and, ultimately, if you can just flat-out do the job, the best agencies will continue to praise and promote you accordingly—with no complaints from anyone.

Good Luck!

▼

RONALD SCHARBO has served as president and chairman of the Atlanta agency, Burton-Campbell, Inc., beginning in 1975. He was previously executive vice president/director of account service at Atlanta's McDonald & Little and has held a number of other agency positions.

A graduate of Duquesne University, he is chairman of the Atlanta Council of the American Association of Advertising Agencies and active in many other professional and civic organizations.

CHAPTER THREE

How to Make Sure You Never Become Disillusioned with Advertising

John V. Chervokas, Executive VP/Chief Creative Officer
Sudler & Hennessey

With your eye-popping spec portfolio, your obvious passion for the business, and your wily use of the advice you're receiving in this book, some day soon you may find yourself hired, actually hired, by an advertising agency. Now what?

As a **copy trainee,** what will you find yourself doing from 9 to 5? Reading strategies...and tagging along. Clipping competitive ads...and tagging along. Writing body copy for a trade ad...and tagging along.

If you are hired as a **junior art director,** you won't be asked to tag along that much. No, but you will be riveted to the drawing board, sketching variations of your boss's lay-out or spacing type for slides for a new business presentation or redesigning the agency's Company Policy handbook.

Eventually you'll drift into the more glamorous crannies of agency creative life, but early on, it will be very easy for you to get your bushy tail down. True, disillusionment with the ad biz is more stereotypically associated with the veterans. We hear of the account man who packs it in for an apple orchard in Vermont or the creative biggie who chucks it all to run a little hotel in Anguilla. Still, disillusionment can also start early on in one's career.

But it also can be avoided both early—and later. And always.

How?

By making a concerted effort, whatever else you are working on, to also be creating advertising for a *pro bono* account. That's free advertising. For a cause. Or a charity. Or a better world.

No matter if you are loaded down with work on a hair spray, a dry beer, or an airline, offering your talent and time for an awareness campaign for a debilitating illness, for a fund-raising effort for the needy, or for a campaign to build a new wing on your local hospital will keep your creative passions stoked—and, more importantly, your book fresh.

ADVERTISING CAREER DIRECTORY

You see, pro bono advertising almost *always* results in advertising you're tickled to slip into your portfolio. That's certainly *not* always true with your paying accounts.

And there's another reason to constantly be doing pro bono advertising. You, and those around you, both in the business and in your home life, will get a better understanding of just how powerful, how *good* this thing called advertising can really be. Pro bono advertising, more than any deep treatise on the economic importance of advertising, justifies the business—and, coincidentally, your involvement with it.

How can you become disillusioned with a career that can actually save lives?

▼

JOHN CHERVOKAS'S latest pro bono campaign is for the American Suicide Foundation, a national organization providing help for survivors of suicide victims as well as funds for suicide prevention research. The extensive print campaign includes a provocative ad which asks, "Is there life after suicide?"

CHAPTER FOUR

Getting Started as a Copywriter

Ron Bacsa, Chief Executive Officer, Creative Director, and Executive Art Director, Ronald Bacsa Advertising, Inc. and Kaye Brinker, Copywriter

Advertising is often defined as the business of persuading the public to buy what your client wants to sell. But before you have a chance to persuade anybody to buy anything, you have to get into the business. And that means persuading someone to take a chance on you.

If you want to be a copywriter, that's not always easy.

Good grades won't do it. Neither will a good school, a good resume, or a "knock-'em-dead" interview. There is only *one* way to get a job as a copywriter. And that's by building a portfolio—a presentation of your work.

The Portfolio—Your Calling Card

Every semester 20 to 30 students enroll in our course in building a portfolio. Some of them are right out of college, others have been working for years. Some majored in communications, others majored in anything from computer science to philosophy. Some have always wanted to write, others are still testing the waters. But no matter how diverse their backgrounds, ages, and abilities, they all know that what counts in getting a job as a copywriter is a portfolio.

Like a salesperson with a sample case, you have to demonstrate what you have to sell. Only in this instance, your sample case is called your portfolio (or, more simply and usually, "your book") and what you have to sell are your ideas—your ability to think strategically and creatively. In fact, being a good thinker is as important as being a good writer.

If you took any advertising courses in college, you may have already started creating ads to put in your portfolio. If you didn't, you should consider taking a course now. Not only will it provide you with professional insights into your work, but it will give you the opportunity to find out if copywriting is what you really want to do.

There are no shortcuts to putting a book together. It will take time. It may take money. But in the end, it will be the most important investment in your career that you can make.

Creating Ads for Your Portfolio

One of the rules of advertising is that there *are* no rules...no absolute way to do things. There are, however, certain generalizations. And generally, the first step in creating an ad is devising a strategy, which simply means asking yourself, "What is the problem?" and "What are the best ways to solve it?"

Looking back at the history of advertising, you would find that in the 1950s, problem solving was often dependent on a Unique Selling Proposition (USP). For example, if you were selling a fountain pen that had a silver tip, you might tell the public that this new pen with a silver tip lets you "write smoother."

The 1960s were known as the "Image Era." One example of this approach was created by David Ogilvy for Hathaway shirts. He used a man wearing a black eye patch in each Hathaway ad.

The 1970s were known as the "Positioning Era." Schaeffer Beer positioned itself as "the one beer to have when you're having more than one." This was clever because 20% of the people consumed 80% of the product.

The 1980s utilized all these approaches.

What happens in the 1990s will be up to you.

In almost every ad, you will see a logo or sponsor signature which identifies who is doing the advertising. This frequently appears in the bottom right hand corner of the page with a phrase, called the **tag line,** that sums up how the sponsor wants the audience to perceive its product or company. Since tag lines are built from strategic thinking, creating your tag line first will sometimes help you create your ad.

From Strategy to Execution

After you've devised a strategy, you have to find a way to execute it. This is what turns a concept or strategy into an ad. This is your opportunity to demonstrate how creative you can be.

Explore every possibility from emotionalism (hitting people where the heart is) to humor to demonstration (showing the product in use) to comparisons. It seems that ads that compare "this" to "that" consistently win awards. An example of this is a campaign created for *Rolling Stone* magazine that was voted one of the top ten of the 80s. It was a trade campaign directed to the advertising industry to get them to consider *Rolling Stone* as a media purchase for their clients.

Each ad was a spread—two facing pages of the magazine. On the left-hand page was the word "Perception." On the right, "Reality."

What's in a Book

Your portfolio has to demonstrate your ability to think strategically, as well as your creativity. Therefore, it should contain three or four campaigns, not just a lot of unrelated ads. A campaign is a continuation of an idea through a series of ads. Your book should also contain a couple of outstanding single ads. If you have an excellent TV storyboard, you may want to include that as well.

And What's Not

Since a book is only as strong as your weakest ad, what you leave out is sometimes as important as what you keep in. You should begin by omitting anything unrelated to advertising—like essays for the college newspaper. Also, omit anything that's cute but does not sell a product. In fact, one good rule to follow is: When in doubt, leave it out. Advertising design portfolio what to exclude

To get across the message that most advertisers probably misperceived who really read *Rolling Stone,* for instance, the picture on the left ("Perception") showed a "hippie" from the 1960s; the right-hand page ("Reality") was a picture of a "yuppie" from the 80s. *Rolling Stone* created an entire campaign by using just these two words and changing the pictures to communicate particular messages about the magazine that they wanted the advertising community to know.

Most important of all, if you have news to tell, tell it. And tell it in the headline. No matter how good a writer you are, most readers don't get past the headline. Your headline must be as intriguing as you can make it. Some writers depend on rhymes, others like alliteration, puns, word twists, or quotations.

Open your mind to every idea. Look at magazines, award annuals at art director clubs, and television. Go to movies, museums, and concerts. Listen to the radio.

Then, when you think you have a great execution, ask yourself: "Is the work on strategy? Does the selling message come through? Is it executed with flair or brilliance or humor or drama? Does it reward the viewer for watching, the listener for listening, the reader for reading?" These are the questions we are asked about the ads we do. If you can answer yes to all the above, chances are you've created a good ad.

Getting Your Portfolio Seen

Since it often takes six months to a year to find a job, make sure you've invested enough time in putting together your book. But once you're satisfied that you have a good book, it's time to get it seen.

Use every approach you can think of to get your book seen. Make a list of any personal contacts you have. Try employment agencies. Although they tend to specialize in middle or senior people, they just might have that job for a junior that you're seeking.

Finally, bring your book to agencies on your own. This means doing a little homework first. Find out who the creative person is that screens books at an agency, then send him or her a resume. This should be followed by a phone call. Most likely, you'll be asked to drop off your book; you have to be willing to do this to get it seen. After all this, if the creative director likes your book and there's an opening, you may be asked to go in for an interview. This is how it works at a large agency. At smaller agencies you may get an interview before someone looks at your book, or at the same time. The only way to become experienced at interviews is to go on them. So go on an many as you can. Each time you will be a little more comfortable.

The Indirect Way to Get Started in Copywriting

Not everyone who has a good book gets hired as a junior copywriter. There are not enough jobs to go around. But there are other ways to enter the creative department. And we think that just about any way you can get a foot in the door is a good way to get started.

These days, both men and women can get jobs as secretaries (sometimes called **creative assistants**) in the creative department. It's not a bad way to get started, since it will give you a chance to find out how an agency works *and* a way to get your work seen by people in a position to help you. Agencies like to hire people they know. So as you become known on the inside for doing a good job at whatever you've been hired to do, you'll also have a better chance of getting hired for an available position than someone from the outside. There are other entry-level positions you might want to explore, but make sure that whatever they are, you'll be dealing with the creative department.

Now What?

If you like to write and like working with people, chances are you'll succeed.

If you're willing to work hard, chances are you'll get ahead.

Finally, if you're willing to take risks and to do what hasn't been done before, there's no limit to how far you can go or how fast you can get there.

Prior to forming his own agency, **Ron Bacsa** was employed at Bozell as creative art supervisor on the Chrysler account. Previous to that, he was with Ally & Gargano and Doyle, Dane Bernbach. He is a graduate of New York City Community College and an active member of the New York Art Director's Club.

Kaye Brinker is currently active as a freelance writer and consultant. Her advertising career also includes employment at Bozell, The Marschalk Company, and Kenyon & Eckhardt. She received her BA degree from the College of New Rochelle and MS from Long Island University.

Ron Bacsa and Kaye Brinker have received many advertising awards. They are also instructors at the School of Visual Arts in New York City.

CHAPTER FIVE

Freelancing, the Kindest or Unkindest Cut of All (Depending on What Day It Is)

Marilyn Bagel

I've often said that only masochists go into advertising. Who else, but maybe actors, would slit themselves open, bare their creative souls, and allow clients to fold, spindle, and mutilate them. Assuming that premise, then only sado-masochists become freelance copywriters.

Making the decision to plunge into the abyss of the advertising freelancer presupposes that a number of factors exist: you have a proven track record as a copywriter, you have friends who owe you favors, and you have always dreamed of not getting paid on a regular basis. When you go to a Chinese restaurant, you can always tell which fortune cookie the copywriter at the table will get. It's the one that says, *"There is money in your future...in 60 days."*

From a practical standpoint, there is something you should be aware of from the start. Freelancers are usually at the end of the line when it comes to getting paid. It is not at all unusual to wait 30, 60, or even 90 days for checks. Though I have a couple of clients that pay within two weeks of receipt of invoice, they are by far the exception. You'll have flush months. You'll have white knuckle months. If you can manage the financial fluctuations and the unknowns—and can click your heels like Dorothy, spin around three times during any crisis and say *"It's only advertising"*—then you, too, can have a career as a freelancer.

The First Commandment of Freelancing

Thou shalt have amassed a strong portfolio of thy work. Like the characters portrayed in the Broadway show, "Chorus Line," you are always "auditioning" for assignments. The only difference is instead of doing a leaps, spins, and all that jazz, your portfolio of ad campaigns, brochures, direct mail, and radio and TV spots is center stage, hoping the prospective client doesn't yell *"get the hook."*

Freelancers are hired for their experience and proven ability to deliver. Oftentimes, a freelancer is called in when the agency is overworked, overwhelmed, and understaffed. You are expected to hit the ground running. Consequently, becoming a freelancer is normally not an option for those just starting out in the advertising copywriting field. If you're established, then it's a different story.

Make Yourself Invaluable

Freelancers are like fireman. When the phone rings, they're ready to jump into action. This brings me to one of the most important qualities of a good freelancer: **reliability.** Clients must know they can count on you every time. If you want to make yourself invaluable, you have to be good, and you have to be fast. You may be on the short end of a deadline because the account executive sat on the assignment an extra few days, or maybe the client has made some unrealistic demands. Regardless, the deadline is the bottom line. Miss one, and you won't get a second chance.

Having been on the hiring end of freelancers when I was on staff at ad agencies, I can tell you that there is no bigger turnoff than someone who tells you he can't take on an assignment because he doesn't want to work over the weekend. As everyone who's ever worked in the trenches can tell you, there is no room for clockwatchers when you have an important campaign to do. Freelancers who share the same sense of urgency and can-do attitude are the ones in the Rolodex.

By far, one of the biggest boons to freelancers has been the fax machine. With the ability to transmit instantaneously, you can give your clients the same time-critical response as if you were working out of their offices. Because most fax machines are kept on 24-hours-a-day, you can fax at any hour day or night. As long as we're talking about technology, it goes without saying that in today's business world, you must be computer literate. Many of my clients request that in addition to hard copy, I submit final approved copy on diskette. It also helps to have knowledge of desktop publishing.

> **Ideas Can Come Any Time!**
>
> Over the years, I've learned to carpe idea-um—seize the creative moment. If I have an idea or inspiration for one of my assignments, even if it's not the next one in line, deadline-wise, I take advantage of the idea flow and quickly jot down headlines or an outline or notes...whatever comes to mind. Then I'll set it aside and turn my attention to the time-critical assignment. When that's done and I go back to my scribbled notes, it's a great feeling to know I have a jumping off point instead of beginning from a cold start.

The Art of Self-Management

If you're contemplating freelancing, an important question to ask yourself is, "Am I disciplined?" You are your own boss. You determine your own schedule. That can be a blessing or a curse, depending on your ability to manage yourself.

It is essential that you have the ability to organize your time well and know how to prioritize. You will probably have a number of balls in the air at any given moment. Sometimes I feel like I'm playing a fast game of tennis at the net. I may have a brochure for a real estate developer in progress while I'm writing a direct mail piece for a trade association and also thinking about a concept for a radio commercial. If your creative juices are in fifth gear, it's exhilarating. If you're having an off day, it can be paralyzing.

With experience, you will learn how your own creative process operates. It's quite fascinating. Your subconscious is at work even when you're not. That's why ideas "fall out of nowhere" at totally unrelated times—in the shower, when sitting in traffic, or while seemingly engrossed in a movie. If I'm just starting a project, I sometimes do background reading at night before I go to sleep. Somehow I feel it gives the information an opportunity to percolate before I begin developing the next morning.

By the way, if you're asked to tackle a project you've never done before, "Just Say Yes", especially if the little voice inside wants to give it a shot. It's your chance to stretch and grow creatively, even if you're terrified in the process. You'll likely be pleasantly surprised with the results.

All Alone by the Telephone

You have to be comfortable with yourself. Freelancing can be a relatively solitary profession when compared with working on staff. In an office, you're usually getting constant feedback, good, bad, or indifferent. As a freelancer, you are the first to know if something is bad, the last to know when something is good. I wrote a direct mail piece for a client, who months later remembered to tell me that it was so successful that the company went into immediate reprintings of the booklet in the offer. Another client I regularly work with rarely communicates results to me unless I ask. This is not an indictment of clients. It is an assessment of reality. Clients are so busy and running at such breakneck pace that, unless there's a problem, they forget to give you feedback. A prime example is when I called in recently about an unrelated matter and the receptionist said, "Congratulations on getting that new account." That's how I found out that the agency had landed a new chunk of business that I had help them pitch the week before.

This isolation can contribute to Freelancer Angst: the affliction of suffering from more highs and lows than staff writers. In fact, I don't know if it's possible for freelancers to feel positive about themselves for more than two weeks in a row. You're up, you're down. You're alternately the best writer in America, or you're on your way to scanning canned prunes as a grocery checker at Safeway.

The Business of Freelancing

So, after all this, let's suppose you've decided to freelance. Who are your clients? How do you get them? Though I've been speaking about advertising agencies, that's just one source. You can work directly for businesses, corporations, and associations. You can work for design studios, which usually do not maintain staff writers. You can work for other freelancers who are designers. You can work for anyone who will pay you.

When I write for design studios or ad agencies, I supply copy and their staff designers do the layout. When I get assignments directly from a company or association, I'll call one of my designer friends, and we team on the project. In return, they call me when they have clients who need copy.

All this brings us to the sixty-four thousand dollar question. How do you get business? There's no easy answer but there are some basics. Probably the single most important avenue is networking. A picture may be worth a thousand words, but a referral can be worth a thousand bucks. The majority of my business results from professional relationships and referrals. As you build your copywriting career, you are also building relationships that can work for you later. Office colleagues may start their own businesses, end up at companies that can use your services, or just put in a good word for you when it counts. Clients you wrote for while on staff may seek you out later to do projects directly.

Professional organizations can be invaluable. Join them. Become active. Be visible. Let people know who you are and what you can do. If your area has a tip club, join it. A tip club is a group of people, representing different professions, who meet monthly and give each other business leads. It can be quite helpful.

When you're trying to build your business, what you don't want is a one-shot deal. You're looking for repeat activity where you can establish on-going relationships with clients. A client recently told me that my phone number was one of those they had programmed on the autodialer of their fax machine. For a freelancer, hearing something is concrete as that is akin to finding out you're getting your own star on the Hollywood Walk of Fame.

You can advertise your services, but that can be expensive, so be selective and be consistent. Try to zero in on the publication that will best reach the business community, whether it is a business publication or a special business section of the newspaper. Targeting is also critical if you send out self-promotional direct mail pieces. Otherwise you're wasting significant amounts of time and money.

Though doing business in a down economy is not easy, there are elements about it that can actually work in your favor. Many companies are rethinking the way they do business. They may be downsizing and reorganizing. Perhaps they are creating their own advertising departments and supplementing them with freelance talent.

Charge of the Write Brigade

Freelancers base their charges on hourly rates which can range from $35 to $75 and up. However, I rarely quote a job to a client by the hour; I use project rates. If you're an experienced copywriter, you know approximately how long it takes you to write a brochure of a given length or how much time you need for a radio spot. Quote a flat price or price range for the project. Quoting hourly rates doesn't mean anything. If you work fast, a higher hourly rate can actually be cheaper to a client than a lower hourly rate. I think all hour rates produce is client anxiety.

ADVICE FROM THE PRO'S

The best defense against having to spend an inordinate amount of time functioning as your own bill collector and nagging slow-pay clients for your money is to do work for people you know or through referral. If it's a first assignment and the company is questionable, request half up front, half upon delivery. The only thing worse than spending gut-wrenching hours on a particularly difficult assignment is not getting paid for it. And there is no one to protect you but you.

So when all is said and done, what do I think of freelancing? I love it. But then, lucky for you, you caught me during a good week. Next week who knows? What if Marilyn Bagel's "Theory of the Five Hundred Creative Ideas" comes to pass: that everyone is born with 500 creative ideas, and I just used my last one today.

▼

MARILYN BAGEL has been an advertising copywriter in the Washington, D.C. area for more than 15 years. She has written collateral, print ads, direct mail, radio, TV, AV, and is also a broadcast producer. Over the years, Marilyn's clients have included local, regional, and national accounts covering every field from finance, healthcare, associations, and real estate, to hospitality, business to business, and retail. Marilyn has been a freelance writer since 1989.

When your last name is "Bagel", you have to be creative. In keeping this appointment with destiny, Marilyn authored *The Bagels' Bagel Book*. Her second book, *The Bagel Bible, the Complete Guide for Bagel Lovers*, is being published by The Globe-Pequot Press, in the fall of 1992. Her feature articles have appeared in *The Miami Herald, Dallas Morning News, The Oregonian,* and *Cleveland Plain Dealer*. She has also written features for a local newspaper.

Marilyn was the show scriptwriter for the 1992 Country Music Gala, emceed by Willard Scott, at the Kennedy Center Concert Hall. The show was performed before a sell-out crowd that included President and Mrs. Bush and starred The Gatlin Brothers, Charley Pride, Hollie Dunn, and many other stars performing on behalf of Joe Gibbs Charities.

Marilyn is a board member of Women in Advertising and Marketing. She is a member of Washington Independent Writers and of American Women's Economic Development. Marilyn lives in Bethesda, Maryland.

CHAPTER SIX

What Your Art School Won't Teach You

Walter Kaprielian, Chairman & Creative Director
Kaprielian/O'Leary Advertising

There isn't a school in the world that can properly prepare you to enter the art directing business. The educational system is not structured to project what really happens in the field.

You'll be mad at *your* school when you find that out. But it's not *their* fault—the business just moves too fast for them to keep up with it.

In school, you're conditioned to work as an individual entity. You earn grades as an individual. You become dependent on your own skills and not the skills of others. You graduate, and one day and one dollar later, you step from being a student to being a professional. From that day on, you start to work with others—and for others—and you'll do better work because of it.

Out of School...Into the Real World

But first, you've got to find a job.

No one goes through that process without a truckload of fears and questions. Mostly about themselves, their portfolio, and this strange industry that has been projected as being so tough, unforgiving, and competitive.

The portfolio has been the center of your life for the past year, and it leaves your hands with nightmares of getting lost or stolen, and, with its loss, your career going down the drain.

The real truth is that entry-level people are no big investment for the hiring party. A great deal of effort is *not* spent in finding a beginner, and, in fact, the task of finding *you* may very well be relegated to an art secretary or assistant.

Why? You're just not that important...yet! Everyone is searching for a diamond in the rough, but not everyone has the ability to recognize one—so what do they look for?

Agencies Are Not Panting to Hire You

First, they really *don't* want to see you. Most would rather have you send your book. Why? So they don't have to spend time talking to someone they might not consider. It's awkward for all concerned. It's also quite disconcerting *for you* to watch someone flip through the pages of your book and glance for three minutes at your seven hundred hours of work. Is that cruel or unfair? Strange as it may seem, you *can* tell a lot about someone without lingering over each page.

But They'll Look at Your Portfolio

What did they see while they "flipped" through your book?

They saw if you were neat or if you were a slob. If hired you *will* touch other people's work. If you don't respect yours, how will you handle *theirs?*

They saw if you had good hands. Do you letter better than you can draw—or vice versa? Do you have any extraordinary skills? They saw if you have a good set of eyes (how are things placed on the page?) and your sense of color, design, taste.

They saw if you have a sense of order. Can you edit?

They saw if you have a good head. Are there ideas behind what you have? Do you think out problems, or are your solutions ordinary and expected? Is there a modicum of unusual thinking in the book?

No one expects a genius, but a glimmer of hope that you *might* be one is nice. You'll probably be judged on the balance between your manual skills and your mental ones. It will be weighted a bit more towards manual. Why? Because the reason most agencies hire a beginner is because they *need* manual help—paste-ups, comp lettering, working on the Macintosh, mechanicals, cutting mats, flaps, anything that saves a higher-priced person's time.

You May Even Get An Interview

If you get called in because your portfolio has stirred some interest, what does the interviewer look for? First of all, he's *not* looking for a person who's late for their interview. Be on time, be presentably dressed, and be pleasant. Most of the people in the business are pretty nice. They know you're on the verge of a nervous breakdown and wouldn't like it if you weren't. Show me a cool, relaxed, under-control, entry-level interviewee, and I'll show you a person who'll probably get canned for long lunch hours and goofing off. Everyone has memories of their first interviews. You'd be surprised at how tolerant and understanding people are of your dilemma. Hopefully, your nervousness will project some of your enthusiasm and eagerness. Remember, all men are *not* created equal; if they were, there would be no need for portfolios and interviews.

Interviews are important even if you *don't* get chosen. The more places you go, the more of a "feel" you'll get for the kind of places there are to work in. Some places project a pulse of what working there would really be like. Seeing the environment and the kind of work done is important. Hard as it might be to believe right now, there are places at which you may choose *not* to work. Be observant. Don't be afraid to trust your instincts.

If you get sent from person to person and place to place, don't get discouraged. It might be a compliment—no one sends a loser to one of his friends.

Should you go to a studio or an ad agency? Who knows? Most of us would have taken the first job that was offered. I know *I* would have.

In every other form of education, you have to pay for post-graduate work. In our field, you get paid for it. If you get your first job in a studio and decide it's not for you, terrific! What better time to change course? The same holds true if your first job is an advertising one.

You Got a Job! Now What?

You just got a job. Oh, my God, what do you do *now*? You do what you would do on any job. You open your eyes wider, your ears get bigger, and your sense of smell gets sharper. Drink in what's going on. If someone doesn't introduce you around, introduce yourself. Find the people who are doing the good work. Throw away your wristwatch—it's not a 9-to-5 world anymore.

Try to understand what responsibilities will be considered yours, and then do them better and more thoroughly than anyone has done them before, no matter *how* unimportant they may seem.

If someone else is overloaded, offer to help. If someone is exceptionally talented, watch how they work. There isn't a book written that will teach you better.

Know who your boss is. Service him or her well. Try to understand the problems he or she faces and how they are solved.

Will you advance? Can you move ahead? The first step in getting a promotion is doing what you were hired to do very well. Would *you* promote anyone incapable of doing what you had hired them to do in the first place?

Always be worth more than you're being paid—it keeps you in the drivers seat. Are there jobs that are below you in status? Sure! Do them! You'd be surprised at how your cooperation can work for you. It allows you to ask for things from others—and your company.

Stop complaining. It's a bore. Everyone knows what's wrong. If you can joke about it, fine. No one needs someone else to depress them. Remember, other people recommend you for promotion. People who you've made feel and look good.

When a disaster looms, try not to panic. Confidence breeds confidence. You'd be surprised at how few people have any.

Always keep an eye out for what's new. Come up with it before anyone else does. Stay young. It has nothing to do with chronological age. It has to do with attitude. When one solution will do, do three. When three are needed, do seven. If everyone is giving photographic answers, take a look at artwork. If everyone is approaching things seriously, consider a cartoon.

Be thought of as someone who takes a fresh approach to things. The first step to fame is being noticed.

ADVICE FROM THE PRO'S

▼ Are You Prepared For This Career?

Does the level of your education matter? Ours is not an industry of MBAs or PhDs. If anyone asks you what school you went to, it's for conversation. If anyone asks you what kind of degree you have, it's even more conversation. This is not to put down higher levels of education. If your heart and head wants it, by all means do it. You probably won't later on. It's just that it's not a prerequisite for consideration.

ADVERTISING CAREER DIRECTORY

Is it Time to Move On?

How long should you stay in one place? I don't know if that is as important as figuring out how long to stay at one *job*. A rut is dangerous. You should watch out for it at any stage in your career.

I worked at BBD&O for eleven years. I stayed because my jobs kept changing...upward. I started as a photostat clerk and left as a group head (with one or two people that I used to order photostats for as part of my group). I left because I got offered twice my salary and didn't know how to refuse it.

I worked at Ketchum Advertising in New York for eighteen years. I came in as an art supervisor and left as president. I didn't have the same position for more than two years. Each change was an upward one. I didn't change agencies, I changed jobs. If the jobs didn't change, I'm sure I would have changed agencies. There really is no single, perfect answer to the question of staying or moving on. The only thing I would say is that a resume with a whole series of six-month positions does tend to indicate a certain amount of instability on your part.

Top Advertising Categories

Based on ad spending
1. Automotive
2. Retail, non-food
3. Food
4. Restaurants
5. Entertainment & media
6. Telephone
7. Beverages, non-alcoholic
8. Cosmetics
9. Airline
10. Beer

Source: *Advertising Age*

It Can Be a Wonderful World

You are not entering a "union" business. Growth in position, income, and job security is very much related to individual value and performance. You *can* lose your job tomorrow, through no real fault of your own. On the other hand, you can double your salary tomorrow, too.

I mentioned before that now—as you're preparing to graduate and find your first agency job—is a time that is filled with fear and questions. Don't be afraid—enjoy every minute of it. You're on the threshold of a life that will not be boring or dull. You really wouldn't want to work 9-to-5 in a supermarket, would you?

Whether you find your first job in an agency or a studio, a small company or a large corporation, the way you work, the enthusiasm with which you perform, and your interest in what you do will play a great role in your success. Go for it. Get rich and famous!

Prior to becoming a partner in his own company, **WALTER KAPRIELIAN** was president and CEO of Ketchum Advertising, New York. His career also includes stays at BBD&O and Grey Advertising.

President of The Art Directors Club Scholarship Fund, and past-president/chairman of the Advisory Board of The Art Directors Club, Mr. Kaprielian is the holder of over 100 awards for creative excellence from numerous industry organizations and competitions. A member of the American Institute of Graphic Arts and The National Academy of Television Arts & Sciences, he also serves on the Advisory Board of New York City Technical College, and has been an instructor at The School of Visual Arts.

CHAPTER SEVEN

Working at a Graphics Design Agency

**Mary Bode Byrd, President
Mary Byrd Productions, Inc.**

The first thing you notice about an advertisement or printed promotion piece is the visual communication. Without strong graphics or a compelling visual appeal, many ads and promotions may be overlooked. What's the point in writing the greatest copy in the world if you can't persuade someone to even look at your work?

At our graphics design agency, we offer solutions to problems. We are visual communicators specializing in print and marketing and we pride ourselves on our creative results-oriented design, layout, type, and illustration as our agency's signature.

At Smaller Agencies You Can Be Involved

Working at a smaller design agency presents you with greater challenges (and rewards!) than working for a large advertising agency. At a design firm, you may be working on accounts that involve fairly small budgets—anywhere from $50,000 to $250,000. What this means is that you will often be doing just as much as the client will let you do. While you may have some tremendous ideas that you know would help the client reach his or her goals, the challenge is to craft these ideas to make them work within the client's budget. There is a great sense of reward when you successfully achieve your client's goals.

While the budgets may be smaller, the diversity in the work you will do is greater. An agency that is a "full-service" design agency will work on dozens of different products or services and utilize every form of advertising available. Once a marketing plan is agreed upon, some or all of the following can be developed for the client—Corporate identity packages, Logos and workmarks, Service/product brochures, Annual reports, Promotional ad campaigns, Catalogs, Publications, Point of purchase designs, Package designs, Newsletters, Direct marketing, and Promotions.

So You Want to Be a Graphics Designer or a Design Account Service Person?

Terrific. We welcome new faces and solutions to problems in this industry. What does that really take, though?

It usually takes a college degree. While this is not always an overriding concern when making a hiring decision, it is often a good indicator of the person's abilities and level of commitment.

Someone hoping to work in this field should also have a commitment of excellence and a desire to see things completed the right way. You should plan on demonstrating strong follow-through—in other words, deliver something when you say you will and deliver more than you promised. Be able to utilize both your left-brain (detail-oriented) and right-brain (creative) skills. Be both energetic and determined to excel in your career goals.

Do Your Research When Finding an Agency

It is important in your research to find out as much about the agency before the interview. Nothing leaves a more unfavorable impression than an interviewee who comes in and says, "Well now, tell me about your agency."

There are some things you can do to prepare for any interview:

1) Pick up the phone and call the agency.

2) Find products or services which the agency is involved with and study them.

Both of these steps will show the agency you are making the extra effort, and are trying to bridge the gap between you, the student, and the agency professional. Once you find a common ground at an interview, a relationship can develop and you can understand what the interviewer wants and he or she can understand what you can offer.

Finally, there is portfolio preparation if you are seeking a design or copywriting position. **Make it clean!** I cannot stress this enough. Make sure your samples are not torn, and you show a consistent level of quality and expertise. Even if you absolutely love the first piece you ever did in art school, leave it out! Take only the pieces related to the ad world and only your best pieces. Know where the company you are applying to comes from and tailor your portfolio as much as possible to meet them there. **Be prepared!** Who knows, maybe the electricity will be out the day you go for your interview and you won't be able to show your slides. If you had a mechanical with you, you would still have work to show. An unlikely example—but stranger things have happened, and you need to be ready for anything. Always follow up your interview within 48 hours. Send or fax a thank you letter and restate the benefit the agency would receive by hiring you.

Internships Can Open the Door

Internships are quite prevalent in this industry. They are an excellent way to learn the business, especially if the agency you intern with views the experience as one that can benefit you and them. At my agency, we try to bring in an intern every summer, and involve them in each aspect of the work in process.

Be Patient and Set Your Goals

In closing, some personal qualities will help you reach your goals in this advertising/promotion business—energy, drive, enthusiasm, and patience. When looking for that first job, make sure your enthusiasm shows at every interview or career fair you attend. If people know you love the work and can't wait to help an agency meet its goals, your first job won't be far behind.

Once you get that first job, be patient. Watch and learn. Do everything thoroughly and don't try to rush your career. Set goals and know where you want to be at each stage of your career.

▼

MARY BODE BYRD is a former designer with Hallmark Cards and the first woman to sell commercial printing in the Metropolitan Washington DC area. Mary has been in business with her own successful design agency for over 17 years having completed major projects for Marriott Hotels and EuroDisney. Other areas of business are financial institutions, healthcare facilities, and associations. Mary is married and the mother of four children under the age of seventeen. She plans to open additional offices in Baltimore and Philadelphia.

CHAPTER EIGHT

How to Prepare Your Portfolio

Shinichiro Tora, Art Director, Popular Photography
Promotion Art Director, American Photo, Popular Photography
Hachette Magazines, Inc.

Art students who have just finished art or design school and have started looking for their first jobs must be prepared to show interviewers a portfolio book that expresses their talents and skills. Assembling your first professional portfolio should be considered your initial, tentative step into the professional world of design.

Why is the portfolio so important? Because it presents your talents and skills in a visual form that requires no further explanation. Employers are always looking for creative talents who will help their businesses. While viewing a portfolio, the employer can objectively weigh each young's artist's potential to perform productively. The portfolio is the *only* way you can prove your artistic talents. It's your sales kit. As such, a neat, well-organized portfolio, showing off your talent and professional skills, is the best way for any artist to promote yourself to potential employers and land that important first job.

Before putting your portfolio together, you must first know something about the business side of the creative world and the types of positions available. Commercial, creative art and design is a large and varied field. Professionals may work in advertising agencies, publishing companies, printing companies, design and photo studios, package design studios, architectural design offices, construction companies, and almost any other industry. Jobs may be found in many different departments—Art, Promotion Art, Creative Arts, Planning Design, Editorial Art, to name a few. As a designer, you can specialize in numerous areas—fashion, graphics, editorial, industrial, architecture, and many more.

Given all these choices, the first step may be the hardest—selecting the particular industry or area in which you want to work. Otherwise, you'll be unable to set up a portfolio which will demonstrate the abilities and skills you possess that are necessary to get an entry-level position in *that* particular field.

Putting Together an Illustration Portfolio

If you are looking for a job as a staff illustrator in an Art department or contemplating freelance illustration, this kind of portfolio is what you need.

First, select your best original drawings, reproduction prints, or proofs (if you have them), about 20 to 30 in all. (That's, I think, the best size for a portfolio presentation.) If your paintings are unusually large (bigger than 30" x 40"), you should make smaller, photographic copies. Otherwise, you probably won't even be able to *carry* your portfolio, and, if you *do* manage to drag it along, interviewers won't have enough room in their offices to spread it out and go through it. You might consider making photographs of *any* canvas paintings, even the small ones. Canvas is just too bulky to fit comfortably in your presentation case.

The photographic copies you intend to use in your portfolio must be faithful, good-quality reproductions. Use black & white film for black & white drawings, color prints or transparencies for color materials. If you plan to make 35mm slides, use slide protector vinyl sheets. They're available at any photographic or art supply store and hold 20 slides each.

Unfortunately, slide projectors are sometimes unavailable and viewing 35mm slides on a light table is an injustice—They're really too small to view the details. I prefer using 8 x 10 or even 11 x 14 color prints or, if you must use slides, 4 x 5 color transparencies for reproducing illustrations. (But, unless they're too large or are 3-D or computer-graphic illustrations, I personally would really rather see the original illustrations, rather than photos.)

You should mount each drawing, printed proof, or photo print on white or black illustration board of uniform size. This will give the portfolio a neat appearance. The preferred size is a maximum of 24 x 18. If you have many small illustrations, you may group more than one on a single board. If your drawing was made on illustration board, don't mount it again, but do try to maintain a uniformity of board size.

When mounting an illustration, leave at least two inches of space all around it. This will protect the painting from fingerprints. You can also put your credit in this border area. In order to protect the painting fully, lay a clear acetate sheet over each board.

The credit for each painting—your name, address, telephone number, and, preferably, the title of the illustration—should always appear *somewhere* on every illustration. If you want to use a rubber stamp, that's all right (though I prefer the title with each in the border area). Paintings may be held for a rather long time and could easily become mixed up with other artists' work, so such identification is mandatory.

Focus Your Portfolio

The portfolio should, therefore, be carefully focused to highlight only the kind of work endemic to either the industry or specific job you're pursuing. Even if you are multi-talented—skilled in a number of disciplines and styles—you can't show off everything in a single portfolio. And you shouldn't try. I've sometimes interviewed persons who have shown me such "unfocused" portfolios. I find them confusing. A person who does a little bit of this and a little bit of that fails to perfect any specific artistic skills. Such portfolios don't provide sufficient samples in my specific areas of interest. So if you have a variety of talents, create a separate portfolio for each major category—illustration, photography, or design.

Putting Together a Photographic Portfolio

The student of photography who is probably aiming to become a professional commercial photographer, art photographer, or photojournalist, needs to create a different portfolio.

There are two ways to break into the professional photography ranks. One is to start as an assistant to an established photographer or in a commercial photo studio. Either job will teach you the special techniques and skills you need to know to sell your work directly to magazines, ad agencies, or stock photo houses.

The second way is to avoid such an apprenticeship and become a professional freelance photographer immediately. I don't recommend it. You need not only quite a bit of talent, but several lucky breaks to even have a chance.

Whether you choose commercial or art photography, you must develop a solid foundation of photographic skills. Shoot, shoot, and *keep* shooting. Practice as much as you can. Photographs can be of a single subject, a series, or any other variation, but they must be sharp, clear images. Then select the best shots from each series or group for your portfolio.

Today, most professionals shoot color, which most advertisers and publications prefer. But black & white prints are still used and a selection of black & white photos should be included in your photographic portfolio. Prints or transparencies are acceptable.

Advertising agencies, generally speaking, tend to prefer large-size (4 x 5 or even 8 x 10) color transparencies; fashion photographers usually use 2 1/4 x 2 1/4 film. Magazines are generally flexible as to format. Stock photo houses prefer 35mm slides.

There are two ways to present a 35mm color portfolio. One is simply to utilize the slide protector sheets mentioned earlier. The other is to organize your slides in a carousel tray (ready for projection) of anywhere from 80 to 140 slides.

A maximum of ten sheets or one carousel tray is probably sufficient for any presentation. If you lean towards the tray method, however, make sure you arrange to have a slide projector available when you make an interview appointment.

To display large-size transparencies, cut black matte board to uniform size. Use 8 1/2 x 11 boards for 4 x 5 film, 11 x 14 for 2 1/4 x 2 1/4 or 8 x 10 transparencies or films. "Gang up" twelve of the 2 1/4 shots per board. Use one board for each 4 x 5 or 8 x 10. To prepare a 2 1/4 presentation board, draw four rules on the back of the board, 1 1/2 inches from each edge. Draw three boxes horizontally, four vertically, each separated by half-inch spaces. Now cut out these box windows. You can then make as many such matte boards as you need.

Put each 2 1/4 transparency in a plastic sleeve and tape each photograph to the back of the matte board so the image shows through the windows you've created. In a similar manner, cut out a single window in the center of the board to mount 4 x 5 or 8 x 10 transparencies. It's also better to mount prints rather than just leaving them loose. Mounting will protect them from fingerprints and other damage and display each photograph in an attractive way.

As previously discussed, make sure each slide or print is fully identified with your name, address and telephone number, especially if you are sending your work to a stock photo agency. Since they handle millions of photos a year, one unnamed slide can very easily get lost in the shuffle. Use 20 to 30 mounted shots in one portfolio case.

Putting Together a Design Portfolio

If you're looking for a job in advertising, editorial, or graphic design at an ad agency, magazine publisher, design studio, or similar media arts firm, you will need to put together a design portfolio. There are two types, depending on where you want to work and the specific kind of design with which you want to be involved—an **advertising design portfolio** and an **editorial design portfolio.** They are distinctly different categories and not at all interchangeable. A portfolio designed for advertising should not be used if you are applying for a publishing job, and vice versa.

An advertising design portfolio should contain concepts for as many of the following as possible: newspaper and/or magazine ads (single ads or entire campaigns for consumer, business, or trade publications), annual reports, booklets or brochures, sales kits, direct mail pieces, record jackets, packages, calendars, letterheads, point-of-purchase materials, corporate identity programs, a sample TV story board, and posters. In other words, sample ads for all the various media and myriad collateral pieces an agency utilizes in its attempt to sell its clients' products or services.

An editorial design portfolio should concentrate on editorial page and layout designs, cover design, book design, and some typographic designs that would be used for presentations.

If at all possible, I would recommend you "customize" each portfolio before the interview with the specific art director you're scheduled to see.

To prepare either type of portfolio, start by collecting as many interesting magazines—new and old—as possible. These will provide you with the raw materials necessary to create your own sample ads or editorial designs. Using these ads and stories as a base, recreate various designs *your* way. At this stage, work freely and don't worry about size and space limitations. Once the concept design is worked out, sketch out each of your ideas and, finally, pick the best ones. Using general magazine sizing and layout formats, turn your sketches into finished mechanicals.

(If you are working on editorial designs, you must furnish keyed layout sheets for the text column format (2, 3, or 4, generally) you are using. This is an important element in editorial design and should, therefore, be carefully prepared and certainly not omitted.)

Now find the photographs or illustrations that fit your designs, either from the magazines you've culled or your own selection of original illustrations or photographs. Advertising agencies especially like to see such original artwork in a design, rather than pictures from cut-up magazines. Set actual headlines by using press type, which is available in a wide variety of typefaces and sizes at most art supply stores. Text can be neatly cut out from your magazine pile. (If you can't find a text section that's long enough for a particular design, just cut out what you have, photocopy it and add the two together.)

If you have some experience in darkroom techniques, you can try 3M color key processing for color lettering on clear acetate, tacking it over the photographic print or illustration. You can also create drop-out lettering on a black background by first using press type on clear acetate and then making a direct print on photo enlargement paper. This can also be colored with magic markers. These and other creative techniques will make your overall presentation far more attractive.

ADVICE FROM THE PRO'S

Your paste-up should be neat and clean. Remove all excess cement. Trim the finished work to magazine size and mount it on uniform-sized white or black boards. For two-page spreads (whether for advertising or editorial), mount them on a single board, just as they would appear in the magazine. Ten to twenty designs are probably sufficient for a solid presentation.

Finally, with portfolio in hand, you start making the rounds, looking for an appointment with the right art director. Good luck!

▼

In addition to his responsibilities as art director at *Popular Photography* and promotion art director for *Popular Photography* and *American Photo,* Hachette Magazines, Inc., SHINICHIRO TORA is an active member of the Society of Illustrators and the Art Directors Club. Since 1974, he has coordinated annual shows in Japan for the latter two organizations. He has chaired numerous association and professional committees and served on the board of directors of the Art Directors Club from 1986-1988. He has received a variety of awards for art direction, illustration, and design annually since 1973, including the 1974 Gold and 1977 Silver Awards from the Society of Publication Designers; the 1980 and 1986 Gold, 1982 and 1986 (two) Silver and 1981 & 1985 Distinctive Merit Awards from the Art Directors Club; and the 1984 Silver and 1986 and 1992 Gold Awards from the Society of Illustrators.

CHAPTER NINE

Great Is Better Than Good

**Sander A. Flaum, President and Chief Executive Officer
Robert A. Becker, Inc.**

The attributes of a "good" account manager in a "good" advertising agency are well documented. A typical job description might read as follows: strong communication skills, both verbal and written; a better-than-average work ethic; personable, well-groomed, and ambitious; a better-than-average IQ.

And if being "average" and working in an "average" agency is where you see yourself, this article is *not* for you.

However, if you are among the minority of individuals who want to leave the realm of mediocrity and strive to be a truly *great* account manager, then I have some advice for you. After 25 years in the industry (eighteen on the client side and seven in the agency business), I think I've learned something about "what makes great!"—that is, those special attributes that enable the "cream" to rise to the top. Consider these ideas and separate yourself from those who would settle to be just "good."

Sit in Your Client's Chair

All of you who enrolled in undergraduate or graduate advertising or marketing programs should realize just how little they have prepared you for the reality of the advertising world. Frankly, your college major isn't in the least important! What *is* significant is your ability to sell—all the time—externally to your client and internally to your management and creative people.

You must be able to communicate effectively via well-written presentations and exciting face-to-face interactions. If public speaking isn't your "cup of tea" and you struggled to pull "C's" on writing assignments, advertising probably is not your niche.

The consensus in this industry is that the needs of the client would be best served if anyone wanting to be an account executive first had to spend several years as a product manager. We have always held the view that the needs of a product manager can be understood best by an account person who has already sat in that chair.

If a product isn't making quota, who cares whether the background of the magazine ad is blue or green? The manager of that product needs a person on the other side of the desk with an understanding of distribution, pricing, packaging, and, of course, marketing and sales strategy.

Working for a client company gives you the opportunity to work with a variety of account people and adopt the characteristics and methods of the exceptional ones. Of course, becoming a corporate product manager—at least for a package goods company—means an MBA degree in many cases.

A positive attitude, a desire to accept coaching (from any level), and a compulsion for detail and follow-up can compensate somewhat for a deficiency in the skills mentioned above.

Be a "Great" Manager

Become Conspicuously Proactive

This term is so difficult to define, yet so pointedly essential to the making of the great account executive. We train our young people to literally shower their clients, on a continuing basis, with fresh ideas to enhance brand performance. We encourage them to think big, think "out-of-the-box" on their brands, think competitively. To become proactive, an account executive must be convinced that the brand competitive to his is taking bread and butter off his table. In other words, we want "hungry" account people.

The concept of proactivity evolved from the notion that if the client is paying a fair hourly rate for marketing counsel and creative thinking, we'd better have account people who stay a half step ahead of their clients. Product managers need another marketing head—an experienced, strategic brain—on the other side of the desk to consult with before "decision time."

One of the qualifications of the "great" agency person is his or her ability to lead people, to manage, and motivate them. While I've read the great books on effective management and have taken the full complement of management courses during my MBA and post-MBA studies at Columbia University's Arden House, I'm still inclined to believe that great managers are born, not made.

Great managers have that charismatic style of getting the big things done faster and better. They are leaders who know inherently how to get the best out of people—at their agency as well as the client company. They have a presence, a respect, a credibility, an obvious posture that makes people want to follow and listen and do. They radiate a silent benign power that everyone wants to be close to. John Kennedy had it; Iaccoca has it; Jessie Jackson has it. Do you?

Great managers are focused people. They have the rare ability to ignore (for the moment) priorities No. 2 to No. 5 when priority No. 1 has to be accomplished...now! They can instantly focus all their energies—creative and active—on the one big task at hand. Other things that are in need of attention but can be put off for a day or a week or a month are put into less critical priority slots and handled only when they need to be.

It takes great mental discipline to stay on that one big project until it's successfully completed. Moving off a "high pressure" project to finish some other task is always tempting. Great managers fight off the temptation and stay with the top priority job until it is done.

Settle for Nothing Less than Excellence

ADVICE FROM THE PRO'S

Great account people are compulsive people. They have an obsession to do each successive task better than the previous one. They strive for excellence. Our theme at Becker is: "If it's not excellent, don't show it!"

The uniquely qualified account executive will not settle for an ad, commercial spot, promotional plan, media proposal, etc., unless it's the *best* it can be. Ernie Lewis, manager of professional advertising at Procter & Gamble, advised agency people recently: "Do it right the first time."

Mr. Lewis' point is well taken. There's *always* time, it seems, to *redo* the storyboard. But there's *never* enough time to get it done properly the *first* time. Our people are instructed never to bring material to the client until they are totally satisfied with the effort.

Great account people will call the client—despite an approaching deadline—and bravely request additional time to "get it right" before bringing it to them. The agency person who really cares about the interests of the client and about his or her brand will argue for more time to bring art, copy, or design to the point of satisfaction—at least from the account person's perspective.

Learn the Business of Our Business

Most account people hesitate talking about fee reconciliation, billing, or post-30 day invoices with their clients. They see themselves as the clients' marketing and advertising consultants and maintain that a discussion of billing would impinge on the sacred "client-agency relationship." Nonsense!

Marketing managers discuss quotas, budgets, billing, the full spectrum of financial matters every day. They pay hourly fees to lawyers, plumbers, electricians, and painters every day. So why would anyone think it wrong for a brand manager to review billing with his agency representative?

The *great* account person considers himself a business manager. He is providing a unique service to his client for which he expects to earn a fair hourly rate and a 20% profit (what any moderately successful business should be able to achieve).

The *exceptional* account executive wants to and should be paid for the dedicated hours his agency team spends on the brand. He is fiscally responsible and responsive to his client—doing hard-bill estimates, revised estimates (when necessary), and on-time billing, with documentation for out-of-pocket expenses.

Thus, a good financial background and understanding of agency finances are a must for the talented, growth-motivated agency account executive.

The importance of being a *good business person* in addition to being a good advertising person, cannot be stressed enough. Neither can the value of embracing your client's business, understanding his point of view, and being sensitive to the daily challenges he faces.

American business has just weathered what, by any measurement, was a serious recession. The advertising industry went through some tough times. As with most adversity, the profession and its people have emerged stronger, and even better prepared for the future. Advertising veterans and beginners alike re-learned what I call the "3 A's" of survival: stay keenly *aware* of trends in the industries you serve; stay *alert* to all opportunities; and keep your *activity* highly focused.

Following these guidelines, the medical advertising business has remained a solid performer with steady growth expected. This suggests another important option to the new advertising professional: *specialization.* While having strong general skills is important, success stories abound of individuals who honed in on specific industries, such as automotive, travel, or health care, did their homework, and became superstars! That's what makes this business fun. No subject matter or area of interest is off limits, and the welcome sign is always out for hard workers.

So That's What Great Is!

Now let's rewrite that job description we started with to reflect the desperate need in this industry for truly *great* account managers: They must possess excellent communications skills, a proactive attitude, leadership, managerial and motivational skills, a drive for excellence, and a solid background in agency finances.

If you are one of those rare individuals who already possesses three out of five of these qualities and is motivated to acquire the remaining two, then you are well on your way to becoming a *great* account manager.

▼

SANDER A. FLAUM joined Robert A. Becker, Advertising Inc. in August 1988. He previously served as executive vice president and director of marketing at Klemtner Advertising, Division of Saatchi & Saatchi. Prior to entering the advertising business, Sander worked for seventeen years as a senior marketing director with Lederle Laboratories, a division of American Cyanamid Company. During his tenure with this major pharmaceutical manufacturer, he served on the task force to take the ethical vitamin line over-the-counter. He also served as task force chairman to launch the Lederle Generic Products Division. As product group director, Sander was responsible for the introductions of most of the important Lederle ethical and biological products from 1974 through 1982. As an advertising account supervisor, he helped launch Calan SR and Lozol.

Sander is also a member of the editorial advisory board of *Pharmaceutical Executive* and an adjunct professor of marketing at New York University Stern School of Business and at the graduate school of business at Fairleigh Dickinson University. He is the author of four published articles and was a featured speaker at two international marketing symposia—Paris in 1982 and Lugano in 1988. He holds a BA from Ohio State University, an MBA (magna cum laude) from Fairleigh Dickinson University, and attended Columbia University's graduate school of business program in advanced marketing studies.

CHAPTER TEN

Measuring Up to a Career in Media

Frank P. McDonald, President
R. J. Palmer, Inc.

There are three things that we're going to talk about in this chapter: what the Media department does, why working in Media is such an interesting career, and, most important, how to secure an entry-level job in this area. As we discuss these three questions, we will also delineate the interests and aptitudes shared by most media people and suggest how these traits may contribute to career advancement.

Let's begin by refuting two commonly held misconceptions about media people.

Myth #1: A media person is a numbers person working in relative isolation—providing answers only when asked, then retreating into the shadows until called upon again.

Though the media person is familiar with the numbers involving the "pull" of the different media and the cost for space or time, his or her job is a totally integrated part of the advertising and marketing process.

Myth #2: Media buying is strictly a dollars and cents business.

If this were true, those media with the lowest costs would corner all the business. Sometimes the *opposite* is true. The "money aspect" is only one element (along with media strategy and synergy) in the complex marketing mix the Media function must construct.

What's Different About the Media Function?

Media is different from any other function within the agency. The media person's contribution is more tangible, more apparent, than that of his or her colleagues. If you prefer to be a specialist rather than a generalist, find it stimulating to talk to clients about their business, and feel comfortable being regarded as an expert whose viewpoint is largely unquestioned, Media may be the right place for you.

What are media people like? They come from a variety of educational backgrounds: economics, mathematics, psychology, to name just a few. Their experience is more diversified, their perspective less fixed, than those in other areas of the agency. Media persons become collectors of disparate pieces of information. They must be familiar with all aspects of the individual accounts assigned to them and have an intimate understanding of the media used as advertising vehicles for those accounts. The media person must have both an **internal** (the different departments of the agency) and an **external** (from agency to clients) focus.

A media person working in either planning or buying can be confident when discussing the effectiveness of media with producers, writers, and editors. Inevitably, these discussions will focus on how a particular medium can work best for an advertiser.

> The media person, naturally, has to be able to make different media work together to deliver an advertising message with memorable frequency and impact, a process called **media synergy**. Creation of a synergistic environment—correlating the client's message and the media environment—can make the difference between effective communication and no communication at all. The key part of this communication, of course, is contained in the message elements—art or copy. But other factors, such as the right medium, the appropriate vehicle (newspaper, magazine, TV program, etc.) within that medium, and the positioning within that environment, can improve performance. Marketing selections like these are the responsibility of the Media department.

A media person's recommendations on how to improve a medium's delivery—make it more audience effective—will receive a fair hearing. These suggestions can range from graphic elements, such as photography or design, to shifts in television programming, even subjects for a mini-series.

What Media Departments Do

Media departments are responsible for two principal functions—planning and buying.

Media Planning

Media planners must possess broad knowledge of all areas of media, a basic understanding of the entire marketing process, and a detailed awareness of each client's marketing position (especially where they stand vis-a-vis competitors). The planner, working with the client and members of the agency account group, plays a key role in formulating the overall marketing and advertising strategies for each client.

The planning process starts with the establishment of media objectives and strategies, proceeds through research to validate the recommended plans and culminates in the construction of a fully-orchestrated media plan.

Once the client approves the plan, the planner places the order for all print media buys, negotiating with magazines, newspapers, and out-of-home media for the best prices and positioning.

The planner is responsible for issuing purchase requests to national and local broadcast buyers, including the amount of advertising **("weight levels")** and timing requirements of the broadcast portions of the media plan.

Though there are exceptions to this, the planner often is responsible for keeping track of budgetary expenditures. The planner regulates expenditures, checking bills to ensure charges are legitimate and that the media budget is not exceeded.

After the buy, the planner files the "post-buy analysis"—a report that includes data ranging from documentation that the advertising actually ran to estimates of audience size.

Media Buying

The second major job responsibility within an agency Media department is that of **media negotiator** (or **buyer**), who purchases time or space, the basic advertising commodities. Most of this activity is now concentrated in the purchase of the electronic media—radio/TV/cable—so at some agencies, the term media buyer has been changed to **broadcast negotiator.**

The media negotiator, like the media planner, works within an area of constant change. The number of commercial messages continues to increase. The time units for these messages come in ever-differing sizes. The buyer has to know the market, the potential for clutter or saturation, and the time units that will work best for his client.

The negotiator has to know whether the market condition is *soft*—so he can bide his time—or *tight*—a condition that might persuade him to buy now. A wise buyer negotiates for the long term, realizing that extracting the last pound of flesh may not be the wisest course when a medium is slipping and its pricing structure soft. He or she will, of course, seek the best price/value relationship but may not try to squeeze out the last penny, fearing a backlash in future negotiations. After all, what goes around comes around—the seller will remember such hardnose policies when the market turns around and *he* is in a position of strength.

The negotiator's judgment of these factors determines the tactical strategy for the ensuing campaign. Other factors such as advertiser positioning (placement on a particular program) or sponsor identifications become at least as important as those of cost.

Like his or her planning counterpart, the media negotiator must possess a general familiarity with all media in order to excel in practicing this specific discipline. The negotiator must be especially sensitive to the marketplace conditions (prices) for each medium he or she appraises as a purchase possibility. Media costs are substantial, and the negotiator has to be versed in all the elements to do the best for his or her client.

The influence of supply and demand on price is a key factor in obtaining the optimum cost/value ratio for dollars invested. When negotiating the media buy, the negotiator isolates the appropriate audience for the advertiser's product. Such demographic parameters as age, sex, income, are vital considerations. Ratings of the particular broadcast vehicle are forecast, and the resulting purchase equation aims to obtain the lowest price for the best positioning within the selected program. Often, the negotiator presses for performance or rating guarantees that insure his client against underdelivery, with provisions for additional commercial announcements or a cash rebate if a station or network doesn't achieve standards agreed upon in advance.

ADVICE FROM THE PRO'S

Buyers must be particularly sensitive to programming opportunities. This means the negotiator must have specific knowledge concerning current competitive data on both a local and national level—what programs are being cancelled, shifted, or added to a schedule. An alert negotiator can apply this information to link the advertising message to the program on a buy-to-buy basis, resulting in a more pertinent, and perhaps more effective delivery of an advertising message.

The basic purchase ingredient of any media buy is not "the audience," but "your client's audience." In order to find this specific ingredient, the negotiator must establish key guidelines.

The media forecast must be accurate. Negotiated price, no matter how favorable, becomes largely academic, and essentially inefficient, if the medium performs below anticipated audience levels. While overestimating performance is a major problem, it is also a serious concern if performance appreciably exceeds estimated levels. In that case, funds that might have been directed to some other activities remain tied up purchasing media weight beyond levels that were necessary.

Media Department Responsibilities

The primary responsibility of an agency's Media department is to place the clients' advertising messages in the most effective and efficient manner.

Before any advertising can be placed, the media person should know answers to the following questions:

- Who are the client's competitors?
- When and where is the product or service used?
- Which audience(s) does the client want to reach?
- Who purchases the product or uses the service?
- Where do these prospects live?
- What are their interests?
- What publications do they read?
- What TV shows do they watch?
- What is the best combination of media to reach them—television and magazines, radio and billboards, etc.?

The agency's goal is to put together the most efficient package within the media budget, one that takes into consideration the answers to all of these questions. The media specialist must rely on his or her own knowledge of available media resources to put together such a plan.

Using Available Research Tools

The **Simmons Market Research Bureau (SMRB)** and **Mediamark Research Inc. (MRI)**—the two major suppliers of syndicated research—measure the demographics of magazine readers and supply secondary data on radio, newspapers, and television and information on product usage and consumption. Using a national projectable sample of 20,000 adults, they extract detailed demographic, media, and marketing information. All of the data is coded and can be cross tabulated to suit a subscriber's needs.

Nielsen, and **Arbitron** produce a wealth of statistics about broadcast media and their audiences, providing a valuable resource for planners. Standard Rate and Data Service (SRDS) volumes supply information about print and broadcast media, including advertising prices and unit availability.

Two widely used systems with specialized approaches to identifying target audiences and their preferences are **PRIZM** and **Cluster Plus** (geodemographic systems).

Essentially, these research tools provide the answers to the questions posed earlier. Once the media specialist can construct a demographic "snapshot" of the target audience and figure out how it can be reached, various media can be selected and combined to reach as much of that audience as efficiently as possible.

There is no such thing as a 100% "right" media plan. Some approaches work; others don't. Research can only serve as a guideline for what is essentially a commonsense process. The media planner must be familiar with the reach and cost efficiency of a broad range of media in order to implement a plan appropriate to each client's needs. While the available research tools are helpful, the work of the media planner is still more art than science.

Media's Relation to Other Agency Departments

Media department staffers use the capabilities of the other agency departments to their advantage; such interaction makes the media specialist's job easier. However, budgetary and technological restraints continue to apply—the most dramatic way of communicating a client's sales message might not be economically sensible or technically feasible. Media must deal on a daily basis with three other key agency departments:

Research Department

Media looks to Research for analyses of demographic data and for specially-conducted research. **Focus groups**—carefully-moderated discussions with consumers about a client's product or product category—are one form of such customized research. Media specialists must familiarize themselves with the techniques used to gather the data—the shortcomings as well as advantages of each—so they can make cogent recommendations to the client.

Creative Department

Media advises **copywriters** and **art directors** of new creative opportunities, such as new print space unit sizes, changes in electronic media, or new advertising vehicles. Not only are media specialists constantly attuned to these developments, but they gauge the impact of these changes on the current media plan. The media special-

---

ADVICE FROM THE PRO'S

Top Media Advertising Categories

Based on ad spending
1. Network TV
2. Spot TV
3. Newspaper
4. Magazine
5. Syndicated TV
6. Cable TV networks
7. National spot radio
8. Network radio
9. Outdoor

Source: *Advertising Age*

ist's recommendation often goes beyond conventional media to such underestimated "sleepers" as in-flight magazines, transit advertisements, direct mail or handbills, and a wide variety of offbeat and unorthodox alternative advertising vehicles, such as sandwich boards, T-shirts, balloons, and skywriting, that *can* sometimes make a measurable difference.

Account Management Department

Account management serves as the "eyes and ears" of the client within the agency. **Account supervisors** are responsible for coordinating the entire advertising effort and providing background to the other departments on such matters as the client's marketing plans and the creative strategies that will be used to implement them.

Media is responsible for ascertaining that the advertising recommended can be implemented and determining available options. For example, skywriting may be a great way to reach large numbers of people with a simple message. But if it's actually to be part of a client's media plan, then the Media department must research detailed weather forecasts for the proposed area at the time of the campaign. If the message gets blown across the sky in a blur, the media budget will have been ineffectively used, and no one will care how good the idea looked on paper.

The Background of an Ideal Media Person

A media person should have good mathematical and analytical skills, though with the increasing use of computers to compile media plans and store data, there is less manual "number crunching" than before. Aspiring media specialists should develop the ability to listen carefully and act on what they have learned. Media is concerned with constantly varying strategies, many different personalities, and ever-changing advertising media opportunities. What might be an effective media plan today may have to be totally reworked tomorrow.

Several academic disciplines provide a good background for a career in Media, including mathematics, psychology, and marketing. But since so much of the work is highly specialized, on-the-job training is necessary no matter how diversified the candidate's educational background.

It is essential to have the ability to work with great attention to detail on projects that may never come to fruition—and not be discouraged. The media person's work can be intense and tedious. The client can switch marketing strategies. Unanticipated fluctuations are bound to occur in the marketplace, forcing the media plan to be recalled and reworked—again. The media staffer accepts these conditions as part of the job. Change is a way of life for media specialists, so people who can adapt quickly to new sets of circumstances are often successful.

The ability to negotiate is another important job requirement. Media negotiators spend a lot of time working to get the best price for their clients. In order to negotiate effectively, intimate knowledge of the various advertising options is imperative. The media negotiator needs to be constantly aware of supply and demand. Both the client and his competitors will be trying to buy advertising time or space in the furthest-reaching, least-expensive media. Demand for effective media, as determined by research, has a significant effect on price.

Media specialists preview upcoming network television schedules and predict which series will succeed, which will fail. While research can provide indications on each program's expected audience demographics, trying to anticipate which new shows are going to be successful and, therefore, a good use of the client's media budget, is still a tricky business. In developing a media plan or completing a negotiation, judgment and intuition are as important as statistical data.

Early on in their careers, media people often assume large amounts of responsibility. When a media planner makes a recommendation, or a buyer executes that plan, a lot of the clients money is involved. It is not unusual for junior media people to be involved in the making of multimillion dollar media decisions. They must be able to fulfill their responsibilities from the outset of their careers.

Making the Most of Your Job Interview

You must be well prepared *before* you set foot inside any advertising agency. Thoroughly research your target agency. Be familiar with the accounts. Look up these accounts' competitors and find out what their advertising agencies are doing. Media rests on the principle of competition—picking effective and efficient advertising vehicles that make your client's advertising work harder at less expense than that of his competitors. It follows that any conversation about what the agency is doing must include an analysis of the competition. How much each client is spending is not usually public knowledge, but a study of the advertising will give you an "amateur's" opinion of its effectiveness.

Before the interview, take some time to really look at the advertising you see on television, in magazines and newspapers, and hear on the radio. The goal of the interview is not to critique this advertising, but to be able to discuss it in general terms, especially in terms of the way it relates to media. A rudimentary knowledge of Nielsen ratings and other demographic techniques would help this discussion.

Agency media people are not professional interviewers, so if the discussion lags, be the sustainer—don't rely on the interviewer to keep the conversation going. Don't be afraid to be wrong. The interviewer may know a fact that disproves your point, but your opinion will provide the beginnings of a meaningful conversation about media. That's what you are there for!

One way to take charge of the interview and show sincere interest in media is to pick several topics and be able to address them in an informed and intelligent manner. These topics may be general—the relative merits of television vs. print advertising—or more specific—split :30 commercials (two 15-second sales messages for two different products in a single, 30-second "pod").

There are few rigid career paths in Media people grow into their positions. So demonstrate a curiosity about the buying process and the specific projects the agency's Media department are working on right from the start.

Once You've Landed a Media Job

After you've landed your first job, can you advance? The answer is "yes"—and in almost any direction. Whether in the planning or buying areas, the ability to make decisions lies at the heart of Media. Though the plan is presented to the client as the agency's recommendation, each member of the Media department must pull a considerable amount of weight in developing and executing that plan.

There are formal training programs available in Media but the real training is on the job. How fast you move up has much to do with your own ability. As a rule of thumb, however, expect to be a trainee for six months to a year after you are hired. After two years in the field, expect to be promoted to media planner. Standards differ widely from agency to agency, so these guidelines are certainly not written in stone.

Whatever agency you choose, whatever their training program, you'll find a career in Media to be exciting, stimulating and rewarding. That's what it is for the thousands of media professionals whose footsteps you'll be tracing.

▼

FRANK P. MCDONALD was elected a senior vice president and named executive media director of N.W. Ayer in 1987, when the nation's oldest advertising agency merged with Cunningham & Walsh. He joined C&W in 1963 as a media buyer. He progressed through the Media Department and was made a vice president/associate media director in 1967. He also served as director of TV programming. He was promoted to director of media services in 1971 and elected a senior vice president in 1972, and in February, 1974, elected to the board of directors. He left N. W. Ayer soon after the merger to accept his current position.

Before joining C&W, Mr. McDonald was responsible for the media planning and buying of all media on the Bristol Myers account at Doherty, Clifford, Steers & Shenfield, Inc. He began his advertising career at Dancer-Fitzgerald-Sample, after receiving his BA degree in 1960 from St. John's University. He is an active member of a number of industry trade associations, especially the various 4A's councils and committees involved with media.

CHAPTER ELEVEN

A Career in Outdoor Advertising Sales: The Billion Dollar Industry You May Have Overlooked!

Robert J. Smith, President
General Outdoor Advertising

This might come as a bit of a shock after 16 years or more of going to school, cramming for exams, and highlighting countless textbooks, but the long-term value of any education—especially college—is not the pure information you glean from books or lectures. Rather, it's the process of learning how to successfully deal and communicate with people.

Don't get me wrong—college courses and curriculum are important. There are some practical courses that can prepare you for positions in sales, accounting, finance, and other specializations. And in terms of preparing for a career in advertising, courses such as journalism, speech, psychology, and sociology (in addition to specific advertising courses) are important. But all of these courses are not "job- or career-specific"—they will help prepare you for most any endeavor. When it comes right down to it, your ability to understand people and communicate with them effectively is the key to success.

Advertising is the business of delivering a message, of communicating, of *persuading*. There are many types of "senders" or "deliverers" of such messages—television (including cable), radio, newspaper, outdoor and direct mail are the primary forms.

The Five Thousand Year-Old Billboard

Outdoor advertising is the oldest form of these messengers, and it's probably the most universally misunderstood and misused. To a great extent, that's probably why it's such an interesting field to be involved in—the business is growing, constantly changing, always challenging.

According to the *Encyclopedia Americana*, "In a sense, advertising began around 3200 B.C. when the Egyptians stenciled inscriptions of the names of kings on the temples being built." Considering that television, radio, newspaper, and direct mail weren't even contemplated then, it can be logically argued that this really marked the beginning of the concept of outdoor advertising.

It was some time before outdoor graduated from these humble beginnings—late in the 19th century, companies began leasing out space on wooden boards for advertising messages or "bills." Hence the term "billboards." Since then, it's grown and evolved not only as an art form, but into a media force.

Today, there are two basic categories of outdoor advertising—**printed or painted bulletins** and **poster panels.** Bulletins are usually 14 x 48 feet, big enough to be visible from relatively far away; these are the billboards you see along expressways and major traffic arteries.

Poster panels are visible along primary and secondary arteries and come in two basic sizes: 12 x 25 feet (a "30-sheet" in industry parlance) or 6 x 12 feet (an "8-sheet").

All three forms—the bulletin, 12 x 25 poster panel and 6 x 12 poster panel—have their place and value in the advertising field and provide alternatives for media placement based on marketing strategy.

Outdoor is probably the purest form of advertising because it's totally involuntary—people don't jump in their cars and drive off to gaze at billboards; you just see them as you drive by. You do, however, turn on a radio to listen to music or the news and, in the process, hear radio advertisements. You turn on the TV and see and hear the commercials. You pick up a newspaper and can't help seeing the ads as you thumb through it.

Outdoor's ability to deliver a strong, brief message at a low cost (relative to the other major media) has caused the industry to grow to close to a billion dollars in sales. The prospects for future growth are excellent—advertisers are always trying to get more "bang for the buck." Obviously, a growing industry offers excellent opportunities for entry-level people.

Best Color Combinations Used in Outdoor Advertising Letter Displays

Based on legibility from a distance
1. Black on yellow
2. Black on white
3. Yellow on black
4. White on black
5. Yellow on blue
6. Green on white
7. Blue on yellow
8. White on green
9. White on brown
10. Brown on yellow

Source: *The Sign User's Guide*

Entry-Level Opportunities

A sales position in the outdoor advertising field requires a person to make face-to-face contact with professionals on many different levels of authority and responsibility.

On the advertising agency side, you may be calling on the media planner, media buyer, account executive, production director, art or creative director, media director, even the president or general manager of the agency. On the client side, you may be dealing with the secretary who can "get you in the door" to see the advertising manager, the director of marketing or president of the company, or anyone in between. Dealing with such a variety of responsible professionals requires an educated, disciplined, creative, persistent, and energetic person. It also means the sales position is constantly changing and ever-challenging.

Though good written and telephone skills are also necessary, face-to-face contact with the decision maker is critical—you must be able to tell your story, both see and hear the response and, most importantly, be a good listener. While direct marketing has it's place and prudent use of both telephone and direct mail contact is all part of the selling process, there still is no substitute for *face-to-face contact.*

The Personality Traits You Need

I personally do not look for a particular "type" when interviewing people for sales positions, though others in my capacity may and do. It's a matter of philosophy—I believe that a successful sales team is one composed of a number of different personalities with different viewpoints who can, despite their differences, work together toward a common goal. Such a diverse group enables me to match the personalities of particular salespeople to those of my clients—some clients are receptive to a friendly extrovert; others prefer a more serious-type who takes a systematic approach. Matching personalities is crucial.

There are, however, basic *traits* I look for, those I feel are key to any candidate becoming not just a successful salesperson, but someone who can eventually move higher in the organization:

1. Honesty
2. Integrity
3. Perseverance
4. Grit
5. Assertiveness
6. Aggressiveness
7. Ability to communicate
8. Need for self esteem
9. Pride in performance
10. Respect and caring for people
11. Loyalty

Not the entire Boy Scout Code, but close!

What You'll Learn

It's easy to get a job in sales and frankly, I think it's easy to *keep* a job in sales if you work at it. Just remember: **There's no such thing as a "born salesperson."** There are however, people who become more successful than others because they possess or develop those traits listed above. There are successful salespeople who lack some of these traits; nevertheless, I believe the more of these you possess, the greater your own chances of success.

While it is important you get proper schooling, the *basis for success* in the outdoor advertising business—in fact, in *all business*—is a willingness to learn, make mistakes, work hard, and be good at what you do.

In addition to a salesperson having a working knowledge of other facets of the business (operations, accounting, etc.), he or she must develop a working knowledge of other media. So you will be trained not only in basic sales techniques applicable to any sales (such as needs/benefits selling), but also "schooled" in the strengths and weaknesses of other media and how they are bought and sold. Therefore, it helps to be creative and imaginative—a critical consideration in outdoor advertising is the creative execution (or design). This does not mean you need to be an artist—you just need to have vision.

I truly believe that a person who is successful in outdoor sales can be successful in *any* form of advertising sales. Because of the divergent nature of the outdoor business, a salesperson is exposed to so many different circumstances and individuals that he or she becomes well prepared to take the next step. I must warn you though: It's easy to get "hooked" on the business, because it's fun, challenging, ever-changing, rewarding, and certainly far from monotonous.

Top 10 Billboards in the United States

Ranked by daily effective circulation
1. Chicago, IL, Kennedy Expressway north of Armitage
2. Los Angeles, CA, Long Beach Freeway at the Santa Ana Freeway
3. Detroit, MI, Chrysler Freeway and Ford Freeway interchange
4. Boston, MA, Central Artery south of Hanover Street
5. San Diego, CA, I-8 at Fairmount
6. New York, NY, Cross-Bronx Expressway
7. Houston, TX, West Loop south of 18th Street
8. Atlanta, GA, I-75 at West Paces Ferry Road
9. Philadelphia, PA, Delaware Expressway at Devereaux
10. Washington, DC, Route 355 south of Gude Drive, Rockville, MD

Source: *Mediaweek*

And What You'll Earn

Compensation plans range from straight commission with no benefits to straight salary with full benefits. Most companies offer a base salary plus commission or bonus for special performance and provide benefits, although the movement in the industry is more toward straight commission sales.

A college graduate with no prior sales or work experience typically will earn $10,000—$20,000 in his or her first full year of employment. Keeping the variety of potential compensation plans in mind, it's still reasonable to say that eventually a person can earn as much as he or she is capable of earning. It is not uncommon for a good salesperson to earn $30,000—$60,000 in just a few years. And if you are really good, you can earn more.

A challenging and rewarding opportunity awaits you in the advertising business, and a special opportunity awaits you in the outdoor advertising business. Join us!

General Outdoor Advertising is a privately owned company based in Gainesville, Georgia. In his present position, **ROBERT J. SMITH** is president and chief operating officer. Prior to this, Mr. Smith was president of Gateway Outdoor Advertising, the largest company of its kind in the outdoor advertising industry. He was previously general manager of Gateway's Chicago office and regional vice president.

A marketing and management graduate of West Virginia University, Mr. Smith successfully operated three different sales territories for Wheeling Corrugating Company and Wheeling-Pittsburgh Steel Company for eight years. In 1978, he switched to advertising sales and quickly became the top performer at Pittsburgh Outdoor Advertising and, subsequently, Foster & Kleiser Outdoor Advertising.

CHAPTER TWELVE

The Not-So-Invisible Promotional Products Industry

Cate Brennan Lisak
Manager of External Communications
Specialty Advertising Association International

The promotional products industry combines advertising and marketing principles with the use of imprinted promotional products. Whether the products are called specialty advertising, premiums, business gifts, or incentives, the one common thread is that a program must include a promotional item, which is often imprinted with the client's name or message and is distributed to a target audience.

There are two primary categories in the promotional products industry: suppliers and distributors. The estimated 2,500 suppliers manufacture, imprint, and sell everything from plastic keytags to trendy pens and T-shirts to leather-bound daily calendars and brass desk items. Suppliers sell, usually nationally, to an independent distributor network. Although there are 15,000 types of products, suppliers generally specialize in a particular product type, like calendars/paper or plastic or fabric products.

Distributors sell more than $5 billion annually in promotional products and programs to end-user clients. Distributors are independent businesspeople who represent on average, 50 suppliers, though they have access to almost all suppliers.

On either side of the sales equation, a college degree is preferred but is not essential. For those with a college degree, an advertising or marketing emphasis is a "double plus." Courses particularly helpful include sales, promotion, advertising, direct marketing, and other marketing and management disciplines.

Both industry segments emphasize a strong work ethic, the ability to work intelligently, a creative approach to problem solving and, most of all, the ability to be a self-starter.

Other than sales and marketing, both suppliers and distributors have career paths in customer service accounting and other administrative functions, plant operations and production, and some engineering.

Sales and marketing people frequently begin their career with a local distributor and then move into supplier sales. Talents refined in the promotional products industry can be transferred to other sales and marketing positions, particularly business-to-business products or services.

Selling philosophy and company (and product line) positioning varies greatly within the promotional products industry. While some distributors and suppliers concentrate on selling products, many others sell solutions to problems. It just so happens that in this industry, those solutions happen to be in the form of a product. For the most part, this chapter will concentrate on the latter, intangible selling approach.

The Distributor Network

Distributors are independent businesspeople who work with the end-user client in developing a promotional program and finding the right product. End-user clients are everyone from large computer companies introducing a new product, ad agencies that want an integrated marketing approach to a campaign, or a local retail store that wants to announce its grand opening.

There are more than 10,000 distributor firms in the United States, most of which are small family-owned companies employing two to five salespeople. These firms tend to have a local or limited regional territory or, less frequently, industry specialization, like health care or travel. Some distributors specialize in a type of promotional program, like safety issues and awareness, recognition programs, or incentive campaigns. Recent years, however, have seen the growth of firms with dozens (sometimes hundreds) of salespeople that operate in many states.

Distributors often use independent contractors instead of employee salespeople. These independent salespeople usually place orders through a specific distributor, but are free to use other distributors. These contractors generally are responsible for purchasing their own sales tools—catalogs and sample kits—and commissions tend to be slightly higher than for employee salespeople.

Distributor salespeople often operate like small ad agencies; they are account executive, copywriter, rough layout artist, and marketing strategist rolled into one. The primary distributor selling (and training) tools are supplier catalogs. The typical sales job title would be account executive, sales coordinator, or "counselor."

Many distributors don't hire recent college graduates until they have a few sales jobs under their belts. But those with sales experience will enter the typical world of sales: cold calling and building their clientele and repeat-order base to increase monthly commissions. Frequently, a promotion to sales manager depends on whether the distributor-owner performs that function.

Income is based on individual ambition, as in any commission sales job. On average, distributors pay 40 to 50 percent commission on products sold. In 1990, the dollar amount of the average order was $400-$499 in 16 percent of orders; $500-$699 in 21 percent; and $700-$999 in 19 percent. Few salespeople are on salary or a combination of salary and commission. In 1990, a minority of distributors charged fees for creative services, though this is changing as end-users look for one-stop distributors.

Top Business Gifts

Based on survey respondents selecting each item
1. Food gifts, with 30%
2. Clocks/watches, 22%
3. Pens/pencils, 20%
4. Calendars/diaries/desk planners, 19%
5. Apparel/caps, 11%
6. Desk sets, 9%
6. Electronic items, 9%
6. Glassware/crystal, 9%
9. Coffee mugs, 8%
9. Wine/liquor, 8%

Source: *Incentive*

The Supplier Side

As with distributor firms, supplier companies run the gamut from small family-owned operations to large international companies (like Rand McNally and Lenox China and Crystal) with retail and special market divisions. Promotional products usually fall under the special markets divisions.

Similar to the distributor side, some suppliers concentrate on selling products while others sell solutions to problems (that happen to be in the form of their products). But whether selling products or solutions to problems, a thorough knowledge of the product line, imprinting methods, and limitations is of the utmost importance.

Most suppliers don't hire recent college graduates unless they have had prior business-to-business selling experience. In fact, one California supplier recommends that salespeople begin their career with a distributor.

In larger supplier companies, outside salespeople usually begin as sales trainees, progress to sales associate or account executive, and then are promoted to regional sales manager (in charge of one or more states depending on population density) for a number of years. Depending on productivity, top salespeople can progress to national sales manager and then to vice president of sales.

In the promotional products industry, inside sales representatives are referred to as customer service representatives. Some telephone sales are done, but customer service reps are primarily order takers. Smaller suppliers without an outside sales force depend more heavily on their inside people to produce additional sales. Suppliers promote customers service reps to outside sales, when appropriate.

Instead of a national sales force, many suppliers employ independent sales representatives, who show and represent numerous noncompeting lines in multistate territories. Sales reps call on distributors in their territory to try to ensure that they are on the "short list" of suppliers most frequently used.

> While most small distributors don't have a formal training program, many offer on-the-job training, industry audiovisual resources, attendance at national or regional association "education days," traveling supplier shows, meetings with supplier representatives, and studying supplier catalogs.

Training outside salespeople can take three to 12 months, with the majority of the time spent in the customer service department. Learning every facet of the myriad of products, complex imprinting methods, shipping methods, and graphic artwork needs is crucial to the success of outside salespeople. Other types of training that may be incorporated are: working with established salespeople and seeing how they present the line; working at national and regional trade shows; and Specialty Advertising Association International resources.

While a college degree is common among salespeople, it isn't absolutely necessary. Instead, business-to-business sales experience almost always is required by suppliers hiring an outside salesperson. But for those with a college degree, an interdisciplinary marketing degree gives salespeople the background to not sell the products, but to sell solutions, says one supplier.

Many suppliers seek salespeople who can present their product line as the solution to a variety of marketing, safety, or incentive problems. Many suppliers seek salespeople who have an understanding of the intangible aspect of promotional programs. This means developing knowledge of the product and appropriate case histories on how the product solved a problem.

Suppliers almost universally agree that an outside salesperson or independent sales rep should: 1) be a self-starter who is outgoing and personable; 2) present a professional image; and 3) be creative and competitive.

Most outside sales people are on salary plus a performance bonus, which can be quarterly, semiannual, or annual. Salary range varies greatly and can't be generalized.

The promotional products industry is unique in advertising and marketing. Those leaving this industry will find the most similarities in representing products used in the premium industry, which often are the same products sold on a mass quantity scale. However, one supplier said that if a person is successful in selling intangible solutions to problems—as in the promotional products industry—then they can easily sell the tangible products in any other industry.

▼

CATE BRENNAN LISAK is manager of external communications for Specialty Advertising Association International. Based in Irving, Texas, SAA International represents more than 5,000 firms that manufacture and distribute promotional products. These firms have sales of more than $5 billion annually. Lisak manages public relations, advertising, and direct marketing programs for the Association. She also directs a speakers bureau program, from which volunteer ambassadors speak to more than 300 student and professional groups annually about the promotional products industry. She has professional experience in newspaper and magazine journalism and general business. She holds a bachelor's degree in journalism from the University of North Texas.

C H A P T E R   T H I R T E E N

Sales Promotion: America's Game

Chris Sutherland, Executive Director
Promotion Marketing Association of America, Inc.

QUESTION: What do basketball, Lee Iacocca, and the sales promotion industry have in common?

ANSWER: Despite their distant roots, each is dynamic, very successful and, most of all, uniquely American. The difference is that while Iacocca and basketball do not offer open-door employment opportunities (unless you can sell Chrysler junk bonds or scrape your head on the ceiling with your feet flat on the floor, respectively), sales promotion is booming with opportunity.

The Surprising Dominance of Sales Promotion

The facts speak for themselves: For every dollar spent on advertising by American consumer product companies, more than *two* dollars is spent on sales promotion. Sales promotion expenditures—over $130 billion—represent the largest single portion of the American marketing budget.

One reason for this surprising dominance lies in the proven ability of sales promotion to motivate purchase. Unlike advertising, which is image-based, sales promotion approaches consumers in ways that have an immediate and measurable impact on their decision to purchase. Advertising suggests...promotion motivates.

Sales promotion exists because consumers have a choice, because price is not the only consideration, and because most major consumer goods are marketed on a national basis. Our system of open competition creates a never-ending need on the part of these manufacturers to get and maintain an edge, and sales promotion is the most powerful single force in this endeavor. While advertising—*aka* "propaganda"—exists in virtually every modern economic environment, sales promotion can only exist in a free enterprise system. In America, consumers celebrate their choice of products, as the seemingly endless flow of product introductions and failures attest.

Perceived quality and brand loyalty are important, but consumers have overwhelmingly demonstrated that they want to be wooed. In supermarkets, for example, studies have shown that fully three out of four purchase decisions are made *after* consumers enter the store! Savvy marketers know that sales promotion is their most effective weapon in the "battle" of the open marketplace.

Putting Promotion into Perspective

So what is a consumer promotion? It is simply a consumer product or service that is combined with a special offer to motivate immediate or continued purchase. To be considered successful, its effect—the amount of "incremental sales" (those over and above the expected norm during a given period) that can be attributed to a specific promotion—must be measurable and its impact significant.

> This newfound recognition of the power of sales promotion has also led to new challenges and opportunities. The need to manage the business of promotion marketing has created opportunities on the corporate side (to manage, track, evaluate, and even create promotions), on the agency side (to create, execute, measure, and analyze), and on the supplier side (everything from "low-tech" fulfillment and point-of purchase services to "high-tech" scanner data and analysis). Even advertising agencies have reluctantly accepted the reality (and overwhelming importance) of promotion marketing by buying or creating their own sales promotion agencies or departments.

Sales promotion creates that "edge" through several recognizable vehicles:

Price Off

This seemingly mundane practice—a temporary reduction in the price of a product or group of products—actually has many applications, depending on the promotion goals:

- **"Sales Price"**—the standard deduction of the regular price, usually communicated through advertising, on the package, or at or near where the product is purchased (known in the trade as "point-of-purchase," e.g., an end aisle display in a supermarket).

- **Modified "Sales Price"**—which usually ties the purchase of several products together to create a sale price. For example, instead of simply saying "25% off any tire purchase," tire dealers might try to encourage multiple purchases by saying "Buy Three, Get One Free." The price off commitment is the same, but a different, more-focused marketing goal is served.

- **Couponing**—Usually delivered through the mail, magazines, or newspapers (e.g. via free-standing inserts—"FSIs"—those glossy inserts that always seem to be the first things that fall out of your Sunday newspaper), coupons are the most common sales promotion tool. They are conceptually identical to a sale price, except that they require a redemption process through the retailer (usually serviced by **fulfillment houses**).

A variation on this theme are *cash rebate programs*, where the consumer must send in product proof-of-purchase (again, administered through a fulfillment house) to receive a rebate check. Because these offers usually involve either multiple purchases or expensive items (e.g., power tools), rebates are generally worth more to the consumer than coupons.

Value Added

As opposed to a price reduction, *"value added"* promotions offer consumers an extra incentive to motivate purchase, one usually not directly related to the product. These promotions may or may not also contain price reductions:

- **Sweepstakes**—possibly the easiest-understood promotion, sweepstakes are simply chance drawings from entries sent in to (guess what?) a fulfillment house, for generally impressive grand prizes of cash, merchandise, or travel.

- **Contests**—essentially sweepstakes, except that the contest requires some level of skill and usually is more complicated. Marketers try to involve consumers quickly through contest devices like "Instant Win" and "Match & Win" formats. Sometimes contests can have secondary benefits, like public relations (e.g., themed essay contests), or cross trial (e.g., "winning" game cards that offer a free coupon for a new product line).

- **Free With Proof-Of-Purchase Offers**—offering a free gift as an incentive to purchase. If a single purchase is all that is required, the gift is usually attached to the packaging in some way. Gifts requiring multiple purchases are usually "fulfilled" like other forms of promotion.

- **"Self Liquidators"**—this intriguing term simply refers to promotions that require a cash outlay on the consumer's part in addition to proofs-of-purchase. Because of this shared responsibility, self-liquidated items are usually more expensive than free gifts. This shared cost is also an attractive consideration to the marketer, because cost liabilities don't become a factor until the item is actually ordered (unless pre-purchase is necessary), hence the term "self liquidator".

There are literally hundreds of variations and combinations of these basic elements, and applications only begin with consumer products. Entries into PMAA's Reggie Awards, symbolic of excellence in promotion marketing, have come from the fields of computers, financial services, airlines, auto parts, even building materials.

In other words, over $100 billion worth of creativity, analysis, management, fulfillment, production, etc. spent by companies that need bright people...people like you!

Finding Your Own Niche in Sales Promotion

Where do you find your start in sales promotion? For starters, there are thousands of consumer products, hundreds of companies that market them, hundreds of agencies that service the companies. Wherever you live or want to work, the opportunities are all around you.

Better still, practically every student starts out equal! That's because there's no M.B.A. in Sales Promotion, no B.A. in Sales Promotion...no degree of any kind in sales promotion. A few universities like Northwestern, Texas, and Syracuse offer courses, but marketing's most important new discipline still waits for its first academic department.

ADVICE FROM THE PRO'S

Opportunities in Corporate Promotion Departments

In the meantime, the college system's loss can be your gain. Just ask Forest Harwood, former Manager of Sales Promotion for Frito-Lay and Chairman Emeritus of the Promotion Marketing Association of America: "Promotion is the 'fun' part of the marketing mix," explains Harwood. "It's a career where your creative abilities can really shine."

But like many corporate promotion executives, Harwood (president of Harwood Marketing Group) looks for a solid business management background along with versatility in entry-level people: "Be prepared to juggle a variety of project aspects at one time. Also, remember: They all have to land together. That takes a lot of careful management, advanced planning and flexible perspective. You need to have a 'think fast, think clear, think-on-your-feet' approach to solutions."

Entry-level corporate salaries in promotion departments are about equal to other marketing department positions. Depending on the company, the part of the country, and your qualifications, starting salaries can range from about $22,000 to $45,000 per year.

At the top end, new ground gets broken literally every day. At this writing, General Mills was reportedly offering an estimated package of $250,000 for their newly created vice president of promotion position.

Opportunities in Marketing Services Agencies

Where corporate promotion departments can provide relative security and control, marketing services agencies typically offer more excitement, more anxiety, and more reward. Under the direction and supervision of corporate promotion managers, sales promotion and related agencies design, create, produce, execute, fulfill, and measure the kinds of promotion programs mentioned earlier.

Entry-level people in these agencies typically work with the "nuts and bolts" of sales promotion. Don Roux, President of Roux Marketing Services, looks for people who can be both creative and detailed at the same time: "Client confidence and respect is our main goal, and even our entry-level account coordinators are key to this effort."

But Roux feels that being this close to the action requires a special kind of person: "The **account coordinator** position is at the center of a fast-paced, high-pressure environment, requiring an energetic, anxious to learn, personable individual."

Starting salaries may seem low at between $18,000 and $25,000, but commission and profit sharing can often supplement the base salary. More importantly, advancement can be rapid, because it is often closely tied to your personal performance.

In fact, Roux specifically looks for candidates with advancement potential: "In five years, you should be at the account executive level, where average earnings are $58,000 plus. After ten years, good account executives can be in the six figure area."

Like Harwood, Roux looks for people with solid marketing credentials, although he will also consider communication and finance majors. But bottom line is again often a matter of client perception, according to Roux, and everyone shares in that responsibility: "I look for people who can talk well on their feet, have the ability to see the big picture, and to converse both 'knee-to-knee' and by telephone."

As Executive Director of the PMAA, a former vice president of a sales promotion firm, and a manager at Pepsi-Cola USA, I have witnessed the growth of promotion marketing firsthand. Simply put, sales promotion in the 1980s is to marketing what computers are to information management.

Even if you're not the next Lee Iacocca or Larry Bird, there's still plenty of room for you at Chrysler or in the NBA. Because people have the choice to buy their products, and because Lee and Larry alone aren't always enough incentive, each uses promotion marketing extensively.

That is truly "America's Game!"

▼

CHRIS SUTHERLAND assumed his current position in September, 1987. Previously, he was vice president at Marketing Equities International, a firm specializing in tie-in promotions, where he worked with Sony, Nabisco, and Coca-Cola. He also headed up Sports Concepts, his own sports marketing consultancy.

From 1982 to 1985, he managed the national sports programs for Pepsi-Cola USA. In the public sector, he was responsible for managing all corporate-sponsored sports programs for Los Angeles (CA) County.

A graduate of California State University at Los Angeles, he and his wife, Arlene, reside in Ossining, NY. They have two children.

CHAPTER FOURTEEN

Think about a Career in Sales Promotion

**Kerry B. Didday, President/Creative Director
Daymark Inc. Sales Promotion+Marketing**

For over ten years, the money being spent in sales promotion has been increasing over that spent for advertising. Today, more than 65% of all budgets are spent in the area of sales promotion.

The definition used to describe sales promotion by the Council of Sales Promotion Agencies is, "The act of influencing perception and behavior to build market share and sales while reinforcing brand image." The magic word in the definition is **behavior.** Where advertising affects and builds image, sales promotion influences behavior and enhances image.

The current elements of sales promotion are:

CONSUMER	TRADE
Tie-ins	Promotional PR
Couponing	Meetings
Refunds	Incentives
Premiums	Sweepstakes
Promotional packaging	Contests
Sweepstakes	Allowances
Contests	Educational programs
Telemarketing	Teleconferencing
Consulting	Sales training
Event marketing	Audio/Visual
Direct mail	Administration
Licensing	Incentive trips
Fulfillment	Product training
Production	Database management

The function of a sales promotion agency is to research, plan, create, and execute complete promotional programs from initial strategy formation through postproduction analysis. The typical services performed by a full-service sales promotion agency include the following:

- Strategic promotional planning
- Promotion pre-testing and analysis
- Tactical and concept development
- Complete creative execution
- Promotional media support
- Promotional materials production
- In-field merchandising and event support
- Post-promotion evaluation

The strategic function of a sales promotion agency, acting in partnership with the client, is to orchestrate the most effective use of the promotion elements or techniques in order to build sales and market share in the short term, while reinforcing brand image and value/positioning in the long term.

Below is a listing of the primary objectives that sales promotion typically addresses:
- Building brand loyalty
- Extending brand image
- Reinforcing advertising
- Generating product trial
- Building repurchase intentions
- Increasing purchase frequency
- Motivating the sales force
- Increasing product usage
- Increasing traffic
- Increasing transactions
- Building/depleting inventories
- Opening new markets
- Expanding customer bases
- Leveraging features
- Leveraging retail displays

The entry-level position in sales promotion usually comes from three major educational disciplines: marketing, communications/journalism, and graphic design. Your college or university can assist you in planning appropriate course selections in order to obtain your desired degree.

Marketing

The entry-level person works in account management as an assistant to a seasoned account executive servicing existing clients and building new clients for the agency or as a team member in the marketing department involved in strategic planning, pre-program testing, and post-promotion evaluation.

Communications/Journalism

This entry-level person works in the media department in a planning capacity or in the creative department as a junior copywriter reporting to a copy director. This person also assists the marketing department in the development of creative strategies, plans, and proposals.

Graphic Design

This entry-level person is a junior-level designer reporting directly to an art director and working as a member of a creative team involved in copywriting, account service, art production, and the marketing of creative strategy presentations.

Regardless of the area in which you may work, the most important ingredients that you can contribute are creativity and idea generation. In this day and age of competitiveness, it can be wise to accept whatever agency job that is made available to you with the idea of looking for ways to present your creative, business building ideas for the agency.

Advancement within an agency is directly related to the growth of the agency and the acquisition of new accounts. This is made possible by effective strategic thinking, creativity, and idea generation. Everyone within the agency can be expected to contribute to the business building effort. The greater the growth, the more opportunities will become available for the standouts of the agency team.

To build an agency and a place for yourself takes a great deal of hard work, dedication, and at times, long hours. A 40-hour workweek would be unusual; you should expect to put in from 50 to 60 hours each week until you have reached a very high level within the organization. Even then, the top management of the agency will put in many 60-hour work weeks. If you're a nine to five person, don't go into the agency business expecting advancement, large pay raises, and bonuses. You might instead consider the large corporate/client environment.

You can expect your typical day to be hectic, action-packed, and high pressured. From putting out fires for the agency and/or clients to brainstorming in a creative session, you can expect to be asked to perform at your highest level, consistently, day in and day out. Your rewards will be to see your ideas come to life in the media and success for the client, the agency, and you.

Entry-level salaries will vary throughout the country. Given my experience in the Midwest, I would place them in the range of $17,000 to $21,000. You can expect to be in the $30,000 range within 5-7 years. Top salaries can be in the six figures.

Many people in sales promotion have worked both the agency side and the client side of the industry, switching from time-to-time. The agency is more rewarding creatively, but with much more competitiveness and pressure. The client side can give you a sense of security and the stability of working for a large corporation.

Listed below are many third party sources that supply both the agency and clients with materials and services. You may want to consider one of them as a source of employment:

Paper supply houses
Art studios and illustrators
Printers
Color separators and film houses
Photographers
Specialty advertising/incentive sources
Typesetters
Telemarketers
Market research firms
Public relation firms
Film production houses
Audio/visual production houses
Media buying services
And many more...

An entry-level person entering the sales promotion industry should possess the following attributes:

Assertiveness
Accuracy and craftsmanship
Creativity

Idea generation
Presentation skills
A sense of the other disciplines involved
A team player
Ability to accept criticism
Dedication and hard work
Sense of responsibility

When available, intern positions can be a valuable way to get your feet wet in the industry. Remember to show your creativity and ability for idea generation. Your resume is your ad, your first contact with your potential employer, so be creative and generate an idea in your resume that will be remembered. One that will create a behavior in your intended audience—of hiring you... for a long term, rewarding career in sales promotion.

▼

KERRY DIDDAY participated in the Cincinnati Milacron Apprentice Program from 1959 to 1961, with a concentration in engineering design. Upon completion, Didday attended the University of Cincinnati and graduated in 1966 with a BS in advertising design. He worked at Cincinnati Milacron as assistant art director until May, 1971, when he opened his own design studio. In 1974, Didday combined his efforts with a partner to form Didday & Branch Inc. The agency showed a steady growth and development in many diversified areas of the advertising industry and developed programs on a local, regional, and national basis. The agency's growth and development enabled Didday & Branch Inc. to be positioned as a full-service sales promotion and marketing agency. After the retirement of Didday's business partner, the agency was renamed Daymark Inc. Sales Promotion+Marketing.

Didday is a member of the Advertising Club of Cincinnati, American Marketing Association, Art Directors Club of Cincinnati/American Advertising Federation, Business/Professional Advertising Association, Council of Sales Promotion Agencies (CSPA), and the Promotional Marketing Association of America.

CHAPTER FIFTEEN

Advertising in the Motor City

**Jim Dale, Chairman of the Board & Chief Executive Officer
W. B. Doner & Company Advertising**

Our agency's largest office is in Detroit, Michigan, which immediately conjures up a singular impression—the automotive industry. No argument—it's a big part of Detroit's reputation and identity.

Admittedly, Detroit doesn't get very good press, and some of that criticism is justified. But it is a superb and affordable area in which to live, the cultural stimuli are marvelous, and there are excellent school systems and recreational facilities in many parts of Greater Detroit.

Detroit is a city bordered on one side by the Great Lakes and on the other by many inland lakes. If you fly low over Northwest Detroit, you will swear there is more water than land.

With few exceptions, our personnel live within 30 minutes of the agency; about half of them are no more than ten minutes away. It's a convenient place to work.

What Makes Our Agency Unique

In a town so identified with a single industry, there always has been a question whether a Detroit-based agency could prosper and grow *without* an automotive account.

We've done it. Of course, it took many years—over 50-55—which seems a long time to someone young enough to be looking for an entry-level position in the advertising business.

But we are a maverick agency in many ways. Nearly 80 accounts, for example, contribute to our $425,000,000 in billing. Obviously, our average account is not huge according to the standards of a J. Walter Thompson, Saatchi & Saatchi, or Young & Rubicam, but we have variety. Creatives don't get burned out because they're stuck on one account.

We are also unusual in that we have used Detroit and Baltimore as our base, developed our talents, and then "distributed" those talents into other parts of North America and overseas. We are like the old vaudevillians who, rather than changing their acts, perfected them and then changed the *audience* by moving from city to city.

W. B. Doner & Co. presently employs about 530 people, 226 of whom are in the Detroit office, 143 in our Baltimore co-headquarters, and the rest in our seven other offices (located in Boston, Cleveland, Dallas, London, Montreal, St. Petersburg, and Toronto).

Emphasis on Retailers

We like retail accounts—perhaps 40% of our billing represents retail advertising.

How do we define retail? Broadly speaking, a retailer is someone who sells through his or her own outlets, rather than distributing through others. According to that definition, not only is a drugstore, a supermarket, or a hardware store a retailer, but so is a bank, an insurance company and a petroleum company.

In representing clients who qualify under the above definition, we have developed a "next-day" business mentality. Retail advertising is the most *accountable* kind of advertising—the product or service either sells or it doesn't. We often say to our retailers that while we must do investigative research and copy research and tracking research, their ultimate research tool is the cash register. Retailers lovingly embrace this theory.

It's natural to think that an agency with retail clients would spend a great deal of its time and talent figuring out ways to run a sale or lay out circulars replete with exclamatory headlines and sunburst price features. But there is another important difference in our agency—more than 80% of our work for retailers is in broadcast. Except to flesh out a theme we have developed for broadcast, we involve ourselves only rarely with retail print advertising.

Even when we do run a sale—or, more importantly, when we're establishing a conceptual theme for a retailer—we apply the same creative juices and the same zest for the right creative thrust as we do for our consumer product manufacturers or financial service clientele.

There are several aspects to our philosophy of advertising:

1. Simple Ideas Have Great Power

There is a seemingly irresistable force to burden an idea with excess baggage, to serve too many masters; solve too many problems. Most advertising is complex, muddy, unfocused, irrelevant to the viewer, and does little more than remind people of a brand's name.

We practice the art and discipline of the simple idea. We gather all the knowledge we can, in order to steep ourselves in background. Once armed, we go about the process of separating the excess from the essential. We distill the input down to its purest form—the simple idea. The one that can pierce apathy and get action.

2. Likeable Advertising Sells

We have proven over and over again that if people like your advertising, they will like you and your product or store...and people like to buy from people they like.

3. In Order to Do Likeable Advertising that Is Effective, You Must Apply the Head, the Heart, and the Funnybone

Some Job Interview Pointers

Let's assume you have decided to apply for a job at Doner. This means you want to be with an agency where the emphasis is on creativity, where, for the most part, you won't begin by working on mega-sized accounts (we only have a few) and where you can be sure you'll work your butt off.

In preparation for a successful job interview at our company, work your butt off *now*. Sit down and cram as if you were going to take one of the most important exams of your life—because you *are*. Learn about our agency—its clients, its creative product, even the reputation of its research, marketing, and media departments.

Know What You Want to Do

While we are not a huge agency, our departmentalization is quite well-defined, something you'll find true of many medium-sized shops and most large ones. So be sure to decide in advance whether you are best suited for copywriting, art directing, print or broadcast production, marketing, research, account service, media planning, media buying, media research, accounting, etc. Don't expect the interviewer to decide where you'd fit.

On the other hand, once in a great while we do succumb to someone who says, "I think I have the ability and the talent, but I want to learn about this business. If you can start me in the mailroom, in the secretarial pool, or anyplace else where I can absorb the atmosphere and the routine of this agency, I'll take anything you've got until you and my department head decide where I can best serve the agency." (In fact, that is how our creative director got started.)

And Learn about Our Industry Now

As for education, we have no rigid rules, but we favor those graduates with a liberal arts foundation and a marketing or advertising major. There are relatively few schools with a serious advertising program, but those few who do make a great contribution to our industry.

I suggest you subscribe to the advertising trade papers, particularly *Advertising Age* and *Adweek*. Canada's *Marketing Magazine* and London's *Campaign* are also useful and fascinating.

Look at advertising continuously. Don't just thumb through magazines and newspapers—*study* the ads, *compare* the ads. Develop your tastes, both from a sales effec-

---

ADVICE FROM THE PRO'S

Getting Your Start in Advertising

What does all of this mean to someone seeking a career in advertising?

After considering our philosophy and account mix, determine for yourself whether you're at all interested in our kind of agency. While I have outlined a few areas in which we are unusual or maverick, that doesn't mean we are absolutely unique. There are other agencies that subscribe to the same or a similar philosophy, even a number of them right here in Detroit. If you don't want to work for an agency like ours, identify the kind(s) of agency you do want to work for and search them out.

tiveness standpoint and an aesthetic one. They are of equal importance.

Whether you're inclined toward the marketing side or the creative side, think about advertising *ideas*. Try them on your friends. Use people in the advertising business as sounding boards.

Find an Internship

If you have the qualifications, you can get a summer internship with us or with other similar-sized agencies. We are not interested in those who want to make a few bucks and keep themselves occupied for the summer. If you don't intend to go into advertising after graduation, then you're a poor investment for us, in terms of both the money we'd pay and the time and energy we'd expend training you.

If you're both good and determined, get in touch with us—virtually anyone who demonstrates a genuine desire to break into advertising can get an interview.

▼

JIM DALE joined W.B. Doner in 1970. In 1981, Jim was made corporate creative director. In 1982, he was named a member of the agency's executive committee, and in 1984, he was promoted to vice chairman—corporate.

Responsible for agency-wide creative, Jim has won every major award for creative excellence...Clio's, The One Show, International Broadcasting Awards, New York Art Director Awards, The London International Advertising Awards, and The Cannes Festival.

He has written some of Doner's most memorable commercials, devised the themes for countless campaigns, and was the first person to ask: "What would you do for a Klondike Bar?". He coaxed seven-year-olds into explaining how electricity works, and picked up a Gold Lion at Cannes for comparing a symphony orchestra to a professional baseball team.

In September of 1990, Jim was named the president and chief operating officer of the agency, and in May of 1992, he moved up to chairman of the board and chief executive officer.

Dale is a member of the American Association of Advertising Agencies' creative committee and has been active in public service work, serving on the boards of the Baltimore Symphony, Maryland Science Center, and Park School.

CHAPTER SIXTEEN

Ad Makin' Town:
The Advertising Scene in Chicago

Hall "Cap" Adams, Jr., Retired Chairman & CEO
Leo Burnett Company, Inc.

Back in 1961, Leo Burnett penned a speech to his employees titled "Ad Makin' Town." It was a dissertation which proclaimed that Chicago was a force to be reckoned with. To quote Mr. Burnett:

"Unlike New York—which was a mythical place—Chicago is *real*. Now I don't intend to argue that Chicago is in any way a worthier city than say, New York. But I *am* suggesting our sod-busting delivery, our loose-limbed stand, and our wide-eyed perspective make it easier for us to create ads that talk turkey to the majority of Americans—that's all."

Hard hitting perhaps, but this chapter is about Chicago. And like me, Leo Burnett was in love with this city.

Chicago is the third largest advertising center in the world, ranked behind New York and Tokyo. But bigger does not necessarily mean better. And Chicago is plenty big enough.

In many ways, Chicago is no different than any other major advertising city, larger or smaller. Chicago advertising agencies create terrific advertising for their clients. Chicago advertising agencies recruit the best people available. And the Chicago advertising business is a tough one to break into.

A lot of noise was made a while back about Chicago's style of advertising. Back in July 1986, a headline from our own *Crain's Chicago Business* states: "If it's friendly and family, it's from Chicago." The story went on to describe the differences in advertising from Chicago, New York, and Los Angeles.

At one time, I might have agreed with the theory of Chicago-style advertising. But today I challenge you to watch a reel of the nation's best advertising and pick out the individual ads produced in New York, Chicago, or Los Angeles!

You see, another look will tell you that Chicago is no longer Carl Sandburg's "hog butchering capital of the world." We're a contemporary, progressive city—that's why major corporations have established worldwide headquarters within our city limits over the years. Furthermore, Chicago agencies service many major national accounts, whether those clients operate out of neighborhood or from distant headquarters, companies like Anheuser Busch, Adolph Coors, General Mills, S.C. Johnson & Son, Kraft, Sears, McDonald's, Procter & Gamble, Philip Morris, and Wrigley. The list goes on and on—you can find it in the *Advertiser Red Book*.

I mention just a few major accounts to emphasize that major advertisers have no reservations about trusting their products to Chicago agencies. If you come to work in this city, you will handle the same demanding national accounts as you would in New York.

What about finding a job in Chicago? The jobs are here. Chicago has more than 200 full-service advertising agencies. Foote Cone & Belding employs more than 600 people in its Chicago office, J. Walter Thompson more than 300, DDB Needham approximately 600, Young & Rubicam approximately 100, just to name a few. Burnett currently employs nearly 2,000 people in its Chicago headquarters.

Most Popular Brands in the United States

Ranking created by Landor Associate's Image Power Survey
1. Coca-Cola
2. Campbell's
3. Disney
4. Pepsi-Cola
5. Kodak
6. NBC
7. Black & Decker
8. Kellogg's
9. McDonald's Corp.
10. Hershey's

Source: *Adweek's Marketing Week*

The same tough expectations exist here as anywhere else advertising is created: If you are looking for a job on the account management side of the business, you are going to need a strong background in liberal arts or business. If you are looking for a job in creative, you're going to need a portfolio full of big ideas.

Of course, dynamic people study all sorts of things in college. What we look for is leadership. People who are active and successful in a lot of different areas.

Chicago is no longer considered the "advertising stepping stone" to the "big time" of New York. If you come to Chicago, come to stay, and come prepared to play in the big leagues.

You might want to consider a few other Chicago realities. We are a city of extremes. Our August temperatures often reach 100 degrees and stay there for days. In January, wind-chill factors send the temperature plummeting, sometimes to more than 50 degrees below zero. However, in spite of such horror stories, Chicago's average temperature is a relatively moderate 49.2 degrees.

There are some other things you should know before you buy your one-way ticket to the Windy City. For one thing, we are *not* the biggest city in the world. While that may mean we're shy one or two major department stores, it also means we're more accessible. Our O'Hare Airport is one the of busiest in the world, and we are serviced by major train and bus lines.

What does that mean? It means that with a couple of bucks and a C.T.A. map, you can get to and from almost any point in our city. That includes most of our suburbs. In addition, because Chicago is smaller, our advertising row is more condensed: Most agencies are lined up along or adjacent to Michigan Avenue's Magnificent Mile.

In other words, pounding Chicago's pavement might be a little easier on your oxfords than in other major cities.

ADVICE FROM THE PRO'S

If you accept a job in Chicago, you can expect to spend an average of 60 minutes commuting daily. Of course, our Lincoln Park people can get to work within minutes. But our Barrington (a far-western suburb) and Indiana employees can spend as much as two hours traveling—one way.

So there you have it: A general overview of Chicago's climate, advertising and otherwise.

Naturally, the location you choose to live in is a matter of strict personal preference.

You should spend some time in any city before you consider settling in.

Talk to the people who live there.

Compare.

Contrast.

Then move to Chicago.

Good luck!

▼

Before his retirement, **HALL "CAP" ADAMS, JR.** was chairman and chief executive officer of Leo Burnett Company, Inc. Prior to that, he was chairman and CEO of the company's USA division, a position he assumed in 1982. Mr. Adams has been a member of the Leo Burnett Company's board of directors since 1977 and serves as chairman of its executive committee.

Mr. Adams, whose entire business career was with Leo Burnett, started as a media research analyst in 1956. He was made vice president in 1969, senior vice president in 1973, group vice president in 1979, and executive vice president/marketing services in 1981.

He is a director of the Advertising Council, the 4A's, the Chicago Council of Foreign Relations, Rush-Presbyterian St. Luke's Medical Center and Junior Achievement of Chicago. He is a member of the Chicago Central Area Committee and Northwestern University Associates, and is serving on the advisory council for the J.L. Kellogg Graduate School of Management.

A graduate of Williams College, Williamstown, Massachusetts, he served in the U.S. Army for two years. He is a resident of Winnetka, Illinois, and is married with two children.

CHAPTER SEVENTEEN

Boston: A City of Tradition in Transition

**George J. Hill III, Chairman/Worldwide Creative Director
Hill, Holliday, Connors, Cosmopulos, Inc.**

There are about 2,250,000 people in the Greater Boston area.

Most of them wouldn't want to be anyplace else.

Because Boston is, above all, a liveable city. But you already knew that.

More importantly, it's a city of tradition that has always been involved in the process of change. Boston is not just liveable—it's adjustable; it's demonstrated over and over how to adjust and prosper in the face of all kinds of social and economic conditions.

This constant change has strengthened the character of native Bostonians, even as it has attracted a steady flow of newcomers into the region.

What's Great About Boston...

Boston is no longer defined by city or county lines. It is a state of mind—an attitude of success—whose work force relies just as strongly on commuters from southern New Hampshire as it does on residents of the Back Bay.

There is a legacy of education that gives Boston a cosmopolitan cultural heritage. On any given night, presidential candidates may be gathering at Harvard's Kennedy School for an evening of political platforming; down the road a bit, at Boston College, a forum on global economic interdependence is about to begin; in the Fens, 300 business leaders from all parts of the country have assembled at Simmons College to evaluate the role women play in industrial management.

It's a typical night in Boston. And, typically, there are also sellout crowds at Symphony Hall, Boston Garden, and Fenway Park.

The movie theaters—current and revival—are offering two evening shows. The bookstores are open late. There are new (affordable) restaurants all around Boston and in the suburbs. Jake Worth's is handing out the same special brew dark beer it has served to generations of Bostonians. At Durgin Park, waitresses are handing out the insults they've featured as a specialite de maison for the last 50 years.

The remarkable fact is that the entire populace will recover from this nighttime spontaneity and arrive at the office bushy-tailed (if not bright-eyed) the next morning.

If you want all the rewards Boston has to offer, you should count yourself among the early risers. The city's universities attract students as well as evening-seminar audiences, and many of the good ones decide they like the place well enough to stick around for a few formative years.

They enter the job market with a head start: Some of them have had internships; they've all been able to make interview appointments and get an early line on some of the better positions. If they pay attention to the local press—Adweek/New England can be found in most school libraries and both the Globe and Herald regularly cover the advertising scene—they already know who's hot (and hiring).

> If there's one characteristic that separates Boston advertising from work done in other parts of the country, it's the superior brand of creative work done for regional accounts. The great work is not just being done for the national advertiser who throws a gargantuan budget at a network television campaign. In New England, the gourmet grocery chain gets terrific work from its local advertising agency, as does the local car dealership association or the hometown newspaper.

...And the Boston Advertising Scene

They also will have learned that Boston is a city of three large agencies and about 30 terrific smaller ones, and they all know each other. In other advertising centers, agency people tend to hang out in small corporate clusters. There's a BBDO bar, a JWT restaurant, an Ogilvy coffee shop. Boston is much looser. With a strong advertising club as an organizational force, there are regular gatherings where names can be attached to faces. After work, a place like Joe's American Bar & Grill will probably have customers from a couple of dozen different agencies. As fierce as their business competition is during the day, by night they're swapping war stories and picking up one another's tab.

The familiarity is not contemptuous. These people from disparate agencies not only unwind together, they've often spent a great deal of time working together. Leaving one agency for another is not an occasion for self-immunization, as it often is in other parts of the world. Indeed, there's a civilized conviviality that allows former colleagues to quietly toast their comrades' successes.

According to the most recent figures, Boston is a young city and one of young businesses—10% of its advertising agencies have been in business less than two years; another one-third were founded after 1980. Only a third of the advertising agencies were around before 1970. As the New England economy has thrived on entrepreneurial energies, so has the agency business. Despite the effects of the recession over the past few years—agency mergers, closings, and staff restructuring—agencies are growing again.

ADVICE FROM THE PRO'S

There has been a flurry of new business presentations during the past few months. In addition, billings in 1991 for the top 50 New England agencies were $1,664,234—and increase of 2.4% over 1990. The dollar volume was generated by a mix of clients that reflects the diversity of the larger New England economy. Boston agencies handle communications services for over 100 of the "Fortune 500" and "Service 500" accounts.

By and large, these agencies are not only Boston-born, but tend to stay in town, too—fewer than 20% of the agencies have any offices outside the city. "This data indicates that agencies operating in the area entered the advertising industry in the Greater Boston area and have remained in the region," the Ad Club notes. "There is an optimism about the ability of the region's economy to provide future growth for agencies serving industries located in the Greater Boston area."

Over 2,000 people are employed by greater Boston area agencies. The majority of the agencies employ fewer than 20 people.

Those are the parameters. But parameters certainly won't get you a job. The fact that the agency business is thriving in Boston doesn't do you much good if you find your only source of remuneration on the unemployment line.

How to Get a Job by the Bay

With your first appointment, make an impression. And that means more than showing up with a resume and a bunch of references from marketing professors.

Study local advertising. Find stuff that you like. Spend an afternoon at the Boston Public Library with *The Standard Directory of Advertisers;* an index at the front of this formidable red tome makes the information inside easily accessible. If you like an ad, use the *Directory* to find out who created it. Come up with a list of advertising agencies you respect, whose work you believe in, whose product most impresses you.

Use that list as your starting point. Then get on the telephone and make some appointments. The larger offices will have personnel offices (sometimes under the heady title of "Human Resources"). The smaller shops will have someone knowledgeable at the switchboard. If you've been particularly impressed for the work they've done for Sam's Restaurant, ask to speak to someone who works on the Sam's account.

By and large, they'll be flattered to learn that the source of your phone call is admiration for their work, not the reference of a second cousin on an account executive's mother's side. Sure, you are bound to get your head chewed off by some people, but they're the ones who've forgotten that they once had to go out and look for a first job.

The lesson is simple: Arrive at an office with more than just a few facts about yourself—show up with an educated interest in your potential employer.

Because the Boston advertising community is tight, a good first impression can take you a long way. If the people who handle Sam's don't have any jobs, they may well know of an agency down the street that has a few openings.

Jot down the name of the agency and head over to the offices of ADWEEK/New England. Treat yourself to a copy of the *ADWEEK Agency Directory.* Learn as much as you can about this other agency down the street. See who their clients are; find out what different kinds of communications services they provide.

You arrive on their doorstep, not just with the recommendation from the people at Sam's agency, but with some smarts...only to find out that they want a writer and you only have a portfolio of art. Don't despair: As long as you keep informed, you'll keep building referrals. And that's a lot more interesting than the unemployment lines or becoming just another worker in industrial management.

▼

A graduate of Harvard, GEORGE J. HILL, III began his career at BBDO. In 1968, he was a founding partner of Hill, Holliday, Connors, Cosmopulos, where he has spent the rest of his career.

CHAPTER EIGHTEEN

Go West, Young Person!

*Phillip Joanou, Chairman and Chief Executive
Dailey & Associates Advertising*

If you live in the West, are interested in advertising, and ask your professors or counselors about how to get started in the agency business, you'll probably be told: Go to New York. Because in New York, such advisors think, you'll find:

- Big league creative;
- Leadership and innovation;
- Major national agencies;
- A fast pace;
- Opportunities to work for major clients.

And, of course, "New York is the advertising center of the world. It's where things start. Others follow..."or so you will be told. "Spend a few years in New York, get an impressive resume. Then, if you wish, return to the West, get a terrific job, and kick back." As if all this weren't enough, you also get to enjoy great museums, wonderful restaurants, fabulous plays, and be with dynamic, charge-ahead people.

All of this, of course, is absolutely true. But if you were to ask *my* advice on where to go to begin your advertising career, I would simply point out that you don't *have* to go to New York to get many (if not all) of the same opportunities and experiences. If you would really prefer to live and work in the West, but feel compelled to go to New York because everyone says that's the smart thing to do, *don't*. Things have changed—if you like the West, stay in the West, because today you will find:

- Big league creative;
- Leadership and innovation;
- Major national agencies;
- A fast pace;
- Opportunities to work for major clients.

There are a few additions I feel make the West special: a great climate, fabulous beaches, mountains and deserts, excellent theater, more championship sports than anywhere in the country; the world's leading trend-setting restaurants, terrific museums, and friendly, outgoing, hard-working people.

Let's look at some of the factors that might influence your decision and help you realize that working in the West is a more than viable career choice.

Western Creative Is Breakthrough

What about major league creative?

Paul Goldberger, architecture critic for *The New York Times,* recently wrote: "Los Angeles is forever destined to be compared to New York, and often in the manner of a child with a talented older sibling. Why does it not do everything correctly, the way its older brother did? Why does it not play by the rules? It is no secret, of course, that the child who goes his own way often turns out, upon maturity, to be the more creative, and so it is with Los Angeles—as an artistic center it is very much coming into its own in this decade, and its creative energies seem nearly limitless. There is less self-consciousness to the Los Angeles, less of a sense of self-importance, less of a sense that there is a set of rules governing the making of architecture. It is right to speak of the architecture being produced here in terms of freestyle. In the hands of its best practitioners it is disciplined, but this discipline is self-imposed, not ordained from above."

Replace the word "architecture" with "advertising" and you have the difference between East and West.

In 1991, *Advertising Age Magazine* presented the Portland-based Wieden & Kennedy with the Agency of the Year award. It was the third year in a row that the winner of this award came from the West. The primary reason for this level of creative excellence is that the West offers a freer, creative climate, one that has produced some of the most innovative, talked-about advertising in recent years. From W&K's work for Nike to Chiat/Day's Energizer Bunny to Foote, Cone & Belding's famous Levis effort, Western shops have truly led the way. And much of the credit for this continuing strong output can be traced to dynamic creative leadership, as the West is home to some of the most highly regarded creative directors in the United States, including Hal Riney of Hal Riney & Partners, Lee Clow of Chiat/Day, and Cliff Einstein of Dailey & Associates.

There are many other powerful, highly creative, strong agencies headquartered in the West whose work holds up with any work being done by *any* agency *anywhere* in the world.

The West Leads in Innovation

Is New York still the center for leadership and innovation? According to *Sunset Magazine,* it's the West that is "worth watching." It has become an aphorism in marketing circles, as auto trends, housing trends, new product trends, and lifestyle trends suddenly seem to sprout in Western soil, take to root and spread, as if by runners, to other parts of the country.

The West is sort of an early-warning system about what's in store for the nation in the next few years. With the new decade, and soon a new century, chances are the West will come under closer scrutiny than ever. In addition, most economists are looking ahead to move and more impact from the burgeoning Pacific region. And the West is the gateway for Pacific trade.

"The Mediterranean is the ocean of the past, the Atlantic the ocean of the present, and the Pacific the ocean of the future."
—Roger Skrentny

The West Is Big Business

What about the size of the Western market?

If the Western states were a separate nation, its GNP of roughly 2 trillion dollars would rank fifth in the world.

Twenty-one of the top 100 advertisers in America are headquartered or have a major division in the West. Large corporations with large advertising budgets demand and expect the highest levels of sophistication and professionalism.

Fortune's listing of the 500 largest companies in the United States shows that 64 are in the West, with 44 in California alone.

According to *Inc. Magazine's* listing of the "500 Fastest-Growing Private Companies," no fewer than 27 of the top 100 are in the West. (Potentially, tomorrow's big new advertising spenders.)

According to the U.S. Census Bureau, California residents have a higher per capita personal income than New York residents. (Advertising salaries in the large Western markets are comparable to New York.)

Unlike much of the country, the West does not depend on older, more vulnerable heavy industry. Rather, it harbors the largest concentration of high technology enterprise in the world and a diversity of other manufacturing and raw materials industries. Such diversity gives the West the capacity to continue to grow.

Westerners control their own commute. Everyone drives. If you want to stay late, you don't worry about trains. You don't have to get cranky and aggressive because you are running out of time. You control time. Results are what count, not frenetic motion. This makes some harassed Easterners believe the pace is slow and easy out here. When people like this come West to manage branches of Eastern agencies, they quite often fail, because, in fact, the competition is fierce, the quality second to none. So if you are not prepared to work very hard to succeed, stay away from the agency business, East or West.

ADVICE FROM THE PRO'S

The Myth of the "Laid Back" West

New York's pace is dictated by commuting schedules, since virtually everyone commutes into "The City." People have to get up very early to get to work late. And leave work early to get home late. This creates a very fast physical pace. Do not, however, confuse motion with action.

The West Has Major Clients

The West offers you chances to work on large national and international clients, too. These major corporations require large, full-service agencies that can provide them with the best advertising available. If they weren't getting the kind and calibre of professional work they needed, it stands to reason that they would simply transfer their accounts East.

Corporations like Carnation, Beatrice Hunt-Wesson, Honda, Mazda, Levi Strauss, Disney, Nike, Lockheed, Atlantic Richfield, Taco Bell, Toyota, Clorox, Apple, Gallo, Hilton, to name just a few, demand the best from their agencies—and they get it. There are more than enough "major league, world class" clients in the West to keep you busy for a lifetime.

Don't misunderstand me. New York is a great city, and if you like it, a great place for an advertising career. But it isn't *better,* just *different.*

Some Pitfalls

There *are* some "downsides" you should be aware of if you're thinking about a West coast advertising career. First, with the exception of Los Angeles and San Francisco, there is less job mobility in most markets. Many people are willing to accept this risk for the lifestyle available in cities like San Diego, Portland, or Seattle. There are good jobs in all of these markets. There are excellent agencies headquartered in the West, but there are *not* a lot of them.

Another possible disadvantage: A good number of agency offices are branches of New York-headquartered companies. In many of these, major decisions are made in New York, so working on the West coast leaves you far away from the real seat of power.

For some of these companies, advancement means moving to corporate headquarters in New York. This, of course, defeats the purpose of building a career in the West.

One thing you would *not* have to give up is money, at least in the Los Angeles market. All surveys I've seen show that salaries in Southern California are equal to those paid in the agency business in New York.

What to Do Next

All the advice in this **Career Directory** that is pertinent to getting an agency job in New York or Chicago or Detroit applies to the agency business out West: Read and use this excellent volume. Get out the *Agency Red Book.* Talk to your professors for advice and leads. Write to agency heads. Follow up with phone calls.

What are the best companies—anywhere—looking for? Intelligence. Honesty. High energy. If you possess these, present yourself well, and don't give up, you *will* find the job you want...*where* you want it.

ADVICE FROM THE PRO'S

PHIL JOANOU is the Chairman and Chief Executive of Dailey & Associates, one of the largest international agencies headquartered in the West. Dailey represents several major occupations including Honda, Nestle, the California State Lottery, Gallo, and Great Western Financial.

A graduate of the University of Arizona, Mr. Joanou has taught undergraduate marketing at the University of Southern California, served as Director of the Institute of Advanced Studies at USC, and has lectured at UCLA, the Art Center, and various professional organizations. He has served as a Governor of the American Association of Advertising Agencies, and on their national board as Director. He was Director of the Los Angeles Advertising Club and Director and President of the Western States Advertising Agencies Association, which named him "Advertising Man Of the Year" in 1983.

In 1972, Mr. Joanou served as Executive Vice President of the November Group, creating the advertising campaign for President Nixon's re-election. He later worked on the presidential campaigns of Gerald Ford and Ronald Reagan.

In 1985, Mr. Joanou created the largest public service campaign in the country's history—the Partnership for a Drug-Free America. The Partnership is a non-profit, private sector coalition of volunteers from the advertising, public relations, production, research, media, and entertainment industries dedicated to reducing demand for illicit drugs in the United States. To date, the partnership for a Drug-Free America has received more than $1 billion in contributed time and space and currently receives donated time at the rate of approximately $1 million per day. Partnership messages are seen and heard on local and network television, newspapers, radio, magazines, outdoor billboards, home video rentals, telephone directories, children's toys, and before feature attractions at movie theaters. For this massive effort, Mr. Joanou was presented the 1987 Award for Private Sector Initiatives by President Ronald Reagan. In 1988, he was presented with the Silver Medal Award for humanitarian and industry contributions by the Advertising club of Los Angeles.

Active in community affairs as well, Mr. Joanou is on the Board of the Art Center College of Design; headed the advertising campaign for United Way; served as President of the La Canada Flintridge Educational Foundation; was Chairman of the Communications Industry for the Music Center Unified Fund; Director of the Arthritis Foundation; as well as other civic and fraternal organizations. He served to captain in the USAR, and is listed in *Who's Who in Advertising, Who's Who in the World,* and *Who's Who in America.*

The Job Search Process

CHAPTER NINETEEN

Getting Started: Self-Evaluation and Career Objectives

Getting a job may be a relatively simple one-step or couple of weeks process or a complex, months-long operation.

Starting, nurturing and developing a career (or even a series of careers) is a lifelong process.

What we'll be talking about in the five chapters that together form our Job Search Process are those basic steps to take, assumptions to make, things to think about if you want a job—especially a first job in an ad agency. But when these steps—this process—are applied and expanded over a lifetime, most if not all of them are the same procedures, carried out over and over again, that are necessary to develop a successful, lifelong, professional career.

What does all this have to do with putting together a resume, writing a cover letter, heading off for interviews and the other "traditional" steps necessary to get a job? Whether your college graduation is just around the corner or a far distant memory, you will continuously need to focus, evaluate and re-evaluate your response to the ever-changing challenge of your future: Just what do you want to do with the rest of your life? Whether you like it or not, you're all looking for that "entry-level opportunity."

You're already one or two steps ahead of the competition—you're sure you want to pursue a career in advertising. By heeding the advice of the many professionals who have written chapters for this *Career Directory*—and utilizing the extensive entry-level job, organization, and career resource listings we've included—you're well on your way to fulfilling that dream. But there are some key decisions and time-consuming preparations to make if you want to transform that hopeful dream into a real, live job.

The actual process of finding the right company, right career path and, most importantly, the right first job, begins long before you start mailing out resumes to potential employers. The choices and decisions you make now are not irrevocable, but this first job will have a definite impact on the career options you leave yourself. To help you make some of the right decisions and choices along the way (and avoid some of the most notable traps and pitfalls), the following chapters will lead you through a series of organized steps. If the entire job search process we are recommending here is properly executed, it will undoubtedly help you land exactly the job you want.

If you're currently in high school and hope, after college, to land a job in advertising, then attending the right college, choosing the right major, and getting the summer work experience many agencies look for are all important steps. Read the section of this *Career Directory* that covers the particular field and/or job specialty in which you're interested—many of the contributors have recommended colleges or graduate programs they favor.

If you're hoping to jump right into any of these fields without a college degree or other professional training, our best and only advice is—don't do it. As you'll soon see in the detailed information included in the **Job Opportunities Databank,** there are not that many job openings for students without a college degree. Those that do exist are generally clerical and will only rarely lead to promising careers.

The Concept of a Job Search Process

As we've explained, a job search is not a series of random events. Rather, it is a series of connected events that together form the job search process. It is important to know the eight steps that go into that process:

1. Evaluating yourself

Know thyself. What skills and abilities can you offer a prospective employer? What do you enjoy doing? What are your strengths and weaknesses? What do you want to do?

2. Establishing your career objectives

Where do you want to be next year, three years, five years from now? What do you ultimately want to accomplish in your career and your life?

3. Creating a company target list

How to prepare a "Hit List" of potential employers—researching them, matching their needs with your skills and starting your job search assault. Preparing company information sheets and evaluating your chances.

4. Networking for success

Learning how to utilize every contact, every friend, every relative, and anyone else you can think of to break down the barriers facing any would-be advertising professional. How to organize your home office to keep track of your communications and stay on top of your job campaign.

5. Preparing your resume

How to encapsulate years of school and little actual work experience into a professional, selling resume. Learning when and how to use it.

6. Preparing cover letters

The many ordinary and the all-too-few extraordinary cover letters, the kind that land interviews and jobs.

7. Interviewing

How to make the interview process work for you—from the first "hello" to the first day on the job.

8. Following up

Often overlooked, it's perhaps the most important part of the job search process.

We won't try to kid you—it is a lot of work. To do it right, you have to get started early, probably quite a bit earlier than you'd planned. Frankly, we recommend beginning this process one full year prior to the day you plan to start work.

So if you're in college, the end of your junior year is the right time to begin your research and preparations. That should give you enough time during summer vacation to set up your files and begin your library research.

Whether you're in college or graduate school, one item may need to be planned even earlier—allowing enough free time in your schedule of classes for interview preparations and appointments. Waiting until your senior year to "make some time" is already too late. Searching for a full-time job is itself a full-time job! Though you're naturally restricted by your schedule, it's not difficult to plan ahead and prepare for your upcoming job search. Try to leave at least a couple of free mornings or afternoons a week. A day or even two without classes is even better.

Otherwise, you'll find yourself, crazed and distracted, trying to prepare for an interview in the ten-minute period between your Advertising Ethics 301 lecture and your Layout and Design seminar. Not the best way to make a first impression and certainly not the way you want to approach an important meeting.

The Self-Evaluation Process

Learning about who you are, what you want to be, what you can be, are critical first steps in the job search process and, unfortunately, the ones most often ignored by job seekers everywhere, especially students eager to leave the ivy behind and plunge into the "real world." But avoiding this crucial self-evaluation can hinder your progress and even damage some decent prospects.

Why? Because in order to land a job with a company at which you'll actually be happy, you need to be able to identify those firms and/or job descriptions that best match your own skills, likes and strengths. The more you know about yourself, the more you'll bring to this process and the more accurate the "match-ups." You'll be able to structure your presentation (resume, cover letter, interviews, follow up) to stress your most marketable skills and talents (and, dare we say it, conveniently avoid your weaknesses?). Later, you'll be able to evaluate potential employers and job offers on the basis of your own needs and desires. This spells the difference between waking up in the morning ready to enthusiastically tackle a new day of challenges and shutting off the alarm in the hopes the day (and your job) will just disappear.

Creating Your Self-Evaluation Form

If your self-evaluation is to have any meaning, you must first be honest with yourself. This self-evaluation form should help you achieve that goal by providing a structured environment to answer these tough questions.

Take a sheet of lined notebook paper. Set up eight columns across the top—Strengths, Weaknesses, Skills, Hobbies, Courses, Experience, Likes, Dislikes.

Now, fill in each of these columns according to these guidelines:

Strengths: Describe personality traits you consider your strengths (and try to look at them as an employer would)—e.g., persistence, organization, ambition, intelligence, logic, assertiveness, aggression, leadership, etc.

Weaknesses: The traits you consider glaring weaknesses—e.g., impatience, conceit, etc. Remember: Look at these as a potential employer would. Don't assume that the personal traits you consider weaknesses will necessarily be considered negatives in the business world. You may be "easily bored," a trait that led to lousy grades early on because teachers couldn't keep you interested in the subjects they were teaching. Well, many entrepreneurs need ever-changing challenges. Strength or weakness?

Skills: Any skill you have, whether you think it's marketable or not. Everything from basic business skills—like typing, word processing, and stenography—to computer, or teaching experience and foreign language literacy. Don't forget possibly obscure but marketable skills like "good telephone voice."

Hobbies: The things you enjoy doing that, more than likely, have no overt connection to career objectives. These should be distinct from the skills listed above, and may include activities such as reading, games, travel, sports and the like. While these may not be marketable in any general sense, they may well be useful in specific circumstances.

Courses: All the general subject areas (history, literature, etc.) and/or specific courses you've taken which may be marketable, you really enjoyed, or both.

Experience: Just the specific functions you performed at any part-time (school year) or full-time (summer) jobs. Entries may include "General Office" (typing, filing, answering phones, etc.), "Creative Writing," "Product Marketing," "Graphic Design," etc.

Likes: List all your "likes," those important considerations that you haven't listed anywhere else yet. These might include the types of people you like to be with, the kind of environment you prefer (city, country, large places, small places, quiet, loud, fast-paced, slow-paced) and anything else which hasn't shown up somewhere on this form. Try to think of "likes" that you have that are related to the job you are applying for. For example, if you're applying for a job at a bank, mention that you enjoy reading the Wall St. Journal. However, try not to include entries which refer to specific jobs or companies. We'll list those on another form.

Dislikes: All the people, places and things you can easily live without.

Now assess the "marketability" of each item you've listed. (In other words, are some of your likes, skills or courses easier to match to a financial job description, or do they have little to do with a specific job or company?) Mark highly marketable skills with an "H." Use "M" to characterize those skills which may be marketable in a particular set of circumstances, "L" for those with minimal potential application to any job.

Referring back to the same list, decide if you'd enjoy using your marketable skills or talents as part of your everyday job—"Y" for yes, "N" for no. You may type 80 words a minute but truly despise typing or worry that stressing it too much will land you on the permanent clerical staff. If so, mark typing with an "N." (Keep one thing in mind—just because you dislike typing shouldn't mean you absolutely won't accept a job that requires it. Almost every professional job today—especially those involving stocks and bonds—requires computer-based work that make typing a plus.)

Now, go over the entire form carefully and look for inconsistencies.

To help you with your own form, consult the sample form on the next page that a job-hunter might complete.

The Value of a Second Opinion

There is a familiar misconception about the self-evaluation process that gets in the way of many new job applicants—the belief that it is a process which must be accomplished in isolation. Nothing could be further from the truth. Just because the family doctor tells you that you need an operation doesn't mean you run right off to the hospital. Prudence dictates that you check out the opinion with another physician. Getting such a "second opinion"—someone else's, not just your own—is a valuable practice throughout the job search process, as well.

So after you've completed the various exercises in this chapter, review them with a friend, relative, or parent—just be sure it's someone who knows you well and cares about you. These second opinions may reveal some aspects of your self description on which you and the rest of the world differ. If so, discuss them, learn from them and, if necessary, change some conclusions. Should everyone concur with your self evaluation, you will be reassured that your choices are on target.

Advertising Career Directory

Strength	Weakness	Skill	Hobby	Course	Experience	Like	Dislike

Marketable?
Enjoy?

Marketable?
Enjoy?

Marketable?
Enjoy?

Establishing Your Career Objective(s)

For better or worse, you now know something more of who and what you are. But we've yet to establish and evaluate another important area—your overall needs, desires and goals. Where are you going? What do you want to accomplish?

If you're getting ready to graduate from college or graduate school, the next five years are the most critical period of your whole career. You need to make the initial transition from college to the workplace, establish yourself in a new and completely unfamiliar company environment, and begin to build the professional credentials necessary to achieve your career goals.

If that strikes you as a pretty tall order, well, it is. Unless you've narrowly prepared yourself for a specific profession, you're probably most ill-prepared for any real job. Instead, you've (hopefully) learned some basic principles—research and analytical skills that are necessary for success at almost any level—and, more or less, how to think.

It's tough to face, but face it you must: No matter what your college, major, or degree, all you represent right now is potential. How you package that potential and what you eventually make of it is completely up to you. It's an unfortunate fact that many companies will take a professional with barely a year or two experience over any newcomer, no matter how promising. Smaller firms, especially, can rarely afford to hire someone who can't begin contributing immediately.

So you have to be prepared to take your comparatively modest skills and experience and package them in a way that will get you interviewed and hired. Quite a challenge.

There are a number of different ways to approach such a task. If you find yourself confused or unable to list such goals, you might want to check a few books in your local library that have more time to spend on the topic of "goal-oriented planning."

But is Advertising Right for You?

Presuming you now have a much better idea of yourself and where you'd like to be, let's make sure some of your basic assumptions are right. We presume you purchased this *Career Directory* because you're considering a career in some area of advertising. Are you sure? Do you know enough about the industry as a whole and the particular part you're heading for to decide whether it's right for you? Probably not. So start your research now—learn as much about your potential career field as you now know about yourself.

Start with the essays in the Advice from the Pro's section—these will give you an excellent overview of advertising, some very specialized (and growing) areas, and some things to keep in mind as you start on your career search. They will also give you a relatively simplified, though very necessary, understanding of just what people who work in all these areas of financial services actually do.

Other sources you should consider consulting to learn more about this business are listed in the **Career Resources** section of this book.

In that section, we've listed trade associations and publications associated with the advertising industry (together with many other resources that will help your job search. Consult the introductory material in the front of this directory for a complete description of the **Career Resources** chapter). Where possible in the association entries, we've included details on educational information they make available, but you should certainly consider writing each of the pertinent associations, letting them know you're interested in a career in their area of specialization and would appreciate whatever help and advice they're willing to impart. You'll find many sponsor seminars and conferences throughout the country, some of which you may be able to attend.

The trade publications are dedicated to the highly specific interests of the various areas of the advertising community. These magazines are generally not available at newsstands, but you may be able to obtain back issues at your local library (most major libraries have extensive collections of such journals) or by writing to the magazines' circulation/ subscription departments. We've also included regional and local magazines.

You may also try writing to the publishers and/or editors of these publications. State in your cover letter what area of advertising you're considering and ask them for whatever help and advice they can offer. But be specific. These are busy professionals and they do not have the time or the inclination to simply "tell me everything you can about becoming a designer."

If you can afford it now, we strongly suggest subscribing to whichever trade magazines are applicable to the specialty you're considering. If you can't subscribe to all of them, make it a point to regularly read the copies that arrive at your local public or college library.

These publications may well provide the most imaginative and far-reaching information for your job search. Even a quick perusal of an issue or two will give you an excellent "feel" for the industry. After reading only a few articles, you'll already get a handle on what's happening in the field and some of the industry's peculiar and particular jargon. Later, more detailed study will aid you in your search for a specific job.

Authors of the articles themselves may well turn out to be important resources. If an article is directly related to your chosen specialty, why not call the author and ask some questions? You'd be amazed how willing many of these professionals will be to talk to you and answer your questions, and the worst they can do is say no. (But *do* use common sense—authors will not *always* respond graciously to your invitation to "chat about the business." And don't be *too* aggressive here.)

You'll find such research to be a double-edged sword. In addition to helping you get a handle on whether the area you've chosen is really right for you, you'll slowly learn enough about particular specialties, companies, the industry, etc., to actually sound like you know what you're talking about when you hit the pavement looking for your first job. And nothing is better than sounding like a pro—except being one.

Advertising Is It. Now What?

After all this research, we're going to assume you've reached that final decision—you really do want a career in some aspect of advertising. It is with this vague certainty that all too many of you will race off, hunting for any firm willing to give you a job. You'll manage to get interviews at a couple and, smiling brightly, tell everyone you meet, "I want a career in advertising." The interviewers, unfortunately, will all ask the same awkward question—"What *exactly* do you want to do at our agency?"—and that will be the end of that.

It is simply not enough to narrow your job search to a specific industry. And so far, that's all you've done. You must now establish a specific career objective—the job you want to start, the career you want to pursue. Just knowing that you "want to get into advertising" doesn't mean anything to anybody. If that's all you can tell an interviewer, it demonstrates a lack of research into the industry itself and your failure to think ahead.

Interviewers will *not* welcome you with open arms if you're still vague about your career goals. If you've managed to get an "informational interview" with an executive whose company currently has no job openings, what is he or she supposed to do with your resume after you leave? Who should he or she send it to for future consideration? Since *you* don't seem to know exactly what you want to do, how's he or she going to figure it out? Worse, that person will probably resent your asking him or her to function as your personal career counselor.

Remember, the more specific your career objective, the better your chances of finding a job. It's that simple and that important. Naturally, before you declare your objective to the world, check once again to make sure your specific job target matches the skills and interests you defined in your self evaluation. Eventually, you may want to state such an objective on your resume, and "To obtain an entry-level position as an as an assistant account executive at a mid-size metropolitan agency," is quite a bit better than "I want a career in advertising." Do not consider this step final until you can summarize your job/career objective in a single, short, accurate sentence.

THE JOB SEARCH PROCESS

CHAPTER TWENTY

Targeting Prospective Employers and Networking for Success

As you move along the job search path, one fact will quickly become crystal clear—it is primarily a process of elimination: your task is to consider and research as many options as possible, then—for good reasons—eliminate as many as possible, attempting to continually narrow your focus.

Your Ideal Company Profile

Let's establish some criteria to evaluate potential employers. This will enable you to identify your target agencies, the places you'd really like to work. (This process, as we've pointed out, is not specific to any industry or field; the same steps, with perhaps some research resource variations, are applicable to any job, any company, any industry.)

Take a sheet of blank paper and divide it into three vertical columns. Title it "Target Agency—Ideal Profile." Call the lefthand column "Musts," the middle column "Preferences," and the righthand column "Nevers."

We've listed a series of questions below. After considering each question, decide whether a particular criteria *must* be met, whether you would simply *prefer* it or *never* would consider it at all. If there are other criteria you consider important, feel free to add them to the list below and mark them accordingly on your Profile. (We have included a sample grid to help you set up your own.)

1. What are your geographical preferences? (Possible answers: U.S., Canada, International, Anywhere). If you only want to work in the U.S., then "Work in United States" would be the entry in the "Must" column. "Work in Canada or Foreign Country" might be the first entry in your "Never" column. There would be no applicable entry for this question in the "Preference" column. If, however, you will consider working in two of the three, then your "Must" column entry might read "Work in U.S. or Canada," your

"Preference" entry—if you preferred one over the other—could read "Work in U.S.," and the "Never" column, "Work Overseas."

2. If you prefer to work in the U.S. or Canada, what area, state(s) or province(s)? If Overseas, what area or countries?

3. Do you prefer a large city, small city, town, or somewhere as far away from civilization as possible?

4. In regard to question 3, any specific preferences?

5. Do you prefer a warm or cold climate?

6. Do you prefer a large or small company? Define your terms (by sales, income, employees, offices, etc.).

7. Do you mind relocating right now? Do you want to work for an agency with a reputation for *frequently* relocating top people?

8. Do you mind travelling frequently? What percent do you consider reasonable? (Make sure this matches the normal requirements of the job specialization you're considering.)

9. What salary would you *like* to receive (put in the "Preference" column)? What's the *lowest* salary you'll accept (in the "Must" column)?

10. Are there any benefits (such as an expense account, medical and/or dental insurance, company car, etc.) you must or would like to have?

11. Are you planning to attend graduate school at some point in the future and, if so, is a tuition reimbursement plan important to you?

12. Do you feel that a formal training program is necessary?

13. If applicable, what kinds of specific accounts would you prefer to work with? What specific products?

It's important to keep revising this new form, just as you should continue to update your Self-Evaluation Form. After all, it contains the criteria by which you will judge every potential employer. Armed with a complete list of such criteria, you're now ready to find all the companies that match them.

Targeting Individual Agencies

To begin creating your initial list of targeted ad agencies, start with the **Job Opportunities Databank** in this directory. We've listed major U.S. ad agencies, many smaller ones, plus selected agencies across Canada, all of which were contacted by telephone for this edition. These listings provide a plethora of data concerning the agencies' overall operations, hiring practices, and other important information on entry-level job opportunities. This latter information includes key contacts (names), the average number of entry-level people they hire each year, along with complete job descriptions and requirements.

One word of advice. You'll notice that some/many of the agencies list "0" under average entry-level hiring. This is more a reflection of the current economic times than a long-range projection. In past editions of this book, these companies did list an average number of new hires, and they will again in the future. We have listed these companies for three reasons: 1) to present you with the overall view of prospective employers; 2) because even companies that don't plan to do any hiring will experience unexpected job openings; and 3) things change, so as soon as the economy begins to pick up, expect entry-level hiring to increase again.

We have attempted to include information on those major agencies that represent most of the entry-level jobs out there. But there are, of course, many other agencies of all sizes and shapes that you may also wish to research. In the Career Resources section, we have listed other reference tools you can use to obtain more information on the companies we've listed, as well as those we haven't.

The Other Side of the Iceberg

You are now better prepared to choose those companies that meet your own list of criteria. But a word of caution about these now-"obvious" requirements—they are not the only ones you need to take into consideration. And you probably won't be able to find all or many of the answers to this second set of questions in any reference book—they are known, however, by those persons already at work in the industry. Here is the list you will want to follow:

Promotion

If you are aggressive about your career plans, you'll want to know if you have a shot at the top. Look for companies that traditionally promote from within.

Training

Look for agencies in which your early tenure will actually be a period of on-the-job training, hopefully ones in which training remains part of the long-term process. As new techniques and technologies enter the workplace, you must make sure you are updated on these skills. Most importantly, look for training that is craft or function-oriented—these are the so-called **transferable skills**, ones you can easily bring along with you from job-to-job, company-to-company, sometimes industry-to-industry.

Salary

Some industries are generally high paying, some not. But even an industry with a tradition of paying abnormally low salaries may have particular agencies or job functions (like sales) within agencies that command high remuneration. But it's important you know what the industry standard is.

Ask the Person Who Owns One

Some years ago, this advice was used as the theme for a highly successful automobile advertising campaign. The prospective car buyer was encouraged to find out about the product by asking the (supposedly) most trustworthy judge of all—someone who was already an owner.

You can use the same approach in your job search. You all have relatives or friends already out in the workplace—these are your best sources of information about those industries. Cast your net in as wide a circle as possible. Contact these valuable resources. You'll be amazed at how readily they will answer your questions. I suggest you check the criteria list at the beginning of this chapter to formulate your own list of pertinent questions. Ideally and minimally you will want to learn: how the industry is doing, what its long-term prospects are, the kinds of personalities they favor (aggressive, low key), rate of employee turnover, and the availability of training.

Benefits

Look for agencies in which health insurance, vacation pay, retirement plans, 401K accounts, stock purchase opportunities, and other important employee benefits are extensive—and company paid. If you have to pay for basic benefits like medical coverage yourself, you'll be surprised at how expensive they are. An exceptional benefit package may even lead you to accept a lower-than-usual salary.

Unions

Make sure you know about the union situation in each industry you research. Periodic, union-mandated salary increases are one benefit nonunion workers may find hard to match.

Making Friends and Influencing People

Networking is a term you have probably heard; it is definitely a key aspect of any successful job search and a process you must master.

Informational interviews and **job interviews** are the two primary outgrowths of successful networking.

Referrals, an aspect of the networking process, entail using someone else's name, credentials and recommendation to set up a receptive environment when seeking a job interview.

All of these terms have one thing in common: Each depends on the actions of other people to put them in motion. Don't let this idea of "dependency" slow you down, however. A job search *must* be a very pro-active process—*you* have to initiate the action. When networking, this means contacting as many people as you can. The more you contact, the better the chances of getting one of those people you are "depending" on to take action and help you out.

So what *is* networking? How do you build your own network? And why do you need one in the first place? The balance of this chapter answers all of those questions and more.

Get your telephone ready. It's time to make some friends.

Not the World's Oldest Profession, But...

As Gordon Gekko, the high-rolling corporate raider played by Michael Douglas, sneers in the movie *Wall Street:* "Any schmuck can analyze stock charts. What separates the players from the sheep is information." Networking is the process of creating your own group of relatives, friends, and acquaintances who can feed you the information you need to find a job—identifying where the jobs are and giving you the personal introductions and background data necessary to pursue them.

If the job market were so well-organized that details on all employment opportunities were immediately available to all applicants, there would be no need for such a process. Rest assured the job market is *not* such a smooth-running machine—most applicants are left very much to their own devices. Build and use your own network wisely and you'll be amazed at the amount of useful job intelligence you will turn up.

While the term networking didn't gain prominence until the 1970s, it is by no means a new phenomenon. A selection process that connects people of similar skills, backgrounds, and/or attitudes—in other words, networking—has been in existence in a variety of forms for centuries. Attend any Ivy League school and you're automatically part of its very special centuries-old network.

Major law firms are known to favor candidates from a preferred list of law schools—the same ones the senior partners attended. Washington, D.C. and Corporate America have their own network—the same corporate bigwigs move back and forth from boardroom to Cabinet Room. The Academia-Washington connection is just as strong—notice the number of Harvard professors who call Washington their second home? No matter which party is in power, certain names just keep surfacing as Secretary of This or Undersecretary of That. No, networking is not new. It's just left its ivory tower and become a well-publicized process *anyone* can and should utilize in their lifelong career development.

And it works. Remember your own reaction when you were asked to recommend someone for a job, club, or school office? You certainly didn't want to look foolish, so you gave it some thought and tried to recommend the best-qualified person that you thought would "fit in" with the rest of the group. It's a built-in screening process.

Creating the Ideal Network

As in most endeavors, there's a wrong way and a right way to network. The following tips will help you construct your own wide-ranging, information-gathering, interview-generating group—*your* network.

Diversify

Unlike the Harvard or Princeton network—confined to former graduates of each school—your network should be as diversified and wide-ranging as possible. You never know who might be in a position to help, so don't limit your group of friends. The more diverse they are, the greater the variety of information they may supply you with.

Don't Forget...

...to include everyone you know in your initial networking list: friends, relatives, social acquaintances, classmates, college alumni, professors, teachers, your dentist, doctor, family lawyer, insurance agent, banker, travel agent, elected officials in your community, ministers, fellow church members, local tradesmen, and local business or social club officers. And everybody they know!

Be Specific

Make a list of the kinds of assistance you will require from those in your network, then make specific requests of each. Do they know of jobs at their company? Can they introduce you to the proper executives? Have they heard something about or know someone at the company you're planning to interview with next week?

The more organized you are, the easier it will be to target the information you need and figure out who might have it. Begin to keep a business card file or case so you can keep track of all your contacts. A small plastic case for file cards that is available at any discount store will do nicely. One system you can use is to staple the card to a 3 x 5 index card. On the card, write down any information about that contact that you might need later—when you talked to them, job leads they provided, specific job search advice, etc. You will then have all the information you need about each company or contact in one easily accessible location.

Learn the Difference...

...between an **informational** interview and a **job** interview. The former requires you to cast yourself in the role of information gatherer; *you* are the interviewer and knowledge is your goal—about an industry, company, job function, key executive, etc. Such a meeting with someone already doing what you soon hope to be doing is by far the best way to find out everything you need to know—before you walk through the door and sit down for a formal job interview, at which time your purpose is more sharply defined: to get the job you're interviewing for.

If you learn of a specific job opening during an informational interview, you are in a position to find out details about the job, identify the interviewer and, possibly, even learn some things about him or her. In addition, presuming you get your contact's permission, you may be able to use his or her name as a referral. Calling up the interviewer and saying, "Joan Smith in your Creative department suggested I contact you regarding openings for assistant designers," is far superior to "Hello. Do you have any job openings in your agency?"

(In such a case, be careful about referring to a specific job opening, even if your contact told you about it. It may not be something you're supposed to know about. By presenting your query as an open-ended question, you give your prospective employer the option of exploring your background without further commitment. If there is a job there and you're qualified for it, you'll find out soon enough.)

Don't Waste a Contact

Not everyone you call on your highly-diversified networking list will know about a job opening. It would be surprising if each one did. But what about *their* friends and colleagues? It's amazing how everyone knows someone who knows someone. Ask—you'll find that someone.

Value Your Contacts

If someone has provided you with helpful information or an introduction to a friend or colleague, keep him or her informed about how it all turns out. A referral that's panned out should be reported to the person who opened the door for you in the first place. Such courtesy will be appreciated—and may lead to more contacts. If someone has nothing to offer today, a call back in the future is still appropriate and may pay off.

The lesson is clear: Keep your options open, your contact list alive. Detailed records of your network—whom you spoke with, when, what transpired, etc.—will help you keep track of your overall progress and organize what can be a complicated and involved process.

Informational Interviews

So now you've done your homework, built your network, and begun using your contacts. It's time to go on your first informational interview.

A Typical Interview

You were, of course, smart enough to include John Fredericks, the bank officer who handled your dad's mortgage, on your original contact list. He knew you as a bright and conscientious college senior; in fact, your perfect three-year repayment record on the loan you took out to buy that '77 Plymouth impressed him. When you called him, he was happy to refer you to his golfing buddy, Bob Jones, creative director at Ad Agency, Inc. Armed with permission to use Fredericks' name and recommendation, you wrote a letter to Bob Jones, the gist of which went something like this:

> *I am writing at the suggestion of Mr. Fredericks at Fidelity National Bank. He knows of my interest in advertising and, given your position at Ad Agency, Inc. thought you may be able to help me gain a better understanding of your field and the career opportunities it presents.*
>
> *While I am majoring in marketing and minoring in English, I know I need to speak with professionals such as yourself to learn how to apply my studies to a work environment. If you could spare a half hour to meet with me, I'm certain I would be able to get enough information about your field to give me the direction I need.*
>
> *I'll call your office next week in the hope that we can schedule a meeting.*

Send a copy of this letter to Mr. Fredericks at the bank—it will refresh his memory should Mr. Jones call to inquire about you. Next step: the follow-up phone call. After you get Mr. Jones' secretary on the line, it will, with luck, go something like this:

> *"Hello, I'm Mr. Paul Smith. I'm calling in reference to a letter I wrote to Mr. Jones requesting an appointment."*
>
> *"Oh, yes. You're the young man interested in our design program. Mr. Jones can see you on June 23rd. Will 10 A.M. be satisfactory?"*
>
> *"That's fine. I'll be there."*

Well, the appointed day arrives. Well-scrubbed and dressed in your best (and most conservative) suit, you are ushered into Mr. Jones' office. He offers you coffee (you decline) and says that it is okay to light up if you smoke (you decline). The conversation might go something like this:

You: "Thank you for seeing me, Mr. Jones. I know you are busy and appreciate your taking the time to talk with me."

You: "As I stated in my letter, my interest in advertising is very real, but I'm having trouble seeing how all of my studies fit into the big picture. I think I'll be much better prepared to evaluate future job offers if I can learn how everything works at an agency such as yours. May I ask you a few questions about the designer function at Ad Agency, Inc.?"

Jones: "Well it's my pleasure since you come so highly recommended. I'm always pleased to meet someone interested in my field."

Jones: "Fire away, Paul".

Mr. Jones relaxes. He realizes this is a knowledge hunt you are on, not a thinly-veiled job interview. Your approach has kept him off the spot—he doesn't have to be concerned with making a hiring decision. You've already gotten high marks for not putting him on the defensive. From this point on, you will be able to ask anything and everything you need to find out—not just about the designer function at agencies in general, but specifically about the training program at Ad Agency, Inc. (which is what you're really interested in).

You: "I have a few specific questions I'd like to ask. First, at an agency such as yours, where does an entry-level person start?"

Jones: "In this company, we rotate new people interested in advertising through all the design areas we work in—graphics, catalogs, and mass mailings. You'd spend about two months in each area, then specialize in the one you're most interested and/or where we need you most."

You: "Where and how fast does someone progress after that?"

Jones: "Obviously, that depends on the person, but given the proper aptitude and ability, that person would simply get more and bigger projects to work with. How well you do all along the way will determine how far and how fast you progress."

You: "What is the work environment like—is it pretty hectic?"

Jones: "We try to keep the work load at an even keel. The comfort of our workers is of prime importance to us. Excessive turnover is costly, you know. But advertising is an exciting business and things change sometimes minute-to-minute. It's not a profession for the faint-hearted!"

You: "If I may shift to another area, I'd be interested in your opinion about the advertising field in general and what you see as the most likely areas of opportunity in the forseeable future. Do you think this is a growth career area, despite the many changes that have occurred in the last 18 months?"

Jones: "Well, judging by the hiring record of our company, I think you'll find it's an area worth making a commitment to. At the entry level, we've hired a number of new people in the past three or four years. There always seems to be opportunities, though it's gotten far more competitive."

You: "Do you think someone with my qualifications and background could get started in sales at a major ad agency? Perhaps a look at my resume would be helpful to you." *(Give it to Mr. Jones.)*

Jones: "Your course work looks appropriate. I especially like the internships you've held every summer. I think you have a real chance to break into this field. I don't think we're hiring right now, but I know a couple of agencies that are looking for bright young people with qualifications like yours. Let me give you a couple of phone numbers." *(Write down names and phone numbers.)*

You: "You have been very generous with your time, but I can see from those flashing buttons on your phone that you have other things to do. Thank you again for taking the time to talk with me."

Jones: "You're welcome."

After the Interview

The next step should be obvious: **Two** thank-you letters are required, one to Mr. Jones, the second to Mr. Fredericks. Get them both out immediately. (And see the next chapter if you need help writing them.)

Keeping Track of The Interview Trail

Let's talk about record keeping again. If your networking works the way it's supposed to, this was only the first of many such interviews. Experts have estimated that the average person could develop a contact list of 250 people. Even if we limit your initial list to only 100, if each of them gave you one referral, your list would suddenly have 200 names. Presuming that it will not be necessary or helpful to see all of them, it's certainly possible that such a list could lead to 100 informational and/or job interviews! Unless you keep accurate records, by the time you're on No. 50, you won't even remember the first dozen!

So get the results of each interview down on paper. Use whatever format with which you're comfortable. You should create some kind of file, folder, or note card that is an "Interview Recap Record." If you have access to a personal computer, take advantage of it. It will be much easier to keep you information stored in one place and well-organized. Your record should be set up and contain something like the following:

Name: Ad Agency, Inc.

Address: 333 Madison Ave., NY, NY 10000

Phone: (212) 666-6666

Contact: Robert L. Jones

Type of Business: Complete design services

Referral Contact: Mr. Fredericks, Fidelity National Bank

Date: June 23, 1992

At this point, you should add a one- or two-paragraph summary of what you found out at the meeting. Since these comments are for your eyes only, you should be both objective and subjective. State the facts—what you found out in response to your specific questions—but include your impressions—your estimate of the opportunities for further discussions, your chances for future consideration for employment.

"I Was Just Calling To..."

Find any logical opportunity to stay in touch with Mr. Jones. You may, for example, let him know when you graduate and tell him your grade point average, carbon him in on any letters you write to Mr. Fredericks, even send a congratulatory note if his company's year-end financial results are positive or if you read something in the local paper about his department. This type of follow up has the all-important effect of keeping you and your name in the forefront of others' minds. Out of sight *is* out of mind. No matter how talented you may be or how good an impression you made, you'll have to work hard to "stay visible."

There Are Rules, Just Like Any Game

It should already be obvious that the networking process is not only effective, but also quite deliberate in its objectives. There are two specific groups of people you must attempt to target: those who can give you information about an industry or career area and those who are potential employers. The line between these groups may often blur. Don't be concerned—you'll soon learn when (and how) to shift the focus from interviewer to interviewee.

To simplify this process, follow a single rule: Show interest in the field or job area under discussion, but wait to be asked about actually working for that company. During your informational interviews, you will be surprised at the number of times the person you're interviewing turns to you and asks, "Would you be interested in...?" Consider carefully what's being asked and, if you *would* be interested in the position under discussion, make your feelings known.

If the Process Scares You

Some of you will undoubtedly be hesitant about, even fear, the networking process. It is not an unusual response—it is very human to want to accomplish things "on your own," without anyone's help. Understandable and commendable as such independence might seem, it is, in reality, an impediment if it limits your involvement in this important process. Networking has such universal application because **there is no other effective way to bridge the gap between job applicant and job.** Employers are grateful for its existence. You should be, too.

▼
Why Should You Network?
- To unearth current information about the industry, company and pertinent job functions. Remember: Your knowledge and understanding of broad industry trends, financial health, hiring opportunities, and the competitive picture are key.
- To investigate each company's hiring policies—who makes the decisions, who the key players are (personnel, staff managers), whether there's a hiring season, whether they prefer applicants going direct or through recruiters, etc.
- To sell yourself—discuss your interests and research activities—and leave your calling card, your resume.
- To seek out advice on refining your job search process.
- To obtain the names of other persons (referrals) who can give you additional information on where the jobs are and what the market conditions are like.

Whether you are a first-time applicant or reentering the work force now that the children are grown, the networking process will more than likely be your point of entry. Sending out mass mailings of your resume and answering the help-wanted ads may well be less personal (and, therefore, "easier") approaches, but they will also be far less effective. The natural selection process of the networking phenomenon is your assurance that water does indeed seek its own level—you will be matched up with agencies and job opportunities in which there is a mutual fit.

Six Good Reasons to Network

Many people fear the networking process because they think they are "bothering" others with their own selfish demands. Nonsense! There are good reasons—six of them, at least—why the people on your networking list will be happy to help you:

1. **Some day you will get to return the favor.** An ace insurance salesman built a successful business by offering low-cost coverage to first-year medical students. Ten years later, these now-successful practitioners remembered the company (and person) that helped them when they were just getting started. He gets new referrals every day.

2. **They, too, are seeking information.** An employer who has been out of school for several years might be interested in what the latest developments in the classroom are. He or she may be hoping to learn as much from you as you are from them, so be forthcoming in offering information. This desire for new information may be the reason he or she agreed to see you in the first place.

3. **Internal politics.** Some people will see you simply to make themselves appear powerful, implying to others in their organization that they have the authority to hire (they may or may not), an envied prerogative.

4. **They're "saving for a rainy day".** Executives know that it never hurts to look and that maintaining a backlog of qualified candidates is a big asset when the floodgates open and supervisors are forced to hire quickly.

5. **They're just plain nice.** Some people will see you simply because they feel it's the decent thing to do or because they just can't say "no."

6. **They are looking themselves.** Some people will see you because they are anxious to do a friend (whoever referred you) a favor. Or because they have another friend seeking new talent, in which case you represent a referral they can make (part of their own continuing network process). You see, networking never does stop—it helps them and it helps you.

Before you proceed to the next chapter, begin making your contact list. You may wish to keep a separate sheet of paper or note card on each person (especially the dozen or so you think are most important), even a separate telephone list to make your communications easier and more efficient. However you set up your list, be sure to keep it up to date—it won't be long before you'll be calling each and every name on the list.

CHAPTER TWENTY-ONE

Preparing Your Resume

Your resume is a one-page summary of you—your education, skills, employment experience and career objective(s). It is not a biography, but a "quick and dirty" way to identify and describe you to potential employers. Most importantly, its real purpose is to sell you to the company you want to work for. It must set you apart from all the other applicants (those competitors) out there.

So, as you sit down to formulate your resume, remember you're trying to present the pertinent information in a format and manner that will convince an executive to grant you an interview, the prelude to any job offer. All resumes must follow two basic rules—excellent visual presentation and honesty—but it's important to realize that different career markets require different resumes. The resume you are compiling for your career in advertising is much different than one you would prepare for a publishing career. As more and more resume " training" services become available, employers are becoming increasingly choosy about the resumes they receive. They expect to view a professional presentation, one that sets a candidate apart from the crowd. Your resume has to be perfect and it has to be specialized—clearly demonstrating the relationship between your qualifications and the job you are applying for.

What does this mean? It means the resume you use to land that first advertising job should demonstrate that you are creative, assertive, able to handle a fast-paced work environment, and are flexible. To offer an example, a woman who knew an advertising agency in Michigan handled accounts for outdoor products and hunting, and fishing equipment, sent her resume in on camouflage-colored paper. She quickly got the job.

An Overview of Resume Preparation

- **Know what you're doing**—your resume is a personal billboard of accomplishments. It must communicate your worth to a prospective employer in specific terms.

- **Your language should be action-oriented,** full of "doing"-type words. And less is better than more—be concise and direct. Don't worry about using complete sentences.

- **Be persuasive.** In those sections that allow you the freedom to do so, don't hesitate to communicate your worth in the strongest language. This does not mean a numbing list of self-congratulatory superlatives; it does mean truthful claims about your abilities and the evidence (educational, experiential) that supports them.

- **Don't be cheap or gaudy.** Don't hesitate to spend the few extra dollars necessary to present a professional-looking resume. Do avoid outlandish (and generally ineffective) gimmicks like oversized or brightly-colored paper.

- **Find an editor.** Every good writer needs one, and you are writing your resume. At the very least, it will offer you a second set of eyes proofreading for embarrassing typos. But if you are fortunate enough to have a professional in the field—a recruiter or personnel executive—critique a draft, grab the opportunity and be immensely grateful.

- **If you're the next Michaelangelo,** so multitalented that you can easily qualify for jobs in different career areas, don't hesitate to prepare two or more completely different resumes. This will enable you to change the emphasis on your education and skills according to the specific career objective on each resume, a necessary alteration that will correctly target each one.

- **Choose the proper format.** There are only three we recommend—chronological, functional, and targeted format—and it's important you use the one that's right for you.

The Records You Need

The resume-writing process begins with the assembly and organization of all the personal, educational, and employment data from which you will choose the pieces that actually end up on paper. If this information is properly organized, writing your resume will be a relatively easy task, essentially a simple process of just shifting data from a set of the worksheets to another, to your actual resume. At the end of this chapter, you'll find all the forms you need to prepare your resume, including worksheets, fill-in-the-blanks resume forms, and sample resumes.

As you will soon see, there is a great deal of information you'll need to keep track of. In order to avoid a fevered search for important information, take the time right now to designate a single location in which to store all your records. My recommendation is either a filing cabinet or an expandable pocket portfolio. The latter is less expensive, yet it will still enable you to sort your records into an unlimited number of more-manageable categories.

Losing important report cards, citations, letters, etc., is easy to do if your life's history is scattered throughout your room or, even worse, your house! While copies of many of these items may be obtainable, why put yourself through all that extra work? Making good organization a habit will ensure that all the records you need to prepare your resume will be right where you need them when you need them.

For each of the categories summarized below, designate a separate file folder in which pertinent records can be kept. Your own notes are important, but keeping actual report cards, award citations, letters, etc. is even more so. Here's what your record-keeping system should include:

Transcripts (Including GPA and Class Rank Information)

Transcripts are your school's official record of your academic history, usually available, on request, from your high school's guidance office or college registrar's office. Your college may charge you for copies and "on request" doesn't mean "whenever you want"—you may have to wait some time for your request to be processed (so **don't** wait until the last minute!).

Your school-calculated GPA (Grade Point Average) is on the transcript. Most schools calculate this by multiplying the credit hours assigned to each course times a numerical grade equivalent (e.g., "A" = 4.0, "B" = 3.0, etc.), then dividing by total credits/ courses taken. Class rank is simply a listing of GPAs, from highest to lowest.

Employment Records

Details on every part-time or full-time job you've held, including:

- Each employer's name, address and telephone number
- Name of supervisor
- Exact dates worked
- Approximate numbers of hours per week
- Specific duties and responsibilities
- Specific skills utilized and developed
- Accomplishments, honors
- Copies of awards, letters of recommendation

Volunteer Activities

Just because you weren't paid for a specific job—stuffing envelopes for the local Republican candidate, running a car wash to raise money for the homeless, manning a drug hotline—doesn't mean that it wasn't significant or that you shouldn't include it on your resume.

So keep the same detailed notes on these volunteer activities as you have on the jobs you've held:

- Each organization's name, address and telephone number
- Name of supervisor
- Exact dates worked

- Approximate numbers of hours per week
- Specific duties and responsibilities
- Specific skills utilized
- Accomplishments, honors
- Copies of awards, letters of recommendation

Extracurricular Activities

List all sports, clubs, or other activities in which you've participated, either inside or outside school. For each, you should include:
- Name of activity/club/group
- Office(s) held
- Purpose of club/activity
- Specific duties/responsibilities
- Achievements, accomplishments, awards

If you were a long-standing member of a group or club, also include the dates that you were a member. This could demonstrate a high-level of commitment that could be used as a selling point.

Honors And Awards

Even if some of these honors are previously listed, specific data on every honor or award you receive should be kept, including, of course, the award itself! Keep the following information in your awards folder:
- Award name
- Date and from whom received
- What it was for
- Any pertinent details

Military Records

Complete military history, if pertinent, including:
- Dates of service
- Final rank awarded
- Duties and responsibilities
- All citations and awards
- Details on specific training and/or special schooling
- Skills developed
- Specific accomplishments

At the end of this chapter are seven **Data Input Sheets**. The first five cover employment, volunteer work, education, activities and awards and are essential to any resume. The last two—covering military service and language skills—are important if, of course, they apply to you. I've only included one copy of each but, if you need to, you can copy the forms you need or simply write up your own using these as models.

Here are some pointers on how to fill out these all-important Data Sheets:

Employment Data Input Sheet: You will need to record the basic information—employer's name, address and phone number, dates of employment and your supervisor's name—for your own files anyway. It may be an important addition to your networking list and will be necessary should you be asked to supply a reference list.

Duties should be a series of brief action statements describing what you did on this job. For example, if you worked as a hostess in a restaurant, this section might read: "Responsible for the delivery of 250 meals at dinner time and the supervision of 20 waiters and busboys. Coordinated reservations. Responsible for check and payment verification."

Skills should enumerate specific capabilities either necessary for the job or developed through it.

If you achieved *specific results*—e.g., "developed new filing system," "collected over $5,000 in previously-assumed bad debt," "instituted award-winning art program," etc.—or *received any award, citation or other honor*—"named Employee of the Month three times," "received Mayor's Citation for Innovation," etc.—make sure you list these.

Prepare one employment data sheet for each of the last three positions you have held; this is a basic guideline, but you can include more if relevant. Do not include sheets for short-term jobs (i.e., those that lasted one month or less).

Volunteer Work Data Input Sheet: Treat any volunteer work, no matter how basic or short (one day counts!), as if it were a job and record the same information. In both cases, it is especially important to note specific duties and responsibilities, skills required or developed and any accomplishments or achievements you can point to as evidence of your success.

Educational Data Input Sheet: If you're in college, omit details on high school. If you're a graduate student, list details on both graduate and undergraduate coursework. If you have not yet graduated, list your anticipated date of graduation. If more than a year away, indicate the numbers of credits earned through the most recent semester to be completed.

Activities Data Input Sheet: List your participation in the Student Government, Winter Carnival Press Committee, Math Club, Ski Patrol, etc., plus sports teams and/or any participation in community or church groups. Make sure you indicate if you were elected to any positions in clubs, groups, or on teams.

Awards And Honors Data Input Sheet: List awards and honors from your school (prestigious high school awards can still be included here, even if you're in graduate school), community groups, church groups, clubs, etc.

Military Service Data Input Sheet: Many useful skills are learned in the armed forces. A military stint often hastens the maturation process, making you a more attractive candidate. So if you have served in the military, make sure you include details in your resume. Again, include any computer skills you gained while in the service.

Language Data Input Sheet: An extremely important section for those of you with a real proficiency in a second language. And do make sure you have at least conversational fluency in the language(s) you list. One year of college French doesn't count, but if you've studied abroad, you probably are fluent or near-fluent. Such a talent could be invaluable, especially in today's increasingly international business climate.

While you should use the Data Input Sheets to summarize all of the data you have collected, do not throw away any of the specific information—report cards, transcripts, citations, etc.—just because it is recorded on these sheets. Keep all records in your files; you'll never know when you'll need them again!

Don't Forget Your Portfolio

When trying to land that first advertising job, your portfolio is just as important as your resume—maybe more so. With that in mind, here is some sound advice on how to put together a portfolio for either a designer or a copywriter position.

The Basics of a Design Portfolio

When shopping for your first portfolio, bite the bullet and buy the largest one that's comfortable for you to carry (look for handles). You'll need the room for oversized samples, page spreads, keeping multiple-part campaigns together, etc.

Acetate pages are best. They let your interviewer take out a piece to examine it more closely, and allow you to easily customize your presentation to your interviewer by removing/adding pages without revamping your whole book.

Since interviewers often expect designers to leave their portfolios behind for more careful perusal or review by others, it's important to label your samples so the book "speaks for you" in your absence. Make sure to have your name and phone number on it, and before you leave, arrange a day and time when you can return to pick it up!

If you're lucky enough to have had designs make it into print, devote a few pages of your portfolio to show a project's progress from original concept through finished piece. Your interviewer will get a better handle on your creative exploration skills if you show a few alternate ideas in thumbnail stage...and your technical skills by seeing how you render type and execute a comprehensive dummy even through camera-ready art. (You'll want to walk the interviewer through any changes that occurred by the time the final piece was printed, putting your negotiation abilities on display.)

Introduce this section with a brief, typewritten creative platform defining your objectives; then annotate (again, label) your samples to show how you achieved them. This will illustrate organization skills, problem-solving, and clear thinking—attributes you'll want to get across in any interview.

If you're thin on printed work, produce a self-promotional piece. Your own brochure (including logo) can communicate a lot about your personal design philosophy—and work ethic!

Get feedback on your portfolio before you hit the pavement—past professors are great; ask peers and nondesigners, too. Not everyone that interviews you will have a graphic arts background, so you want to make sure your book is easily understood by all.

How to Make Your Writing Portfolio Shine

To present your writing samples, choose a portfolio with protective acetate pages large enough to accommodate both single- and multiple-page pieces—from advertising tear-sheets to brochures—without gluing them down. (A pocket in the cover that can hold larger samples, like catalogs, annual reports, or magazines is useful too.) This serves a two-fold purpose: first, it lets you customize your presentation for different interviews or situations; secondly, it lets your prospect take out a piece to examine it more closely (which, by the way, is an excellent sign).

Put your best stuff first. In the ideal interview, you'll never make it all the way through the book. And, while you should try to show diversity, select samples you think will most interest your interviewer. If you've done your homework, you'll know the types of accounts his or her agency handles—try to have your portfolio reflect this.

If you're new to the job market and are "thin" on printed or published samples, here are two suggestions. Use writing samples from your college courses (advertising or otherwise) and accompany each with a **creative platform**—if you can define your objectives in writing then show how you achieved them, the battle is half won. Another way to showcase your skills is to choose a few published ads from magazines or direct mail pieces from your mailbox and rewrite them **better.** (Here, of course, you'll want to select products or services relevant to your interviewer's interests, being careful not to rewrite any of his or her pet projects.)

Creating Your First Resume

There are many options that you can include or leave out. In general, we suggest you always include the following data:

1. Your name, address and telephone number
2. Pertinent educational history (grades, class rank, activities, etc.) Follow the grade point "rule of thumb"—mention it only if it is above 3.0.
3. Pertinent work history
4. Academic honors
5. Memberships in organizations
6. Military service history (if applicable)

You have the option of including the following:

1. Your career objective
2. Personal data
3. Hobbies
4. Summary of qualifications

5. Feelings about travel and relocation (Include this if you know in advance that the job you are applying for requires it. Often times, for future promotion, job seekers **must** be willing to relocate.

And you should never include the following:

1. Photographs or illustrations (of yourself or anything else) unless they are required by your profession—e.g., actors' composites

2. Why you left past jobs

3. References

4. Salary history or present salary objectives/requirements (if salary history is specifically requested in an ad, it may be included in your cover letter)

Special note: There is definitely a school of thought that discourages any mention of personal data—marital status, health, etc.—on a resume. While I am not vehemently opposed to including such information, I am not convinced it is particularly necessary, either.

As far as hobbies go, I would only include such information if it were in some way pertinent to the job/career you're targeting, or if it shows how well-rounded you are. Your love of reading is pertinent if, for example, you are applying for a part-time job at a library. But including details on the joys of "hiking, long walks with my dog and Isaac Asimov short stories" is nothing but filler and should be left out.

Maximizing Form and Substance

Your resume should be limited to a single page if possible. A two-page resume should be used **only** if you have an extensive work background related to a future goal. When you're laying out the resume, try to leave a reasonable amount of "white space"—generous margins all around and spacing between entries. It should be typed or printed (not Xeroxed) on 8 1/2" x 11" white, cream, or ivory stock. The ink should be black. Don't scrimp on the paper quality—use the best bond you can afford. And since printing 100 or even 200 copies will cost only a little more than 50, if you do decide to print your resume, *over*estimate your needs and opt for the highest quantity you think you may need. Prices at various "quick print" shops are not exorbitant and the quality look printing affords will leave the impression you want.

Use Power Words for Impact

Be brief. Use phrases rather than complete sentences. Your resume is a summary of your talents, not a term paper. Choose your words carefully and use "power words" whenever possible. "Organized" is more powerful than "put together;" "supervised" better than "oversaw;" "formulated" better than "thought up." Strong words like these can make the most mundane clerical work sound like a series of responsible, professional positions. And, of course, they will tend to make your resume stand out. Here's a starter list of words that you may want to use in your resume:

achieved	developed	issued	researched
administered	devised	launched	reviewed
advised	directed	lectured	revised
analyzed	established	litigated	reorganized
applied	evaluated	lobbied	regulated
arranged	executed	managed	selected
budgeted	formulated	negotiated	solved
calculated	gathered	operated	scheduled
classified	generated	organized	supervised
communicated	guided	overhauled	systematized
completed	implemented	planned	taught
computed	improved	prepared	tested
conceptualized	initiated	presented	trained
coordinated	instituted	presided	updated
critiqued	instructed	programmed	utilized
delegated	introduced	promoted	
determined	invented	recommended	

Choose the Right Format

There is not much mystery here—your background will generally lead you to the right format. For an entry-level job applicant with limited work experience, the chronological format, which organizes your educational and employment history by date (most recent first) is the obvious choice. For older or more experienced applicants, either the functional—which emphasizes the duties and responsibilities of all your jobs over the course of your career, may be more suitable. If you are applying for a specific position in one field, the targeted format is for you. While I have tended to emphasize the chronological format in this chapter, one of the other two may well be the right one for you.

A List of Do's and Don't's

In case we didn't stress them enough, here are some rules to follow:

- **Do** be brief and to the point—Two pages if absolutely necessary, one page if at all possible. Never longer!
- **Don't** be fancy. Multicolored paper and all-italic type won't impress employers, just make your resume harder to read (and easier to discard). Use plain white or ivory paper, blue or black ink and an easy-to-read standard typeface.
- **Do** forget rules about sentences. Say what you need to say in the fewest words possible; use phrases, not drawn-out sentences.
- **Do** stick to the facts. Don't talk about your dog, vacation, etc.
- **Don't** ever send a resume blind. A cover letter should always accompany a resume and that letter should always be directed to a specific person.
- **Don't** have any typos. Your resume must be perfect—proofread everything as many times as necessary to catch any misspellings, grammatical errors, strange hyphenations, or typos.

ADVERTISING CAREER DIRECTORY

- **Do** use the spell check feature on your personal computer to find errors, and also try reading the resume backwards—you'll be surprised at how errors jump out at you when you do this. Finally, have a friend proof your resume.
- **Do** use your resume as your sales tool. It is, in many cases, as close to you as an employer will ever get. Make sure it includes the information necessary to sell yourself the way you want to be sold!
- **Do** spend the money for good printing. Soiled, tattered or poorly reproduced copies speak poorly of your own self-image. Spend the money and take the time to make sure your resume is the best presentation you've ever made.
- **Do** help the reader, by organizing your resume in a clear-cut manner so key points are easily gleaned.
- **Don't** have a cluttered resume. Leave plenty of white space, especially around headings and all four margins.
- **Do** use bullets, asterisks, or other symbols as "stop signs" that the reader's eye will be naturally drawn to.

On the following pages, I've included a "fill-in-the-blanks" resume form so you can construct your own resume right away, plus a couple of samples of well-constructed student resumes.

EMPLOYMENT DATA INPUT SHEET

Employer name: _____

Address: _____

Phone: _____ Dates of employment: _____

Hours per week: _____ Salary/Pay: _____

Supervisor's name and title: _____

Duties: _____
_____
_____

Skills utilized: _____
_____
_____

Accomplishments/Honors/Awards: _____
_____
_____

Other important information: _____
_____
_____

ADVERTISING CAREER DIRECTORY

VOLUNTEER WORK DATA INPUT SHEET

Organization name: _____

Address: _____

Phone: _____ Dates of activity: _____

Hours per week: _____

Supervisor's name and title: _____

Duties: _____
_____
_____

Skills utilized: _____
_____
_____
_____

Accomplishments/Honors/Awards: _____
_____
_____
_____

Other important information: _____
_____
_____

HIGH SCHOOL DATA INPUT SHEET

School name: _____

Address: _____

Phone: _____ Years attended: _____

Major studies: _____

GPA/Class rank: _____

Honors: _____

Important courses: _____

_____

_____

_____

OTHER SCHOOL DATA INPUT SHEET

School name: _____

Address: _____

Phone: _____ Years attended: _____

Major studies: _____

GPA/Class rank: _____

Honors: _____

Important courses: _____

_____

_____

ADVERTISING CAREER DIRECTORY

COLLEGE DATA INPUT SHEET

College: _____

Address: _____

Phone: _____   Years attended: _____

Degrees earned: _____ Major: _____ Minor: _____

Honors: _____

Important courses: _____

_____

_____

_____

_____

GRADUATE SCHOOL DATA INPUT SHEET

College: _____

Address: _____

Phone: _____   Years attended: _____

Degrees earned: _____ Major: _____ Minor: _____

Honors: _____

Important courses: _____

_____

_____

_____

_____

MILITARY SERVICE DATA INPUT SHEET

Branch: _____

Rank (at discharge): _____

Dates of service: _____

Duties and responsibilities: _____
_____
_____
_____

Special training and/or school attended: _____
_____
_____
_____

Citations or awards: _____
_____
_____
_____

Specific accomplishments: _____
_____
_____
_____

ADVERTISING CAREER DIRECTORY

ACTIVITIES DATA INPUT SHEET

Club/activity: _____ Office(s) held: _____

Description of participation: _____

_____

_____

Duties/responsibilities: _____

_____

Club/activity: _____ Office(s) held: _____

Description of participation: _____

_____

_____

Duties/responsibilities: _____

_____

Club/activity: _____ Office(s) held: _____

Description of participation: _____

_____

_____

Duties/responsibilities: _____

_____

AWARDS AND HONORS DATA INPUT SHEET

Name of Award or Citation: _____

From Whom Received: _____ Date: _____

Significance: _____

_____

Other pertinent information: _____

_____

Name of Award or Citation: _____

From Whom Received: _____ Date: _____

Significance: _____

_____

Other pertinent information: _____

_____

Name of Award or Citation: _____

From Whom Received: _____ Date: _____

Significance: _____

_____

Other pertinent information: _____

_____

ADVERTISING CAREER DIRECTORY

LANGUAGE DATA INPUT SHEET

Language: _____

___Read ___Write ___Converse

Background (number of years studied, travel, etc.) _____

_____

_____

_____

Language: _____

___Read ___Write ___Converse

Background (number of years studied, travel, etc.) _____

_____

_____

_____

Language: _____

___Read ___Write ___Converse

Background (number of years studied, travel, etc.) _____

_____

_____

_____

FILL-IN-THE-BLANKS RESUME OUTLINE

Name: _____

Address: _____

City, state, ZIP Code: _____

Telephone number: _____

OBJECTIVE: _____

_____

_____

_____

_____

SUMMARY OF QUALIFICATIONS: _____

_____

_____

_____

EDUCATION

GRADUATE SCHOOL: _____

Address: _____

City, state, ZIP Code: _____

Expected graduation date: _____ Grade Point Average: _____

Degree earned (expected): _____ Class Rank: _____

ADVERTISING CAREER DIRECTORY

Important classes, especially those related to your career: _____
_____
_____
_____
_____
_____
_____

COLLEGE: _____

Address: _____

City, state, ZIP Code: _____

Expected graduation date: _____ Grade Point Average: _____

Class rank: _____ Major: _____ Minor: _____

Important classes, especially those related to your career: _____
_____
_____
_____
_____
_____
_____

HIGH SCHOOL: _____

Address: _____

City, state, ZIP Code: _____

Expected graduation date: _____ Grade Point Average: _____

Class rank: _____

Important classes, especially those related to your career: _____
_____
_____
_____
_____
_____
_____
_____

HOBBIES AND OTHER INTERESTS (OPTIONAL) _____
_____
_____
_____
_____

EXTRACURRICULAR ACTIVITIES (Activity name, dates participated, duties and responsibilities, offices held, accomplishments): _____

_____
_____
_____
_____
_____
_____
_____
_____

AWARDS AND HONORS (Award name, from whom and date received, significance of the award and any other pertinent details): _____

_____
_____
_____
_____
_____
_____
_____
_____

WORK EXPERIENCE. Include job title, name of business, address and telephone number, dates of employment, supervisor's name and title, your major responsibilities, accomplishments, and any awards won. Include volunteer experience in this category. List your experiences with the most recent dates first, even if you later decide not to use a chronological format.

_____

_____

_____

_____

_____

_____

_____

_____

_____

_____

_____

_____

_____

_____

_____

_____

_____

REFERENCES. Though you should *not* include references in your resume, you do need to prepare a separate list of at least three people who know you fairly well and will recommend you highly to prospective employers. For each, include job title, company name, address, and telephone number. Before you include anyone on this list, make sure you have their permission to use their name as a reference and confirm what they intend to say about you to a potential employer.

1. _____

2. _____

3. _____

4. _____

5. _____

Creative Cover Sheet for Advertising

MOTIVATED

CREATIVE

FLEXIBLE

ENERGETIC

COLLEGE GRADUATE

Seeking Position

Sample Resume: Targeted

DONNA B. MARIE

Local Address:
4240 Hill Road
Los Angeles, CA 90410
(213) 555-0100

Permanent Address:
80 Stemmons
Dallas, TX 87540
(214) 555-0000

GOAL **Marketing Research** position within the faced-paced Advertising Industry demanding quality performance and offering a challenge.

EDUCATION
U.C.L.A., West L.A., CA
Bachelor of Science in **Marketing**, June 1993
Summa Cum Laude
Current Graduate Study:
*Sales Management, Consumer Behavior

Relevant Skills:
*Knowledge of Marketing and Advertising Theory.
*Participated in Statistical Analysis Research Project for Chamber of Commerce as Class Assignment.
*Statistical computer software, Word Perfect, Excel.

RELATED EXPERIENCE

Summer, 1992 — Jim Cannon, Inc., Los Angeles, CA
Administrative Assistant in Research Department
Responsible for record keeping, expense reports, public relations lab report dissemination, and correspondence.
Key Result: Trained in behavioral research techniques.

Summer, 1990-91 — Kischtronics, San Diego, CA
Sales and Management Trainee
Duties included billing, inventory control, shipping and distribution, lab maintenance and delivery schedules.
Key Result: Experienced in all aspects of a major research and development facility.

HONORS/ ACTIVITIES
Marketing Club, Treasurer, 1991
United Way, Head Fund Raiser
National Honor Society, President
Track Athlete of the Year, 1989

Sample Resume: Functional

ROBERT DANIEL SMITH
76 Spruce St.
New York, NY 10017
(212) 555-1111

CAREER OBJECTIVE
Entry level position within an aggressive **Advertising Agency** demanding Ability, Motivation, and Creativity.

EDUCATION
University State	New York	Bachelor of Arts
Advertising Major	June 1993	Cum Laude

PRODUCTION/EDITING
*Assisted traffic coordinator in facilitating ad production.
*Wrote effective ad script for University paper.

COMMUNICATIONS
*Interfaced with various ad departments including legal, video, and creative.
*Scheduler for cable programming; required excellent telephone skills.
*Supervised staff of three salespersons.

HIGHLY MOTIVATED
*Earned "Outstanding Intern" Award, University State, 1992.
*National Honor Society, President, Cortland High School.

TECHNICAL EXPERTISE
*Orchestrated complete cable "spot" entitled *"Fall Fashion: What They're Wearing"* including script writing, stage design/set-up, selecting session host, filming/editing.
*Layout and design using PageMaker/CorelDraw.

PROFESSIONAL EXPERIENCE

Summer, 1991	Summer, 1992
Brown Associates, Inc., NY, NY	Burton Cable, Inc, Englewood, NJ
Co-op Traffic Assistant	**Cable Assistant/Intern**

HONORS/ACTIVITIES
Dean's List; Advertising Club of New York
<u>University State News</u>, Advertising Coordinator, 1992
Fluent in Spanish; Willing to relocate

REFERENCES/PORTFOLIO/VIDEOS
Available Upon Request

Sample Resume: Chronological

CHRISTOPHER F. GREEN

367 Warrington Road
East Lansing, MI 48824
(517) 555-1111

****

OBJECTIVE	To obtain a position offering a challenge in the **Advertising Industry**.
EDUCATION	Michigan State University East Lansing, MI Bachelor of Arts in **Advertising**, June, 1993 Cumulative GPA: 2.9 Major GPA: 3.5 (Financed 75% of college expense through employment)
EMPLOYMENT EXPERIENCE	Admissions Department East Lansing, MI 9/91 - Present **Clerk:** Responsibilities include preparing promotional items for prospective students; clerical duties; use of Lotus 1-2-3 for accurate tracking. Creativity-By-Design, Inc. Lansing, MI Summer, 1991 **Advertising Intern:** Responsibilities included business-to-business brochures, including art design; hands-on experience with desktop publishing; cold calling of prospective clients. Montgomery Ward Lansing, MI 9/90 - 5/91 **Sales Associate:** Duties included assisting customers, supervising 6 workers as group leader during store renovation.
HONORS	Scholastic Art Award, 1991-92 Partial Art Scholarship
ACTIVITIES	Advertising Club MSU Concert Band President - 1992 Campus Tour Guide Membership - 1991 Freelance Artist
REFERENCES/ WORK SAMPLES	Available Upon Request

****

CHAPTER TWENTY-TWO

Writing Better Letters

Stop for a moment and review your resume draft. It is undoubtedly (by now) a near-perfect document that instantly tells the reader the kind of job you want and why you are qualified. But does it say anything personal about you? Any amplification of your talents? Any words that are ideally "you?" Any hint of the kind of person who stands behind that resume?

If you've prepared it properly, the answers should be a series of ringing "no's"—your resume should be a mere sketch of your life, a bare-bones summary of your skills, education, and experience.

To the general we must add the specific. That's what your letters must accomplish—adding the lines, colors, and shading that will help fill out your self-portrait. This chapter will cover the kinds of letters you will most often be called upon to prepare in your job search. There are essentially nine different types you will utilize again and again, based primarily on what each is trying to accomplish. I've included at least one well-written example of each at the end of this chapter.

Answer these Questions

Before you put pencil to paper to compose any letter, there are five key questions you must ask yourself:

- Why are you writing it?
- To Whom?
- What are you trying to accomplish?
- Which lead will get the reader's attention?
- How do you organize the letter to best accomplish your objectives?

Why?

There should be a single, easily definable reason you are writing any letter. This reason will often dictate what and how you write—the tone and flavor of the letter—as well as what you include or leave out.

Have you been asked in an ad to amplify your qualifications for a job and provide a salary history and college transcripts? Then that (minimally) is your objective in writing. Limit yourself to following instructions and do a little personal selling—but very little. Including everything asked for and a simple, adequate cover letter is better than writing a "knock 'em, sock 'em" letter and omitting the one piece of information the ad specifically asked for.

If, however, you are on a networking search, the objective of your letter is to seek out contacts who will refer you for possible informational or job interviews. In this case, getting a name and address—a referral—is your stated purpose for writing. You have to be specific and ask for this action.

You will no doubt follow up with a phone call, but be certain the letter conveys what you are after. Being vague or oblique won't help you. You are after a definite yes or no when it comes to contact assistance. The recipient of your letter should know this. As they say in the world of selling, at some point you have to ask for the order.

Who?

Using the proper "tone" in a letter is as important as the content—you wouldn't write to the owner of the local meat market using the same words and style as you would employ in a letter to the director of personnel of a major company. Properly addressing the person or persons you are writing to is as important as what you say to them.

Some hints to utilize: the recipient's job title and level, his or her hiring clout (correct title and spelling are a **must**), the kind of person they are (based on your knowledge of their area of involvement), etc. (Even if you know the letter is going through a screening stage instead of to the actual person you need to contact, don't take the easy way out. You have to sell the person doing the screening just as convincingly as you would the actual contact, or else you might get passed over instead of passed along! Don't underestimate the power of the person doing the screening.)

For example, it pays to sound technical with technical people—in other words, use the kinds of words and language which they use on the job. If you have had the opportunity to speak with them, it will be easy for you. If not, and you have formed some opinions as to their types then use these as the basis of the language you employ. The cardinal rule is to say it in words you think the recipient will be comfortable hearing, not in the words you might otherwise personally choose.

What?

What do you have to offer that company? What do you have to contribute to the job, process or work situation that is unique and/or of particular benefit to the recipient of your letter.

For example, if you were applying for a sales position and recently ranked number one in a summer sales job, then conveying this benefit is logical and desirable. It is a factor you may have left off your resume. Even if it was listed in your skills/accomplishment section of the resume, you can underscore and call attention to it in your letter. Repetition, when it is properly focused, can be a good thing.

Which?

Of all the opening sentences you can compose, which will immediately get the reader's attention? If your opening sentence is dynamic, you are already fifty percent of the way to your end objective—having your entire letter read. Don't slide into it. Know the point you are trying to make and come right to it. One word of caution: your first sentence **must** make mention of what led you to write—was it an ad, someone at the company, a story you saw on television? Be sure to give this point of reference.

How?

While a good opening is essential, how do you organize your letter so that it is easy for the recipient to read in its entirety. This is a question of *flow*—the way the words and sentences naturally lead one to another, holding the reader's interest until he or she reaches your signature.

If you have your objective clearly in mind, this task is easier than it sounds: Simply convey your message(s) in a logical sequence. End your letter by stating what the next steps are—yours and/or the reader's.

One More Time

Pay attention to the small things. Neatness still counts. Have your letters typed. Spend a few extra dollars and have some personal stationery printed.

And most important, make certain that your correspondence goes out quickly. The general rule is to get a letter in the mail during the week in which the project comes to your attention or in which you have had some contact with the organization. I personally attempt to mail follow-up letters the same day as the contact; at worst, within 24 hours.

When to Write

- To answer an ad
- To prospect (many companies)
- To inquire about specific openings (single company)
- To obtain a referral
- To obtain an informational interview
- To obtain a job interview
- To say "thank you"
- To accept or reject a job offer
- To withdraw from consideration for a job

In some cases, the letter will accompany your resume; in others, it will need to stand alone. Each of the above circumstance is described in the pages that follow. I have included at least one sample of each type of letter at the end of this chapter.

Answering an Ad

Your eye catches an ad in the Positions Available section of the Sunday paper for an assistant designer. It tells you that the position is in a large ad agency and that, though some experience would be desirable, it is not required. Well, you possess *those* skills. The ad asks that you send a letter and resume to a Post Office Box. No salary is indicated, no phone number given. You decide to reply.

Your purpose in writing—the objective (why?)—is to secure a job interview. Since no person is singled out for receipt of the ad, and since it is a large company, you assume it will be screened by Human Resources.

Adopt a professional, formal tone. You are answering a "blind" ad, so you have to play it safe. In your first sentence, refer to the ad, including the place and date of publication and the position outlined. (There is a chance that the company is running more than one ad on the same date and in the same paper, so you need to identify the one to which you are replying.) Tell the reader what (specifically) you have to offer that agency. Include your resume, phone number, and the times it is easiest to reach you. Ask for the order—tell them you'd like to have an appointment. (A sample of this and other letter types is included at the end of this chapter.)

Blanket Prospecting Letter

In June of this year you will graduate from a four-year college with a degree in advertising. You seek a position (internship or full-time employment) in a major agency's creative department. You have decided to write to 50 top agencies, sending each a copy of your resume. You don't know which, if any, have job openings.

Such blanket mailings are effective given two circumstances: 1) You must have an exemplary record and a resume which reflects it; and 2) You must send out a goodly number of packages, since the response rate to such mailings is very low.

A blanket mailing doesn't mean an impersonal one—you should always be writing to a specific executive. If you have a referral, send a personalized letter to that person. If not, do not simply mail a package to the Human Resources department; identify the department head and *then* send a personalized letter. And make sure you get on the phone and follow up each letter within about ten days. Don't just sit back and wait for everyone to call you. They won't.

Just Inquiring

The inquiry letter is a step above the blanket prospecting letter; it's a "cold-calling" device with a twist. You have earmarked a company (and a person) as a possibility in your job search based on something you have read about them. Your general research tells you that it is a good place to work. Although you are not aware of any specific openings, you know that they employ entry-level personnel with your credentials.

While ostensibly inquiring about any openings, you are really just "referring yourself" to them in order to place your resume in front of the right person. This is what I would call a "why not?" attempt at securing a job interview. Its effectiveness depends on their actually having been in the news. This, after all, is your "excuse" for writing.

Networking

It's time to get out that folder marked "Contacts" and prepare a draft networking letter. The lead sentence should be very specific, referring immediately to the friend, colleague, etc. "who suggested I write you about..." Remember: Your objective is to secure an informational interview, pave the way for a job interview, and/or get referred to still other contacts.

This type of letter should not place the recipient in a position where a decision is necessary; rather, the request should be couched in terms of "career advice." The second paragraph can then inform the reader of your level of experience. Finally, be specific about seeking an appointment.

Unless you have been specifically asked by the referring person to do so, you will probably not be including a resume with such letters. So the letter itself must highlight your credentials, enabling the reader to gauge your relative level of experience. For entry-level personnel, education, of course, will be most important.

For an Informational Interview

Though the objectives of this letter are similar to those of the networking letter, they are not as personal. These are "knowledge quests" on your part and the recipient will most likely not be someone you have been referred to. The idea is to convince the reader of the sincerity of your research effort. Whatever selling you do, if you do any at all, will arise as a consequence of the meeting, not beforehand. A positive response to this type of request is in itself a good step forward. It is, after all, exposure, and amazing things can develop when people in authority agree to see you.

Thank-You Letters

Although it may not always seem so, manners do count in the job world. But what counts even more are the simple gestures that show you actually care—like writing a thank-you letter. A well-executed, timely thank-you note tells more about your personality than anything else you may have sent, and it also demonstrates excellent follow-through skills. It says something about the way you were brought up—whatever else your resume tells them, you are, at least, polite, courteous and thoughtful.

Thank-you letters may well become the beginning of an all-important dialogue that leads directly to a job. So be extra careful in composing them, and make certain that they are custom made for each occasion and person.

The following are the primary situations in which you will be called upon to write some variation of thank-you letter:

1. After a job interview
2. After an informational interview
3. Accepting a job offer
4. Responding to rejection: While optional, such a letter is appropriate if you have been among the finalists in a job search or were rejected due to limited experience. Remember: Some day you'll *have* enough experience; make the interviewer want to stay in touch.

THE JOB SEARCH PROCESS

5. Withdrawing from consideration: Used when you decide you are no longer interested in a particular position. (A variation is usable for declining an actual job offer.) Whatever the reason for writing such a letter, it's wise to do so and thus keep future lines of communication open.

IN RESPONSE TO AN AD

10 E. 89th Street
New York, NY 10028
August 10, 1992

The New York Times
PO Box 7520
New York, NY 10128

Dear Sir or Madam:

This letter is in response to your advertisement for an assistant publicist which appeared in the July 20th issue of the *New York Times*.

I have the qualifications you are seeking. I graduated magna cum laude from Emerson Junior College with a degree in advertising and a minor in journalism.

I wrote for the Emerson newspaper--the *Collegian*--during all four years. During my senior year, when I was editor-in-chief, we won four awards for editorial excellence--three more than Emerson had ever won before.

For the past three summers, I have worked for Johnson Advertising, a firm specializing in publishing accounts. This position has provided me with hands-on experience in the advertising field, as well as the chance to use and hone my writing, communication and interpersonal skills.

My resume is enclosed. I would like to have the opportunity to meet with you personally to discuss your requirements for the position. I can be reached at (212) 785-1225 between 8:00 a.m. and 5:00 p.m. and at (212) 785-4221 after 5:00 p.m. I look forward to hearing from you.

Sincerely,

Karen Weber

Enclosure: Resume, Clips

PROSPECTING LETTER

Kim Kerr
8 Robutuck Hwy.
Hammond, IN 54054
515-555-2392

August 10, 1992

Mr. Fred Jones
Vice President--Account Management
Alcott & Alcott
One Lakeshore Drive
Chicago, IL 60606

Dear Mr. Jones:

The name of Alcott & Alcott continually pops up in our classroom discussions of outstanding advertising firms. Given my interest in advertising as a career and account management as a specialty, I've taken the liberty of enclosing my resume.

As you can see, I have just completed a very comprehensive four years of study at Warren University majoring in advertising, with an emphasis on agency financing. Though my resume does not indicate it, I will be graduating in the top 10% of my class, with honors.

I will be in the Chicago area on August 29 and will call your office to see when it is convenient to arrange an appointment.

Sincerely yours,

Kim Kerr

INQUIRY LETTER

42 7th Street
Ski City, VT 85722
September 30, 1992

Mr. Michael Maniaci
President
Pinnacle Ad & PR, Inc.
521 West Elm Street
Indianapolis, IN 83230

Dear Mr. Maniaci:

I just completed reading the article in the October issue of *Fortune* on your company's record-breaking quarter. Congratulations!

Your innovative approach to recruiting minorities is of particular interest to me because of my background in advertising and minority recruitment.

I am interested in learning more about your work as well as the possibilities of joining your firm. My qualifications include:

- B.A. in Communications
- Research on minority recruitment
- Advertising Seminar participation (Univ. of Virginia)
- Reports preparation on creative writing, education and minorities

I will be in Indiana during the week of October 10 and hope your schedule will permit us to meet briefly to discuss our mutual interests. I will call your office next week to see if such a meeting can be arranged.

I appreciate your consideration.

Sincerely yours,

Ronald W. Sommerville

NETWORKING LETTER

Richard A. Starky
42 Bach St.
Musical City, IN 20202
317-555-1515

November 14, 1992

Ms. Michelle Fleming
Vice President
Creative Planning Associates
42 Jenkins Avenue
Fulton, MS 23232

Dear Ms. Fleming:

Sam Kinney suggested I write you. I am interested in an entry-level account management position with an advertising firm. Sam felt it would be mutually beneficial for us to meet and talk.

I have been educated and trained as an accountant and have just over two years part-time experience in bookkeeping, accounting, auditing, and tax work. But I also worked in the advertising department of my college newspaper throughout my undergraduate career. I am particularly interested in finding a way to mesh my interests.

I know from Sam how similar our backgrounds are--the same training, the same interests. And, of course, I am aware of how successful you have managed to mesh these interests--fourteen awards in fifteen years!

As I begin my job search during the next few months, I am certain your advice would help me. Would it be possible for us to meet briefly? My resume is enclosed.

I will call your office next week to see when your schedule would permit such a meeting.

Sincerely,

Richard A. Starky

TO OBTAIN AN INFORMATIONAL INTERVIEW

16 NW 128th St.
Raleigh, NC 75775
December 2, 1992

Mr. Johnson B. McClure
Vice President
Goldmine Promotion, Inc.
484 Smithers Road
Awkmont, NC 76857

Dear Mr. McClure:

I'm sure a good deal of the credit for your company's 23% jump in accounts last year is attributable to the highly-motivated sales promotion staff you have recruited during the last three years. I hope to obtain an entry-level position for a company just as committed to growth.

I have four years of sterling sales results to boast of, experience acquired while working my way through college. I believe my familiarity with consumer markets and buying trends, sales experience and Bachelor's degree in marketing from American University have properly prepared me for a career in sales promotion.

As I begin my job search, I am trying to gather as much information and advice as possible before applying for positions. Could I take a few minutes of your time next week to discuss my career plans? I will call your office on Monday, December 6, to see if such a meeting can be arranged.

I appreciate your consideration and look forward to meeting you.

Sincerely,

Karen R. Burns

AFTER AN INFORMATIONAL INTERVIEW

Lazelle Wright
921 West Fourth Street
Steamboat Springs, CO 72105
303-555-3303

November 21, 1992

Mr. James R. Payne
Account Manager
Bradley Finch, Inc.
241 Snowridge
Ogden, UT 72108

Dear Mr. Payne:

Jinny Bastienelli was right when she said you would be most helpful in advising me on a
career in advertising.

I appreciated your taking the time from your busy schedule to meet with me. Your advice was most helpful and I have incorporated your suggestions into my resume. I will send you a copy next week.

Again, thanks so much for your assistance. As you suggested, I will contact Joe Simmons at Creative Concepts, Inc. next week in regard to a possible opening with his company.

Sincerely,

Lazelle Wright

AFTER A JOB INTERVIEW

1497 Lilac Street
Old Adams, MA 01281
October 15, 1992

Mr. Rudy Delacort
Director of Personnel
Grace Advertising, Inc.
175 Boylston Avenue
Ribbit, MA 02857

Dear Mr. Delacort:

Thank you for the opportunity to interview yesterday for the junior art director position. I enjoyed meeting with you and Cliff Stoudt and learning more about Grace.

Your organization appears to be growing in a direction which parallels my interests and goals. The interview with you and your staff confirmed my initial positive impressions of Grace, and I want to reiterate my strong interest in working for you.

I am convinced my prior experience as ad design director for my school's newspaper, and my summer internship working with a variety of products would enable me to progress steadily through your training program and become a productive member of your art department.

Again, thank you for your consideration. If you need any additional information from me, please feel free to call.

Yours truly,

Harold Beaumont

cc: Mr. Cliff Stoudt
   New Projects Unit

ADVERTISING CAREER DIRECTORY

ACCEPTING A JOB OFFER

1497 Lilac Street
Old Adams, MA 01281
October 7, 1992

Mr. Rudy Delacort
Director of Personnel
Grace Advertising, Inc.
175 Boylston Avenue
Ribbit, Massachusetts 01281

Dear Mr. Delacort:

I want to thank you and Mr. Stoudt for giving me the opportunity to work for Grace. I am very pleased to accept the position as a junior art director with your New Projects Unit. The position entails exactly the kind of work I want to do, and I know that I will do a good job for you.

As we discussed, I shall begin work on December 5, 1992. In the interim, I shall complete all the necessary employment forms, obtain the required physical examination and locate housing.

I plan to be in Ribbit within the next two weeks and would like to deliver the paperwork to you personally. At that time, we could handle any remaining items pertaining to my employment. I'll call next week to schedule an appointment with you.

Sincerely yours,

Harold Beaumont

cc: Mr. Cliff Stoudt
    New Projects Unit

WITHDRAWING FROM CONSIDERATION

1497 Lilac Street
Old Adams, MA 01281
October 7, 1992

Mr. Rudy Delacort
Director of Personnel
Grace Advertising, Inc.
175 Boylston Avenue
Ribbit, MA 01281

Dear Mr. Delacort:

It was indeed a pleasure meeting with you and Mr. Stoudt last week to discuss your needs for a junior art director in your New Projects Unit. Our time together was most enjoyable and informative.

As I discussed with you during our meetings, I believe one purpose of preliminary interviews is to explore areas of mutual interest and to assess the fit between the individual and the position. After careful thought, I have decided to withdraw from consideration for the position.

I want to thank you for interviewing me and giving me the opportunity to learn about your needs. You have a fine staff and I would have enjoyed working with them.

Yours truly,

Harold Beaumont

cc: Mr. Cliff Stoudt
    New Projects Unit

IN RESPONSE TO REJECTION

ADVERTISING CAREER DIRECTORY

1497 Lilac Street
Old Adams, MA 01281
October 7, 1992

Mr. Rudy Delacort
Director of Personnel
Grace Advertising, Inc.
175 Boylston Avenue
Ribbit, Massachusetts 01281

Dear Mr. Delacort:

Thank you for giving me the opportunity to interview for the junior art director position. I appreciate your consideration and interest in me.

Although I am disappointed in not being selected for your current vacancy, I want you to know that I appreciated the courtesy and professionalism shown to me during the entire selection process. I enjoyed meeting you, Cliff Stoudt, and the other members of your staff. My meetings confirmed that Grace would be an exciting place to work and build a career.

I want to reiterate my strong interest in working for you. Please keep me in mind if a similar position becomes available in the near future.

Again, thank you for the opportunity to interview and best wishes to you and your staff.

Sincerely yours,

Harold Beaumont

cc: Mr. Cliff Stoudt
    New Projects Unit

CHAPTER TWENTY-THREE

Questions for You, Questions for Them

You've finished your exhaustive research, contacted everyone you've known since kindergarten, compiled a professional-looking and sounding resume, and written brilliant letters to the dozens of companies your research has revealed are perfect matches for your own strengths, interests and abilities. Unfortunately, all of this preparatory work will be meaningless if you are unable to successfully convince one of those firms to hire you.

If you were able set up an initial meeting at one of these companies, your resume and cover letter obviously peaked someone's interest. Now you have to traverse the last minefield—the job interview itself. It's time to make all that preparation pay off.

This chapter will attempt to put the interview process in perspective, giving you the "inside story" on what to expect and how to handle the questions and circumstances that arise during the course of a normal interview—and even many of those that surface in the bizarre interview situations we have all sometimes experienced.

Why Interviews Shouldn't Scare You

Interviews shouldn't scare you. The concept of two (or more) persons meeting to determine if they are right for each other is a relatively logical idea. As important as research, resumes, letters, and phone calls are, they are inherently impersonal. The interview is your chance to really see and feel the company firsthand—"up close and personal," as Howard Cosell used to crow—so think of it as a positive opportunity, your chance to succeed.

That said, many of you will still be put off by the inherently inquisitive nature of the process. Though many questions *will* be asked, interviews are essentially experiments in chemistry. Are you right for the company? Is the company right for you? Not just on paper—*in the flesh.*

If you decide the company is right for you, your purpose is simple and clear-cut—to convince the interviewer that you are the right person for the job, that you will fit in, and that you will be an asset to the company now and in the future. The interviewer's purpose is equally simple—to decide whether he or she should buy what you're selling.

This chapter will focus on the kinds of questions you are likely to be asked, how to answer them and the questions you should be ready to ask of the interviewer. By removing the workings of the interview process from the "unknown" category, you will reduce the fear it engenders.

But all the preparation in the world won't completely eliminate your sweaty palms, unless you can convince yourself that the interview is an important, positive life experience from which you will benefit—even if you don't get the job. Approach it with enthusiasm, calm yourself, and let your personality do the rest. You will undoubtedly spend an interesting hour, one that will teach you more about yourself. It's just another step in the learning process you've undertaken.

What to Do First

Start by setting up a calendar on which you can enter and track all your scheduled appointments. When you schedule an interview with a company, ask them how much time you should allow for the appointment. Some require all new applicants to fill out numerous forms and/or complete a battery of intelligence or psychological tests—all before the first interview. If you've only allowed an hour for the interview—and scheduled another at a nearby firm ten minutes later—the first time you confront a three-hour test series will effectively destroy any schedule.

Some companies, especially if the first interview is very positive, like to keep applicants around to talk to other executives. This process may be planned or, in a lot of cases, a spontaneous decision by an interviewer who likes you and wants you to meet some other key decision makers. Other companies will tend to schedule such a series of second interviews on a separate day. Find out, if you can, how the company you're planning to visit generally operates. Otherwise, especially if you've traveled to another city to interview with a number of firms in a short period of time, a schedule that's too tight will fall apart in no time at all.

If you need to travel out-of-state to interview with a company, be sure to ask if they will be paying some or all of your travel expenses. (It's generally expected that you'll be paying your own way to firms within your home state.) If they don't offer—and you don't ask—presume you're paying the freight.

Even if the company agrees to reimburse you, make sure you have enough money to pay all the expenses yourself. While some may reimburse you immediately, the majority of firms may take from a week to a month to forward you an expense check.

Research, Research, and More Research

The research you did to find these companies is nothing compared to the research you need to do now that you're beginning to narrow your search. If you followed our detailed suggestions when you started targeting these firms in the first place, you've already amassed a great deal of information about them. If you didn't do the research *then,* you sure better decide to do it *now.* Study each company as if you were going to be tested on your detailed knowledge of their organization and operations. Here's a complete checklist of the facts you should try to know about each company you plan to visit for a job interview:

The Basics

1. The address of (and directions to) the office you're visiting
2. Headquarters location (if different)
3. Some idea of domestic and international branches
4. Relative size (compared to other similar companies)
5. Annual billings, sales and/or income (last two years)
6. Subsidiary companies; specialized divisions
7. Departments (overall structure)
8. Major accounts, products, or services

The Subtleties

1. History of the firm (specialties, honors, awards, famous names)
2. Names, titles and backgrounds of top management
3. Existence (and type) of training program
4. Relocation policy
5. Relative salaries (compared to other companies in field or by size)
6. Recent developments concerning the company and its products or services (from your trade magazine and newspaper reading)
7. Everything you can learn about the career, likes, and dislikes of the person(s) interviewing you

The amount of time and work necessary to be this well prepared for an interview is considerable. It will not be accomplished the day before the interview. You may even find some of the information you need is unavailable on short notice.

Is it really so important to do all this? Well, somebody out there is going to. And if you happen to be interviewing for the same job as that other, well-prepared, knowledgeable candidate, who do you think will impress the interviewer more?

As we've already discussed, if you give yourself enough time, most of this information is surprisingly easy to obtain. In addition to the reference sources covered in the Career Resources chapter, the company itself can probably supply you with a great deal of data. A firm's annual report—which all publicly-owned companies must publish yearly for their stockholders—is a virtual treasure trove of information. Write each company and request copies of their last two annual reports. A comparison of sales, income, and other data over this period may enable you to discover some interesting things about their overall financial health and growth potential. Many libraries also have collections of annual reports from major corporations.

Attempting to learn about your interviewer is hard work, the importance of which is underestimated by most applicants (who then, of course, don't bother to do it). Being one of the exceptions may get you a job. Use the biographical references covered previously. If he or she is listed in any of these sources, you'll be able to learn an awful lot about his or her background. In addition, find out if he or she has written any articles that have appeared in the trade press or, even better, books on his or her area(s) of expertise. Referring to these writings during the course of an interview, without making it too obvious a compliment, can be very effective. We all have egos and we all like people to talk about us. The interviewer is no different from the rest of us. You might also check to see if any of your networking contacts worked with him or her at his current (or a previous) company and can help "fill you in."

Selection vs. Screening Interviews

The process to which the majority of this chapter is devoted is the actual **selection interview,** usually conducted by the person to whom the new hire will be reporting. But there is another process—the **screening interview**—which many of you may have to survive first.

Screening interviews are usually conducted by a member of the personnel department. Though they may not be empowered to hire, they are in a position to screen out or eliminate those candidates they feel (based on the facts) are not qualified to handle the job. These decisions are not usually made on the basis of personality, appearance, eloquence, persuasiveness, or any other subjective criteria, but rather by clicking off yes or no answers against a checklist of skills. If you don't have the requisite number, you will be eliminated from further consideration. This may seem arbitrary, but it is a realistic and often necessary way for corporations to minimize the time and dollars involved in filling even the lowest jobs on the corporate ladder.

Remember, screening personnel are not looking for reasons to *hire* you; they're trying to find ways to *eliminate* you from the job search pack. Resumes sent blindly to the personnel department will usually be subjected to such screening; you will be eliminated without any personal contact (an excellent reason to construct a superior resume and not send out blind mailings).

If you are contacted, it will most likely be by telephone. When you are responding to such a call, keep these three things in mind: 1) It is an interview, be on your guard; 2) Answer all questions honestly; 3) Be enthusiastic; and 4) Don't offer any more information than you are asked for. Remember, this is another screening step, so don't say anything that will get you screened out before you even get in. You will get the standard questions from the interviewer—his or her attempts to "flesh out" the information included on your resume and/or cover letter. Strictly speaking, they are seeking out any negatives which may exist. If your resume is honest and factual (and it should be), you have no reason to be anxious, because you have nothing to hide.

Don't be nervous—be glad you were called and remember your objective: to get past this screening phase so you can get on to the real interview.

The Day of the Interview

On the day of the interview, wear a conservative (not funereal) business suit—*not* a sports coat, *not* a "nice" blouse and skirt. Shoes should be shined, nails cleaned, hair cut and in place. And no low-cut or tight-fitting clothes.

It's not unusual for resumes and cover letters to head in different directions when a company starts passing them around to a number of executives. If you sent them, both may even be long gone. So bring along extra copies of your resume and your own copy of the cover letter that originally accompanied it.

Whether or not you make them available, we suggest you prepare a neatly-typed list of references (including the name, title, company, address, and phone number of each person). You may want to bring along a copy of your high school or college transcript, especially if it's something to brag about. (Once you get your first job, you'll probably never use it—or be asked for it—again, so enjoy it while you can!)

On Time Means Fifteen Minutes Early

Plan to arrive fifteen minutes before your scheduled appointment. If you're in an unfamiliar city or have a long drive to their offices, allow extra time for the unexpected delays that seem to occur with mind-numbing regularity on important days.

Arriving early will give you some time to check your appearance, catch your breath, check in with the receptionist, learn how to correctly pronounce the interviewer's name, and get yourself organized and battle ready.

Arriving late does not make a sterling first impression. If you are only a few minutes late, it's probably best not to mention it or even excuse yourself. With a little luck, everybody else is behind schedule and no one will notice. However, if you're more than fifteen minutes late, have an honest (or at least serviceable) explanation ready and offer it at your first opportunity. Then drop the subject as quickly as possible and move on to the interview.

The Eyes Have It

When you meet the interviewer, shake hands firmly. People notice handshakes and often form a first impression based solely on them.

Try to maintain eye contact with the interviewer as you talk. This will indicate you're interested in what he or she has to say. Eye contact is important for another reason—it demonstrates to the interviewer that you are confident about yourself and your job skills. That's an important message to send.

Sit straight. Body language is also another important means of conveying confidence.

Should coffee or a soft drink be offered, you may accept (but should do so only if the interviewer is joining you).

Keep your voice at a comfortable level, and try to sound enthusiastic (without imitating Charleen Cheerleader). Be confident and poised, and provide direct, accurate and honest answers to the trickiest questions.

And, as you try to remember all this, just be yourself, and try to act like you're comfortable and almost enjoying this whole process!

Don't Name Drop...Conspicuously

> ### You Don't Have to Say a Word
>
> "Eighty percent of the initial impression you make is nonverbal," asserts Jennifer Maxwell Morris, a New York-based image consultant, quoting a University of Minnesota study. Some tips: walk tall, enter the room briskly while making eye contact with the person you're going to speak to, keep your head up, square your shoulders and keep your hand ready for a firm handshake that involves the whole hand but does not pump.
>
> Source: *Working Woman*

A friendly relationship with other company employees may have provided you with valuable information prior to the interview, but don't flaunt such relationships. The interviewer is interested only in how you will relate to him or her and how well he or she surmises you will fit in with the rest of the staff. Name dropping may smack of favoritism. And you are in no position to know who the interviewer's favorite (or least favorite) people are.

On the other hand, if you have established a complex network of professionals through informational interviews, attending trade shows, reading trade magazines, etc., it is perfectly permissible to refer to these people, their companies, conversations you've had, whatever. It may even impress the interviewer with the extensiveness of your preparation.

Fork on the Left, Knife on the Right

Interviews are sometimes conducted over lunch, though this is not usually the case with entry-level people. If it does happen to you, though, try to order something in the middle price range, neither filet mignon nor a cheeseburger.

Do not order alcohol—ever! If your interviewer orders a carafe of wine, politely decline. You may meet another interviewer later who smells the alcohol on your breath, or your interviewer may have a drinking problem. It's just too big a risk to take after you've come so far. Just do your best to maintain your poise, and you'll do fine.

The Importance of Last Impressions

There are some things interviewers will always view with displeasure: street language, complete lack of eye contact, insufficient or vague explanations or answers, a noticeable lack of energy, poor interpersonal skills (i.e., not listening or the basic inability to carry on an intelligent conversation), and a demonstrable lack of motivation.

Every impression may count. And the very *last* impression an interviewer has may outweigh everything else. So, before you allow an interview to end, summarize why you want the job, why you are qualified, and what, in particular, you can offer their company.

Then, take some action. If the interviewer hasn't told you about the rest of the interview process and/or where you stand, ask him or her. Will you be seeing other people that day? If so, ask for some background on anyone else with whom you'll be interviewing. If there are no other meetings that day, what's the next step? When can you expect to hear from them about coming back?

Ask for a business card. This will make sure you get the person's name and title right when you write your follow-up letter. You can staple it to the company file for easy reference as you continue networking. When you return home, file all the business cards, copies of correspondence, and notes from the interview(s) with each company in the appropriate files. Finally, but most importantly, ask yourself which firms you really want to work for and which you are no longer interested in. This will quickly determine how far you want the process at each to develop before you politely tell them to stop considering you for the job.

Immediately send a thank-you letter to each executive you met. These should, of course, be neatly-typed business letters, not handwritten notes (unless you are most friendly, indeed, with the interviewer and want to stress the "informal" nature of your note). If you are still interested in pursuing a position at their company, tell them in no uncertain terms. Reiterate why you feel you're the best candidate and tell each of the executives when you hope (expect?) to hear from them.

> A new style of interview called the "situational interview," or low-fidelity simulation, asks prospective employees what they would do in hypothetical situations, presenting illustrations that are important in the job opening. Recent research is encouraging employers to use this type of interview approach, because studies show that what people say they would do is pretty much what they will do when the real-life situation arises.
> Source: *Working Woman*

On the Eighth Day God Created Interviewers

Though most interviews will follow a relatively standard format, there will undoubtedly be a wide disparity in the skills of the interviewers you meet. Many of these executives (with the exception of the Personnel staff) will most likely not have extensive interviewing experience, have limited knowledge of interviewing techniques, use them infrequently, be hurried by the other duties, or not even view your interview as critically important.

Rather than studying standardized test results or utilizing professional evaluation skills developed over many years of practice, these nonprofessionals react intuitively—their initial (first five minutes) impressions are often the lasting and over-riding factors they remember. So you must sell yourself—fast.

The best way to do this is to try to achieve a comfort level with your interviewer. Isn't establishing rapport—through words, gestures, appearance common interests, etc.—what you try to do in *any* social situation? It's just trying to know one another better. Against this backdrop, the questions and answers will flow in a more natural way.

The Set Sequence

Irrespective of the competence levels of the interviewer, you can anticipate an interview sequence roughly as follows:

- Greetings
- Social niceties (small talk)
- Purpose of meeting (let's get down to business)
- Broad questions/answers
- Specific questions/ answers
- In-depth discussion of company, job, and opportunity
- Summarizing information given & received
- Possible salary probe (this should only be brought up at a second interview)
- Summary/indication as to next steps

When you look at this sequence closely, it is obvious that once you have gotten past the greeting, social niceties and some explanation of the job (in the "getting down to business" section), the bulk of the interview will be questions—yours and the interviewer's. In this question and answer session, there are not necessarily any right or wrong answers, only good and bad ones. Be forewarned, however. This sequence is not written in stone, and some interviewers will deliberately **not** follow it. Some interviewers will try to fluster you by asking off-the-wall questions, while others are just eccentric by nature. Be prepared for anything once the interview has started.

It's Time to Play Q & A

You can't control the "chemistry" between you and the interviewer—do you seem to "hit it off" right from the start or never connect at all? Since you can't control such a subjective problem, it pays to focus on what you *can* control—the questions you will be asked, your answers and the questions you had better be prepared to ask.

Not surprisingly, many of the same questions pop up in interview after interview, regardless of company size, type, or location. I have chosen the 14 most common—along with appropriate hints and answers for each—for inclusion in this chapter. Remember: There are no right or wrong answers to these questions, only good and bad ones.

Substance counts more than speed when answering questions. Take your time and make sure that you listen to each question—there is nothing quite as disquieting as a lengthy, intelligent answer that is completely irrelevant to the question asked. You wind up looking like a programmed clone with stock answers to dozens of questions who has, unfortunately, pulled the wrong one out of the grab bag.

Once you have adequately answered a specific question, it is permissible to go beyond it and add more information if doing so adds something to the discussion and/or highlights a particular strength, skill, course, etc. But avoid making lengthy speeches just for the sake of sounding off. Even if the interviewer asks a question that is right up your "power alley", one you could talk about for weeks, keep your answers short. Under two minutes for any answer is a good rule of thumb.

Study the list of questions (and hints) that follow, and prepare at least one solid, concise answer for each. Practice with a friend until your answers to these most-asked questions sound intelligent, professional and, most important, unmemorized and unrehearsed.

"Why do you want to be in this field?"

Using your knowledge and understanding of the particular field, explain why you find the business exciting and where and what role you see yourself playing in it.

"Why do you think you will be successful in this business?"

Using the information from your self-evaluation and the research you did on that particular company, formulate an answer which marries your strengths to their's and to the characteristics of the position for which you're applying.

"Why did you choose our company?"

This is an excellent opportunity to explain the extensive process of education and research you've undertaken. Tell them about your strengths and how you match up with their firm. Emphasize specific things about their company that led you to seek an interview. Be a salesperson—be convincing.

"What can you do for us?"

Construct an answer that essentially lists your strengths, the experience you have which will contribute to your job performance, and any other unique qualifications that will place you at the head of the applicant pack. Use action-oriented words to tell exactly what you think you can do for the company—all your skills mean nothing if you can't use them to benefit the company you are interviewing with. Be careful: This is a question specifically designed to *eliminate* some of that pack. Sell yourself. Be one of the few called back for a second interview.

"What position here interests you?"

If you're interviewing for a specific position, answer accordingly. If you want to make sure you don't close the door on other opportunities of which you might be unaware, you can follow up with your own question: "I'm here to apply for your design program. Is there another position open for which you feel I'm qualified?"

If you've arranged an interview with a company without knowing of any specific openings, use the answer to this question to describe the kind of work you'd like to do and why you're qualified to do it. Avoid a specific job title, since they will tend to vary from firm to firm.

If you're on a first interview with the personnel department, just answer the question. They only want to figure out where to send you.

"What jobs have you held and why did you leave them?"

Or the direct approach: "Have you ever been fired?" Take this opportunity to expand on your resume, rather than precisely answering the question by merely recapping your job experiences. In discussing each job, point out what you liked about it, what factors led to your leaving, and how the next job added to your continuing professional education. If you have been fired, say so. It's very easy to check.

"What are your strengths and weaknesses?"

Or **"What are your hobbies (or outside interests)?"** Both questions can be easily answered using the data you gathered to complete the self-evaluation process. Be wary of being too forthcoming about your glaring faults (nobody expects you to volunteer every weakness and mistake), but do not reply, "I don't have any." They won't believe you and, what's worse, you won't believe you. After all, you did the evaluation—you know it's a lie!

Good answers to these questions are those in which the interviewer can identify benefits for him or herself. For example: "I consider myself to be an excellent planner. I am seldom caught by surprise and I prize myself on being able to anticipate problems and schedule my time to be ahead of the game. I devote a prescribed number of hours each week to this activity. I've noticed that many people just react. If you plan ahead, you should be able to cut off most problems before they arise."

You may consider disarming the interviewer by admitting a weakness, but doing it in such a way as to make it relatively unimportant to the job function. For example: "Higher mathematics has never been my strong suit. Though I am competent enough, I've always envied my friends with a more mathematical bent. In sales, though, I haven't found this a liability. I'm certainly quick enough in figuring out how close I am to monthly quotas and, of course, I keep a running record of commissions earned."

"Do you think your extracurricular activities were worth the time you devoted to them?"

This is a question often asked of entry-level candidates. One possible answer: "Very definitely. As you see from my resume, I have been quite active in the Student Government and French Club. My language fluency allowed me to spend my junior year abroad as an exchange student, and working in a functioning government gave me firsthand knowledge of what can be accomplished with people in the real world. I suspect my marks would have been somewhat higher had I not taken on so many activities outside of school, but I feel the balance they gave me contributed significantly to my overall growth as a person."

"What are your career goals?"

Interviewers are always seeking to probe the motivations of prospective employees. Nowhere is this more apparent than when the area of ambition is discussed. The high key answer to this question might be: "Given hard work, company growth, and personal initiative, I'd look forward to being in a top executive position by the time I'm 35. I believe in effort and the risk/reward system—my research on this company has shown me that it operates on the same principles. I would hope it would select its future leaders from those people who displaying such characteristics."

"At some future date would you be willing to relocate?"

Pulling up one's roots is not the easiest thing in the world to do, but it is often a fact of life in the corporate world. If you're serious about your career (and such a move often represents a step up the career ladder), you will probably not mind such a move. Tell the interviewer. If you really *don't* want to move, you may want to say so, too—though I would find out how probable or frequent such relocations would be before closing the door while still in the interview stage.

Keep in mind that as you get older, establish ties in a particular community, marry, have children, etc., you will inevitably feel less jubilation at the thought of moving once a year or even "being out on the road." So take the opportunity to experience new places and experiences while you're young. If you don't, you may never get the chance.

"How did you get along with your last supervisor?"

This question is designed to understand your relationship with (and reaction to) authority. Remember: Companies look for team players, people who will fit in with their hierarchy, their rules, their ways of doing things. An answer might be: "I prefer to work with smart, strong people who know what they want and can express themselves. I learned in the military that in order to accomplish the mission, someone has to be the leader and that person has to be given the authority to lead. Someday I aim to be that leader. I hope then my subordinates will follow me as much and as competently as I'm ready to follow now."

"What are your salary requirements?"

If they are at all interested in you, this question will probably come up, though it is more likely at a second interview. The danger, of course, is that you may price yourself too low or, even worse, right out of a job you want. Since you will have a general idea of industry figures for that position (and may even have an idea of what that company tends to pay new people for the position), why not refer to a range of salaries, such as $25,000 - $30,000?

If the interviewer doesn't bring up salary at all, it's doubtful you're being seriously considered, so you probably don't need to even bring the subject up. (If you know you aren't getting the job or aren't interested in it if offered, you may try to nail down a salary figure in order to be better prepared for the next interview.)

"Tell me about yourself"

Watch out for this one! It's often one of the first questions asked. If you falter here, the rest of the interview could quickly become a downward slide to nowhere. Be prepared, and consider it an opportunity to combine your answers to many of the previous questions into one concise description of who you are, what you want to be, and why that company should take a chance on you. Summarize your resume—briefly—and expand on particular courses or experiences relevant to the firm or position. Do not go on about your hobbies or personal life, where you spent your summer vacation, or anything that is not relevant to securing that job. You may explain how that particular job fits in with your long-range career goals and talk specifically about what attracted you to their company in the first place.

"Do You Have Any Questions?"

It's the last fatal question on our list, often the last one an interviewer throws at you after an hour or two of grilling. Even if the interview has been very long and unusually thorough, you *should* have questions—about the job, the company, even the industry. Unfortunately, by the time this question off-handedly hits the floor, you are already looking forward to leaving and may have absolutely nothing to say.

Preparing yourself for an interview means more than having answers for some of the questions an interviewer may ask. It means having your own set of questions—at least five or six—for the interviewer. The interviewer is trying to find the right person for the job. You're trying to find the right job. So you should be just as curious about him or her and the company as he or she is about you. Be careful with any list of questions prepared ahead of time. Some of them were probably answered during the course of the interview, so to ask that same question at this stage would demonstrate poor listening skills. Listening well is becoming a lost art, and its importance cannot be stressed enough. (See the box on this page for a short list of questions you may consider asking on any interview).

Your Turn to Ask the Questions

1. What will my typical day be like?
2. What happened to the last person who had this job?
3. Given my attitude and qualifications, how would you estimate my chances for career advancement at your company?
4. Why did you come to work here? What keeps you here?
5. If you were I, would you start here again?
6. How would you characterize the management philosophy of your firm?
7. What characteristics do the successful employees at your company have in common?
8. What's the best (and worst) thing about working here?

The Not-So-Obvious Questions

Every interviewer is different and, unfortunately, there are no rules saying he or she has to use all or any of the "basic" questions covered above. But we think the odds are against his or her avoiding all of them. Whichever of these he or she includes, be assured most interviewers do like to come up with questions that are "uniquely theirs." It may be just one or a whole series—questions developed over the years that he or she feels help separate the wheat from the chaff.

You can't exactly prepare yourself for questions like, "What would you do if...(fill in the blank with some obscure occurrence)?," "What do you remember about kindergarten?," or "What's your favorite ice cream flavor?" Every interviewer we know has his or her favorites and all of these questions seem to come out of left field. Just stay relaxed, grit your teeth (quietly), and take a few seconds to frame a reasonably intelligent reply.

The Downright Illegal Questions

Some questions are more than inappropriate—they are illegal. The Civil Rights

Act of 1964 makes it illegal for a company to discriminate in its hiring on the basis of race, color, religion, sex, or national origin. It also means that any interview questions covering these topics are strictly off-limits. In addition to questions about race and color, what other types questions can't be asked? Some might surprise you:

- Any questions about marital status, number and ages of dependents, or marriage or child-bearing plans.
- Any questions about your relatives, their addresses, or their place of origin.
- Any questions about your arrest record. If security clearance is required, it can be done after hiring but before you start the job.

A Quick Quiz to Test Your Instincts

After reading the above paragraphs, read through the 10 questions below. Which ones do you think would be legal to ask at a job interview? Answers provided below.

1. Confidentially, what is your race?
2. What kind of work does your spouse do?
3. Are you single, married, or divorced?
4. What is your native language?
5. Who should we notify in case of an emergency?
6. What clubs, societies, or organizations do you belong to?
7. Do you plan to have a family?
8. Do you have any disability?
9. Do you have a good credit record?
10. What is your height and weight?

The answers? Not a single question out of the ten is legal at a job interview, because all could lead to a discrimination suit. Some of the questions would become legal once you were hired (obviously a company would need to know who to notify in an emergency), but none belong at an interview.

Now that you know what an interviewer can't ask you, what if he or she does? Well, don't lose your cool, and don't point out that the question may be outside the law—the nonprofessional interviewer may not realize such questions are illegal, and such a response might confuse, even anger, him or her.

Instead, whenever any questions are raised that you feel are outside legal boundaries, politely state that you don't understand how the question has bearing on the job opening and ask the interviewer to clarify him or herself. If the interviewer persists, you may be forced to state that you do not feel comfortable answering questions of that nature. Bring up the legal issue as a last resort, but if things reach that stage, you probably don't want to work for that company after all.

Testing and Applications

Though not part of the selection interview itself, job applications, skill tests, and psychological testing are often part of the pre-interview process. You should know something about them.

The job application is essentially a record-keeping exercise—simply the transfer of work experience and educational data from your resume to a printed application forms. Though taking the time to recopy data may seem like a waste of time, some companies simply want the information in a particular order on a standard form. One difference: Applications often require the listing of references and salary levels achieved. Be sure to bring your list of references with you to any interview (so you can transfer the pertinent information), and don't lie about salary history; it's easily checked.

Many companies now use a variety of psychological tests as additional mechanisms to screen out undesirable candidates. Although their accuracy is subject to question, the companies that use them obviously believe they are effective at identifying applicants whose personality makeups would preclude their participating positively in a given work situation, especially those at the extreme ends of the behavior spectrum.

Their usefulness in predicting job accomplishment is considered limited. If you are normal (like the rest of us), you'll have no trouble with these tests and may even find them amusing. Just don't try to outsmart them—you'll just wind up outsmarting yourself.

Stand Up and Be Counted

Your interview is over. Breathe a sigh of relief. Make your notes—you'll want to keep a file on the important things covered for use in your next interview. Some people consider one out of ten (one job offer for every ten interviews) a good score—if you're keeping score. We suggest you don't. It's virtually impossible to judge how others are judging you. Just go on to the next interview. Sooner than you think, you'll be hired. For the right job.

Job Opportunities Databank

CHAPTER TWENTY-FOUR

Job Opportunities Databank

The Job Opportunities Databank contains listings for more than 200 advertising agencies in the United States and Canada that offer entry-level hiring and/or internships, including the top 50 agencies in the United States (based on revenue). It is divided into two sections: Entry-Level Job and Internship Listing, which provides full descriptive entries for agencies in the United States and Canada; and Companies Supply No Further Information, which includes name, address, and telephone information only for agencies that did not respond to our inquiries. For complete details on the information provided in this chapter, please consult the introductory material at the front of this directory.

Entry-Level Job and Internship Listings

AC&R Advertising Inc.
Saatchi & Saatchi USA Affiliates
16 E. 32nd St.
New York, NY 10016
Phone: (212)685-2500

Employees: 180.

Average Entry-Level Hiring: 5-10.

Opportunities: Account coordinator—college degree required; typing proficiency and word processing skills a plus. Media planner—college degree required; should be good with figures and possess strong communication skills.

Human Resources: Robin Michaels, VP of Human Resources.

Application Procedures: Send resume and cover letter.

▶ **Internships**

Type: Limited number of internship(s) available. Contact the company for more information.

Ackerman Advertising
1 Huntington Quad.
Melville, NY 11747
Phone: (516)249-2121

Employees: 35.

Average Entry-Level Hiring: 0.

Opportunities: This small company seldom hires outside of the company.

Human Resources: Skip Ackerman, President.

ADVERTISING CAREER DIRECTORY

Application Procedures: Send resume and cover letter to contact.

Ackerman, Hood & McQueen, Inc.
1600 Rhode Island Ave., NW
Washington, DC 20036
Phone: (202)223-8270

Employees: 8.

Average Entry-Level Hiring: 0.

Opportunities: College graduates (usually majoring in public relations or journalism) may begin as a secretary and move on to account manager after approximately one year.

Human Resources: Lynn Dahlstron, Application Contact.

> "Just why advertising works is an enduring mystery," claims *Newsweek's* Robert J. Samuelson. "A lot of it is ignored and (rightfully) deplored. In regular public surveys, about 30 percent of respondents label TV ads misleading and about 20 percent say the ads are offensive, reports Video Storyboard Tests, a polling service in New York. But somehow, advertising triumphs over its limitations. It helps create and preserve markets." Martin Mayer observes in the 1991 book *Whatever Happened to Madison Avenue?* that "If greater advertising over time doesn't generate greater profits, there's something seriously wrong with the fellows who make up the budgets."

Application Procedures: Send resume and cover letter to contact.

▶ **Internships**

Contact: Ed Klecka, Vice Pres. Public Relations.

Type: Offers paid internship(s), and nonpaid internship(s) that earn college credit. **Number Available Annually:** 1-2. **Applications Received:** 80-100.

Duties: Will travel with full-time staff to special events. Writing assignments include news releases, feature material, sports, and general news. Will participate as a media liaison with local, regional, and national media.

Application Procedure: Send resume and cover letter to contact.

Application Deadline: Two to three months in advance.

Ackerman, Hood & McQueen, Inc.
8023 E. 63rd Pl.
Tulsa, OK 74133
Phone: (918)250-9511

Employees: 35.

Average Entry-Level Hiring: 5-10.

Opportunities: Traffic—college degree preferred; no other requirements specified.

Application Procedures: Send resume and cover letter to the appropriate department head.

▶ **Internships**

Contact: Nancy Martin, Creative Department Mgr.

Type: Credit (through college). **Number Available Annually:** 1-3.

Duties: Varies according to departmental needs.

Application Procedure: Call or send resume and cover letter.

Application Deadline: Ongoing.

Ackerman, Hood & McQueen, Inc.
600 Commerce Tower
545 E. John Carpenter Fwy.
Irvin, TX 75062
Phone: (214)444-9000

Employees: 18.

Average Entry-Level Hiring: Varies.

Opportunities: Opportunities available for receptionists, secretaries, account coordinators, and traffic coordinators—college degree and experience preferred.

Human Resources: Tom Millweard, Sr. VP Management Supervisor.

Application Procedures: Send resume and cover letter.

▶ **Internships**

Contact: Mr. Robin Doss, Account Coordinator.

Type: Offers nonpaid internship(s) for college credit. **Number Available Annually:** 5.

Duties: Varies according to department needs.

Application Procedure: Send resume and cover letter to contact.

Application Deadline: Ongoing.

Ackerman, Hood & McQueen, Inc.
1601 NW Expressway, Ste. 1100
Oklahoma City, OK 73118
Phone: (405)843-7777

Human Resources: Christy Tebow, Manager Traffic Operations.

Application Procedures: Send resume and cover letter to contact.

▶ **Internships**

Contact: Christy Tebow, Mgr. of Traffic Operations.

Type: Nonpaid. Earned college credit. **Number Available Annually:** 10.

Duties: Varies with department of interest.

Application Procedure: Call for more information.

Application Deadline: Ongoing.

Advanswers
10 S. Broadway
St. Louis, MO 63102
Phone: (314)444-2100
Fax: (314)444-2219

Average Entry-Level Hiring: 10-15.

Human Resources: Christine Moeller, Exec. Sec.

Application Procedures: Send resume and cover letter to Ms. Moeller.

▶ **Internships**

Type: The company does not offer an internship program.

Advertising Development Specialists
1025 E. Swallow, No. 200
Fort Collins, CO 80525
Phone: (303)223-1743

Employees: 6.

Average Entry-Level Hiring: 0.

Opportunities: Office/Administrative—college degree (liberal arts preferred); typing, Word Star experience. Account executive—college degree (business and/or marketing preferred).

Human Resources: Linda Roesener, Personnel Dir.

Application Procedures: Send resume and cover letter.

▶ **Internships**

Type: Offers nonpaid internships that can be used for college credit. **Number Available Annually:** 2-3. **Applications Received:** 30.

Duties: Clerical and other work, as needed.

Application Procedure: Send resume and cover letter to contact.

Ally & Gargano, Inc.
805 3rd Ave.
New York, NY 10022
Phone: (212)688-5300

Employees: 260.

Average Entry-Level Hiring: 0-5.

Opportunities: Applicants with experience only.

Human Resources: Paulette Barlanera, VP of Personnel.

Application Procedures: Places newspaper advertisements for certain openings. Send resume and cover letter to contact.

Aloysius, Butler & Clark, Inc.
110 S. Poplar St.
Wilmington, DE 19801
Phone: (302)655-1552

Employees: 30.

Average Entry-Level Hiring: 0.

Opportunities: Account service—college degree. No other requirements specified.

Human Resources: John Hawkins, CEO & Pres.

Application Procedures: Send resume and cover letter to contact.

▶ **Internships**

Type: The company does not offer an internship program.

Andrew/Mautner, Inc.
600 N. Broadway
Milwaukee, WI 53202
Phone: (414)272-4482

Employees: 20.

ADVERTISING CAREER DIRECTORY

Average Entry-Level Hiring: 1-2.

Opportunities: Opportunities available for media assistant and assistant account executive—college degree (B.A./B.S.) required. Two to three years experience preferred.

Human Resources: Christopher M. Vernon, Exec. VP.

Application Procedures: Very seldom hires; may send resume and cover letter.

> Advertising slogans form part of our shared mass-culture lexicon. They're stashed in our language bank, although we made no effort to deposit them there. Our awareness of these simple but ingenious advertising lines means that their creators were successful. The truth behind the jingle you find yourself humming all day—even when you hate the product, the ad, or both—is simple. A good slogan gets under your skin.
>
> Source: *Every Bite a Delight and Other Slogans*

Auger, Babuex, McKim Advertising Ltd.
225 Roy E., Ste. 100
Montreal, PQ, Canada H2W 1M5
Phone: (514)499-1963

Average Entry-Level Hiring: 1-2.

Human Resources: Serge Babeux, Manager.

Application Procedures: Send resume, cover letter, and samples of the artists' work.

→ N.W. Ayer Inc.
Worldwide Plaza
825 8th Ave.
New York, NY 10019-7498
Phone: (212)474-5000

Average Entry-Level Hiring: 20.

Opportunities: Opportunities available for group assistants—college degree preferred but not required. Must type 40 wpm.

Application Procedures: Accepts unsolicited resumes and applications. Contact the Employment Manager. Applications and/or resumes kept on file for two years. Some hiring is done through an employment agency.

▶ **Internships**

Type: The company does not offer an internship program.

Backer Spielvogel Bates Worldwide Inc.
405 Lexington Ave.
New York, NY 10174
Phone: (212)297-7000

Business Description: Engaged in advertising operations.

Officers: John N. Citron, Exec. VP of Finance; Carl Spielvogel, CEO & Chairman of the Board.

Employees: 6,739.

Human Resources: Carol DeCosta, Personnel Admin.

Application Procedures: Places newspaper advertisements for certain openings. Send resume and cover letter to the attention of Carol DeCosta, Personnel Admin.

Bader Rutter & Assoc.
13555 Bishop's Ct.
Brockfield, WI 53005
Phone: (414)784-7200

Employees: 100.

Application Procedures: Send resume and cover letter to the attention of Personnel.

▶ **Internships**

Contact: Lyle E. Orwig, VP & Director of Public Rel.

Type: Paid. **Number Available Annually:** 2-3. **Applications Received:** 10-15.

Duties: Varies according to the accounts to which an intern is assigned.

Application Procedure: Send resume and cover letter.

Application Deadline: Two to three months before the internship starts.

Barnhart & Co.
455 Sherman, Ste. 500
Denver, CO 80203
Phone: (303)744-3211

Employees: 48.

Average Entry-Level Hiring: 2-3.

Opportunities: Receptionist—college degree. Word processor—college degree; word processing/computer training. Traffic runner—high school diploma. "Initial contact made with letter and resume. If positions are open, we set up interview. We average 10 resumes per day, so we aren't able to interview everyone. Resumes are kept on hand for six months and are referred to when positions become available. We have very little turnover!"

Human Resources: Liz Long, Office Mgr.

Application Procedures: Send resume and cover letter.

▶ Internships

Contact: Steve Sanders, VP Accts. Services Dir.

Type: Offers nonpaid internships. **Number Available Annually:** 1. **Applications Received:** 100.

Duties: Varies according to departmental needs.

Application Procedure: Send resume and cover letter to contact.

Base Brown & Partners Ltd.
512 King St., E.
Toronto, ON, Canada M5A 1M2
Phone: (416)364-5044

Employees: 20.

Average Entry-Level Hiring: 5.

Opportunities: Account executive, secretary, clerical, receptionist, and graphic artist—no requirements specified.

Human Resources: Harold Bradshaw, Dir. of Finance.

Application Procedures: Send resume and cover letter.

▶ Internships

Type: The company does not offer an internship program.

BBDO Worldwide
1285 Avenue of the Americas
New York, NY 10019
Phone: (212)459-5000
Fax: (212)459-6645

Business Description: Engaged in the operation of advertising agencies.

Officers: Philip B. Dusenberry, CEO & Chairman of the Board.

Employees: 5,520.

Application Procedures: Places newspaper advertisements for certain openings. Some hiring is done through an employment agency. Send resume and cover letter to the attention of Human Resources.

BCP Advertising
1000 Sherbrooke St. W., 21st Fl.
Montreal, PQ, Canada H3A 3G9
Phone: (514)285-1414

Employees: 140.

Average Entry-Level Hiring: 1-2.

Human Resources: Prefontaine Chrftane, Personnel Representative.

Application Procedures: Copywriter, art director, and marketing opportunities. For marketing, one needs a bachelor's degree in marketing. For copywriting and art direction, one needs French-language skills and a marketing or communications degree. Send resume and cover letter stating position of interest.

After World War II advertising demonstrated America's move to the suburbs with increased print space occupied by ads from construction firms, builders of superhighways, and automakers. General Motors displaced Procter & Gamble as the nation's largest advertiser.

Source: *Fortune*

Beckman Associates Advertising Agency, Inc.
382 Broadway
Albany, NY 12207
Phone: (518)465-4573

Employees: 35.

Average Entry-Level Hiring: 1-3.

Opportunities: Copywriter—college degree. Account executive—college degree; two to three years experience. Administrative assistant—typing, other basic office skills. Art—college degree; experience preferred.

Advertising Career Directory

Human Resources: Judy Arnold, Human Resources.

Application Procedures: Send resume and cover letter to contact.

▶ **Internships**

Contact: Lisa Callucci, Acct. Exec.

Type: Offers nonpaid internship(s). **Number Available Annually:** Two per semester. **Applications Received:** 200.

Duties: Varies according to department in which intern is needed.

Application Procedure: Send resume and cover letter to contact; specify your job interests.

Application Deadline: Two to three months before starting.

Chicago-based advertising legend Leo Burnett, creative genius of the 1950s, claimed that ads should "convey a feeling of sodbuster honesty" and in mid-decade brought such folksy creations as the Marlboro man and Tony the Tiger to consumers.

Source: *Fortune*

William R. Biggs-Gilmore Associates Inc.
200 E. Michigan
Kalamazoo, MI 49007
Phone: (616)349-7711
Fax: (616)349-3051

Business Description: Engaged in the operation of advertising agencies.

Officers: Ron Davis, President; Don De Groot, Treasurer & Sec.; Don De Groot, Sr. VP of Data Processing; Jeff White, Sr. VP of Mktg.

Employees: 110.

Human Resources: Joyce Peterman, VP of Human Resources.

▶ **Internships**

Contact: Mike Gersen, General Mgr.

Type: Non-salaried, college credit internships available year-round. Departments include public relations and account services. Housing is provided. **Number Available Annually:** 1.

Duties: Interns will act as entry-level employees, assisting the account executives with the day-to-day operations and learning to follow a job through all the phases.

Qualifications: College student (any year). Many interns in the past have been marketing or public relations majors. Interns are chosen based on their academic performance. The company recruits at Western Michigan University.

Application Procedure: Contact the company for more information.

Application Deadline: On-going.

The Bloom Cos.
3500 Maple
Dallas, TX 75219
Phone: (214)443-9900

Employees: 200.

Average Entry-Level Hiring: 1-2.

Opportunities: No specific titles or requirements other than four-year college degree. Using campus recruiting to look for advertising majors.

Human Resources: Debbie Lockhart, Personnel Dir.

Application Procedures: Send resume and cover letter to contact.

Bolt Advertising, Inc.
3512 Brambleton Ave., SW, Ste. 6
Roanoke, VA 24018
Phone: (703)989-2881

Employees: 10.

Average Entry-Level Hiring: 0-1.

Opportunities: This small company seldom needs to hire.

Human Resources: Pete Ostaseski, President.

Application Procedures: Send resume and cover letter to contact.

Bronson Communications, Inc.
1 Freedom Park Pl.
Bangor, ME 04401
Phone: (207)848-5725
Fax: (207)848-5727

Employees: 10.

Average Entry-Level Hiring: 1.

Opportunities: Opportunities available in graphic arts. College degree (B.A./B.S.)

required. Some experience preferred. Candidates should demonstrate graphics ability.

Human Resources: Richard B. Bronson, CEO.

Application Procedures: Send resume and cover letter.

▶ Internships

Type: Offers paid internship(s). **Number Available Annually:** 1.

Duties: Varies.

Application Procedure: Send resume and cover letter.

Application Deadline: Two to three months in advance.

T. Stewart Brown & Company, Ltd.
207 W. Hastings St., Ste. 1111
Vancouver, BC, Canada V6B 1H7
Phone: (604)683-7667

Employees: 6.

Average Entry-Level Hiring: Unknown. Freelancers only.

Opportunities: Freelance artists—portfolio required. Freelance copywriters—samples required.

Human Resources: Mr. Brown, President.

Application Procedures: Send resume and cover letter. Only experienced need apply; no training or entry-level positions available.

▶ Internships

Type: The company does not offer an internship program.

Broyles, Allebaugh & Davis Inc.
31 Denver Technological Ctr.
8231 E. Prentice Ave.
Englewood, CO 80111
Phone: (303)770-2000

Employees: 30.

Average Entry-Level Hiring: 0.

Opportunities: Due to the size of our organization and the performance skills required, we do not hire entry-level people. When a vacancy occurs, or staff additions are required, we seek out experienced professionals, and each department hires individually. At some point in the future we may be in a position to hire entry-level people, but that course of action is not contemplated at this time. The company does not offer an internship program.

Application Procedures: Send resume and cover letter. No entry-level positions are offered.

Leo Burnett Company Inc.
35 W. Wacker Dr.
Chicago, IL 60601
Phone: (312)220-5959
Fax: (312)220-3299

Business Description: An advertising agency network with clients worldwide.

Officers: Hall Adams, CEO & Chairman of the Board; Richard B. Fizdale, Pres. & Chairman of the Board; John C. Kraft, VP of Finance.

Employees: 5,653.

Average Entry-Level Hiring: Unknown.

Opportunities: Media or research trainee—B.S./B.A. (liberal arts or other degree). Client service trainee—M.B.A. (Some undergraduates accepted, but this is rare). Art director and copywriter—based on portfolio.

Human Resources: Dorothy Evans, Supervisor of Nonexempt Employment; Wayne Johnson.

Application Procedures: Interview decisions for all entry-level candidates are based on resume. Creative candidates must have a portfolio. Places newspaper advertisements for certain openings. Send resume and cover letter to the attention of Dorothy Evans, Supervisor of Nonexempt Employment.

Cabot Communications
One Constitution Plaza
Boston, MA 02129
Phone: (617)242-6200

Employees: 125.

Average Entry-Level Hiring: 20.

Opportunities: Account management—college degree (B.A./B.S.); some marketing and media background; outgoing, hard worker, strong social skills. The company does not offer an internship program.

Human Resources: Janet Haugh, Personnel Dept.

Application Procedures: Faxed resumes are accepted. Send resume and cover letter to the attention of Janet Haugh, Personnel Dept. Phone: (617)242-6305.

ADVERTISING CAREER DIRECTORY

Campbell-Mithun-Esty Advertising Minneapolis Branch
222 S. 9th St.
Minneapolis, MN 55402
Phone: (612)347-1000

Employees: 430.

Average Entry-Level Hiring: Unknown.

Opportunities: Entry-level creative openings rarely occur. Account assistant (account services)—future openings are unpredictable. Media analyst (planning), broadcast assistant (broadcast buying)—future openings are unpredictable. Requirements for the previous positions—bachelor degree, possibly master degree or equivalent work experience. The company does not offer an internship program.

Human Resources: Bob Sepen, Human Resources Dir.

Application Procedures: Phone calls not accepted. Send resume and cover letter to the attention of Bob Seper, Human Resources Dir. Phone: (612)347-1318.

A dvertising in the tradition of the "unique selling proposition" singles out a product's key attribute and hammers it home through repetition. For decades, consumer-products companies such as Procter & Gamble used this strategy to peddle laundry detergent, disposable diapers, and the like. The 1980s saw the dominance of the "high-concept" campaigns that spend big bucks to conjure up images and values linking a product to the customer. But in the 1990s many companies want more ads that get results fast, and they're abandoning the subtler pitch for cheaper and simpler messages that stress price, product, and competition.

Source: *Business Week*

Campbell-Mithun-Esty Advertising New York Branch
405 Lexington Ave.
New York, NY 10174
Phone: (212)856-4500

Employees: 185.

Average Entry-Level Hiring: Varies.

Opportunities: Rarely available, entry-level openings tend to be in the areas of accounting and media.

Human Resources: Patricia Shores, Human Resources Dir.

Application Procedures: Applications can be filled out on site, or send resume and cover letter to the attention of Patricia Shores, Human Resources Dir. Phone: (212)856-4940.

Chiat/Day/Mojo Inc.
320 Hampton Dr.
Venice, CA 90291
Phone: (213)314-5000

Business Description: Engaged in the operation of advertising agencies.

Officers: Steve Alburty, Info. Systems Mgr.; Jay Chiat, CEO & Chairman of the Board; Pete de Vaux, Exec. VP & CFO.

Employees: 1,368.

Human Resources: Sharon Stanley, Sr. VP of Admin.

Colle & McVoy Inc.
7900 International Dr., Ste. 700
Minneapolis, MN 55425
Phone: (612)851-2500

Employees: 90.

Average Entry-Level Hiring: 2-4.

Opportunities: Account coordinator and assistant account executive positions—undergraduate or graduate degrees in journalism, public relations, advertising, or marketing preferred. Internships are advantageous. Entry-level positions in creative areas are rarely available.

Human Resources: Jon Andersoner, Exec. Creative Dir.; Debby Becker, VP & Dir. of Public Relations.

Application Procedures: "We suggest sending a cover letter and resume to contact. Exploratory interviews are conducted as time permits. When an opening occurs, resume file is the first source used to identify candidates for interviews. Agency conducts monthly informational meetings for public relations and account services entry-level candidates." Bob Hettlinger, VP & Dir. of Human Resources.

▶ **Internships**

Contact: Bob Hettlinger, VP & Dir. of Human Resources.

Type: The company offers an internship program; positions are filled locally.

Coons Corker & Associates

W. 621 Mallon Ave.
Spokane, WA 99201
Phone: (509)326-8310

Employees: 11.

Average Entry-Level Hiring: 3.

Opportunities: Asst. account executive—college degree (marketing, advertising preferred). Copy-writer—college degree; good credentials. Support personnel—no requirements specified. Experience (1-2 years) preferred for all positions.

Human Resources: Steve Corker, President.

Application Procedures: Send resume and cover letter to the attention of Steve Corker, President.

▶ **Internships**

Contact: Steve Corker.

Type: The company offers an internship program for college credits. **Number Available Annually:** 2.

Duties: Duties include copywriting and account executive work.

Application Procedure: Send resume and cover letter to the attention of Steve Corker.

Application Deadline: Beginning of each school semester.

Frank J. Corbett Inc.

211 E. Chicago Ave., Ste. 1100
Chicago, IL 60611
Phone: (312)664-5310

Employees: 80.

Average Entry-Level Hiring: Low.

Opportunities: Any position would require a degree in marketing, advertising or communications.

Application Procedures: Employment contacts depend on specific departments. Recruits through private firms.

Cramer Krasselt

733 N. Van Buren St.
Milwaukee, WI 53202
Phone: (414)227-3500

Officers: Paul Bentley; Neil Casey; Donald Pom.

Employees: 75.

Average Entry-Level Hiring: 1-2.

Opportunities: Copy—college degree; creative writing ability. Art—college or art school degree; layout and mechanical skills. Research—college degree; organizational and analytical skills. Account services—college degree (B.A. or M.B.A.); people and organizational skills. Media—positions available for both college graduates with people/organizational skills and high school graduates (mainly clerical).

Human Resources: Paul Counsell, CEO.

Application Procedures: Send resume and cover letter to the attention of Paul Counsell, CEO.

▶ **Internships**

Type: The company offers an internship program. Contact the company for more information.

Two decades ago, most commercials bore the signature styles of their creators. The joke then was that a client asked three agencies what time it was. David Ogilvy insisted that his agency's famed research department could nail it down. Rosser Reeves, of the relentless Ted Bates agency, snapped, "It's three o'clock, three o'clock, three o'clock, goddamnit." And obliging Marion Harper, founder of Interpublic, asked, "Well, sir, what time do you want it to be?"

Source: *New York*

CTS Advertising

1 Park Ln.
Dearborn, MI 48126
Phone: (313)336-0077

Employees: 8.

Average Entry-Level Hiring: 2.

Human Resources: Tom Scholl, President.

Application Procedures: Send resume and cover letter to the attention of Tom Scholl, President.

ADVERTISING CAREER DIRECTORY

CV Advertising
1 Englingon Ave. E., Ste. 500
Toronto, ON, Canada M4P 3A1
Phone: (416)486-6695

Employees: 48.

Average Entry-Level Hiring: As needed.

Opportunities: Account executive, clerical—no requirements specified.

Application Procedures: Send resume and other appropriate letters, portfolio, etc. The information is distributed to department heads who will contact applicant if interested. Contact the company for more information.

Looking for a job is largely a mind game—you're the one who defines the goal and how to get there—and flexibility has to be part of the strategy. For instance, announcements of many openings never turn up outside the employer's offices, since most companies prefer to hire from within. The trick, then, is to get inside. One way is to put your ego on hold and take a job as a clerical worker. "You need to gain employment first," says L. Patrick Sheetz, director of Michigan State University's Collegiate Employment Research Institute. "You gain promotion from there."

Source: *U.S. News & World Report*

Dailey & Associates
3055 Wilshire Blvd.
Los Angeles, CA 90010
Phone: (213)386-7823

Employees: 200.

Average Entry-Level Hiring: 3.

Opportunities: Account management—college degree (four-year). Writers—writing skills and portfolio. Art director—art school graduate; demonstrated ability with portfolio. Media—college degree (four-year).

Human Resources: Toby J. Burke, Dir. of Personnel Administration.

Application Procedures: Send resume and cover letter.

D'Arcy Masius Benton & Bowles Inc.
1675 Broadway
New York, NY 10019-5809
Phone: (212)468-3622
Fax: (212)468-4385

Business Description: Engaged in the operation of advertising agencies.

Officers: Roy J. Bostock, CEO & Pres.; Craig Brown, Exec. VP & CFO.

Employees: 360.

Human Resources: Judith Kemp, Personnel Dir.

Application Procedures: Some hiring is done through an employment agency. Send resume and cover letter to the attention of Judith Kemp, Personnel Dir.

▶ **Internships**

Contact: Lauren Gold, Personnel Dir.

Number Available Annually: 1-2.

Qualifications: Second year MBA students.

Application Procedure: Send resume and cover letter to contact.

DCA Advertising
114 Avenue of the Americas
New York, NY 10036
Phone: (212)869-8350

Average Entry-Level Hiring: Unknown.

Human Resources: Blanche Goodman, Manager.

Application Procedures: Send resume and cover letter.

▶ **Internships**

Contact: Blanche Goodman, Manager.

Type: Paid. **Number Available Annually:** 2.

Duties: Duties depend on specific Department.

Application Procedure: Send resume and cover letter to the attention of Blanche Goodman.

Application Deadline: May 15.

DDB Needham Worldwide Inc.
437 Madison Ave.
New York, NY 10022
Phone: (212)415-2000
Fax: (212)415-3520

Business Description: An advertising agency.

Officers: Gerald Germain, Exec. VP & CFO; Keith L. Reinhard, CEO & Chairman of the Board.

Employees: 5,951.

Human Resources: Mariam Saytell, Human Resources Representative.

Application Procedures: Places newspaper advertisements for certain openings. Send resume and cover letter to the attention of Human Resources Department.

▶ **Internships**

Contact: Ms. Mariann Saytell.

Type: Non-salaried, summer internships available for all departments. Internships last 10-12 weeks. **Number Available Annually:** 5. **Applications Received:** 50-100.

Duties: Assist in all areas. Good chance for interns to return as full-time employees after graduation.

Qualifications: Undergraduate seeking a career in advertising must have strong academic background and leadership ability.

Application Procedure: Send resume and cover letter to the attention of Ms. Mariann Saytell, Human Resources Representative.

Application Deadline: March 31. **Decision Date:** May 15.

Deacon Day Advertising
20 Richmond St. E., 7th Fl.
Toronto, ON, Canada M5C 2R9
Phone: (416)362-8600

Employees: 22.

Average Entry-Level Hiring: Unknown.

Opportunities: Account secretary, junior, copywriter, junior art director—college degree required. Receptionist, account coordinator—no specific information available.

Human Resources: Peter Johnson, Human Resources; Maureen Williamson, Human Resources.

Application Procedures: Send resume and cover letter.

▶ **Internships**

Type: The company does not offer an internship program.

Della Femina, McNamee WCRS
500 N. Michigan Ave.
Chicago, IL 60611
Phone: (312)222-1313

Employees: 45.

Average Entry-Level Hiring: Varies.

Opportunities: Account coordinator—college degree required. Accounting—no experience necessary. Copywriter, art director—college degree and at least two-three years required. Media—college degree required; experience preferred.

Human Resources: Arlene Hamilton, Office Mgr.

Application Procedures: Send resume and cover letter to the attention of Arlene Hamilton, Office Mgr.

Lotto newspaper ads run at the beginning and end of the week, when people are most attuned to fantasy. This is an example of media mapping, tracking people's media use to reach them most effectively. Media mapping requires different ads for different publications: Dial soap, for example, is promoted as a "noseguard" in *Sports Illustrated*, as a "stress management" tool in *Fortune*, and as a "self-esteem booster" in *Parents*.

Source: *New York*

Detrow & Underwood
1126 Cottage St.
Ashland, OH 44805
Phone: (419)289-0265

Average Entry-Level Hiring: Minimal turnover.

Opportunities: Graphic designer—college degree or art school; marketing and sales skills. Jr. account executive—college degree; marketing/sales business skills.

Application Procedures: Send resume and cover letter to the attention of. Mike W. Detrow, Exec. VP.

Advertising Career Directory

Discovery Music
5554 Calhoun Ave.
Van Nuys, CA 91401
Phone: (818)782-7818
Toll-free: 800-782-7817
Fax: (818)782-7817

Business Description: Children's record company with openings in advertising and marketing.

▶ **Internships**

Contact: Kirstie Salamanikas, Marketing Assistant.

Type: Nonpaid positions in the promotion/advertising and marketing departments. College credit can be arranged. **Number Available Annually:** 2.

Duties: The promotions/advertising position will involve implementing information gathering and research strategies. Some work on special projects will also be available. The marketing position will learn the basics of implementing marketing strategies. Will also provide secretarial support, so accurate typing, proofreading, and office skills are required. Good phone skills are a must for both positions.

Application Procedure: Contact Kirstie Salamanikas to request an application.

According to the Minneapolis-based consulting firm Personnel Decisions, women managers are slightly less satisfied with the nature of their work than men, are more likely to be critical of the way promotions are determined, and are more pessimistic than men about moving up. In addition, while 63% of men at the executive level think they work for top-notch managers, only 42% of women at the same level agreed.

Source: *Working Woman*

Dodson, Craddock & Born
4711 Scenic Hwy.
PO Drawer A
Pensacola, FL 32581
Phone: (904)433-8314

Employees: 10.

Average Entry-Level Hiring: 1.

Opportunities: Artist—college degree (B.A.); one year experience, copywriter—college degree; one year experience.

Human Resources: Mary Nolan, VP of Employee Relations.

Application Procedures: Applications can be filled out on site, or send resume and cover letter.

W.B. Doner & Company Advertising
25900 Northwestern Hwy.
Southfield, MI 48075
Phone: (313)354-9700

Employees: 575.

Average Entry-Level Hiring: Unknown.

Opportunities: Jr. copywriter—college degree required, previous internship helpful, and portfolio required. Jr. art director—college degree required and portfolio required. Assistant account executive—college degree required and internship helpful. Broadcast traffic coordinator—college degree required. Assistant media planners and buyers—college degree required and internship helpful.

Human Resources: Susan Ciuchna, Creative Recruiter.

Application Procedures: Send resume and cover letter to the attention of Ms. Susan Ciuchna, Creative Recruiter. Phone: (313)827-8456.

▶ **Internships**

Type: Company may offer an internship program.

Dudreck, Depaul, Ficco and Morgan
200 1st Ave.
Pittsburgh, PA 15222
Phone: (412)261-2580

Average Entry-Level Hiring: Unknown.

Human Resources: Albert W. Dudreck, Chairman of the Board.

Application Procedures: Send resume and cover letter to the attention of John DePaul.

Dugan Farley Communications
600 E. Cressant Ave.
Upper Saddle River, NJ 07458
Phone: (201)934-0720

Employees: 65.

Average Entry-Level Hiring: Unknown.

Opportunities: Traffic, jr. account executive, account coordinators, bookkeeping, administrative assistants—college degree preferred; experience is a must.

Human Resources: Ginny Raimann, Office Mgr.

Application Procedures: Send resume and cover letter to the attention of Ms. Ginny Raimann, Office Mgr.

Earle Palmer Brown
100 Colony Sq., Ste. 2400
Atlanta, GA 30361
Phone: (404)881-8585

Average Entry-Level Hiring: Varies.

Application Procedures: Send resume and cover letter to the attention of Personnel Department. To contact, phone (301)657-6000.

Edelmann Scott Inc.
629 E. Main St., Ste. 1104
Richmond, VA 23219
Phone: (804)643-1931

Employees: 15.

Average Entry-Level Hiring: Unknown.

Opportunities: Research—college degree (B.A./B.S.). Public relations—college degree (journalism preferred). Bookkeeping—college degree (accounting preferred).

Human Resources: Richard J. Scott, CEO.

▶ **Internships**

Contact: Ed Edelmann.

Type: College credit. **Number Available Annually:** 1.

Duties: Duties are related to department of interest.

Application Procedure: Send resume and cover letter to the attention of Ed Edelmann.

Application Deadline: None.

Evans Communications
4 Triad Ctr.
Salt Lake City, UT 84180
Phone: (801)364-7000

Employees: 289.

Average Entry-Level Hiring: 1.

Human Resources: Evonne Marsala, VP of Admin. Services.

Application Procedures: Send resume and cover letter to the attention of. Ms. Evonne Marsala, VP of Admin. Services.

> Ad agencies suffering from mid-life crises are waging guerrilla warfare. By and large, these "sales creation" or "admotion" (advertising and promotion) firms—as they might be more appropriately called—have stopped producing the dazzlingly creative work that was the hallmark of the sixties. The goal now is to generate sales in any way possible: promotion (which now accounts for 60% of the average marketing budget), distribution, in-store activities, and other marketing techniques.
>
> Source: *New York*

Evans-San Francisco
690 5th St.
San Francisco, CA 94107
Phone: (415)957-0300

Employees: 37.

Average Entry-Level Hiring: Minimal turnover.

Opportunities: Account coordinator, media assistant—college degree (B.A./B.S.); 2 years experience preferred. The company does not offer an internship program.

Human Resources: Bernard J. Cummins, VP of Employee Relations.

Application Procedures: Send resume and cover letter to the attention of Bernard J. Cummins, Jr., VP of Employee Relations.

FCB/Ronalds-Reynolds
1500 W. Georgia, Ste. 1500
Vancouver, BC, Canada V6G 2Z6
Phone: (604)684-8311

Employees: 30.

Average Entry-Level Hiring: Varies.

JOB OPPORTUNITIES DATABANK

Opportunities: Account coordinator—college degree preferred; some sales and marketing experience. Media buyer—two/three years experience preferred. Product coordinator—some experience required.

Human Resources: Don Panton, Vice Pres.

Application Procedures: Send resume and cover letter.

▶ **Internships**

Contact: Cameron Moriarty, Human Resources.

A new breed of advertising professionals is known in the trade as "ethnographers." Adapted from the anthropological practice of recording human culture, ethnography emphasizes observing consumers in their natural habitat—and incorporating those observations into advertising. Explains Barbara Feigin, an executive vice president at Grey Advertising in New York, "You want people to feel that the brand understands them—where they live, not just in their minds, but in their hearts and their guts."

Source: *Newsweek*

Foote, Cone & Belding
1255 Battery St.
San Francisco, CA 94111
Phone: (415)398-5200

Employees: 300.

Average Entry-Level Hiring: Unknown.

Opportunities: Assistant media planner, assistant account coordinator, and secretarial positions—college degree preferred. No other requirements specified.

Human Resources: Sue Poulter, Personnel Mgr.

Application Procedures: Send resume and cover letter to contact.

▶ **Internships**

Contact: Barney Ansell, Human Resources Dir.

Type: Offers paid internships during the summer. **Number Available Annually:** Varies.

Duties: Varies according to departments.

Foote, Cone & Belding
11601 Wilshire Blvd.
Los Angeles, CA 90025

Employees: 185.

Average Entry-Level Hiring: Low.

Opportunities: Account group secretary—college degree preferred; typing 50-60 wpm; word processing knowledge helpful. Assistant media planner—college degree required; computer knowledge; skill with numbers.

Human Resources: Melissa Germaine, Personnel Admin.

Application Procedures: Send resume and cover letter to contact.

Francis, Williams & Johnson Ltd.
10405 Jasper Ave., Ste. 1790
Edmonton, AB, Canada T5J 3N4
Phone: (403)423-1546

Employees: 15.

Average Entry-Level Hiring: 0-1.

Opportunities: Account managers, supervisors, and coordinators; art and media directors; recruitment coordinators; accountants—no requirements specified. Seminars and on-the-job training depending on departmental needs.

Human Resources: John Francis, President.

Application Procedures: Send resume and cover letter.

▶ **Internships**

Contact: Mark Johnson, VP of Operations.

Type: Paid internships available. **Number Available Annually:** 2-3.

Application Procedure: Send resume and cover letter stating your desire for an advertising degree.

Application Deadline: Open.

Francis, Williams & Johnson Ltd.
635 6th Ave. SW, Ste. 500
Calgary, AB, Canada T2P 0T5
Phone: (403)266-7061

Employees: 35.

Average Entry-Level Hiring: Unknown.

Human Resources: Jerry Pasely, Human Resources.

Application Procedures: Send resume and cover letter. For creative positions, a work sample should be included.

Franklin Advertising Associates Inc.
88 Needham St.
Newton, MA 02161
Phone: (617)244-8368

Employees: 10.

Average Entry-Level Hiring: 1, low turnover.

Opportunities: Account coordinator—college degree preferred. Art assistant—college degree preferred.

Human Resources: Harriet L. Wiggin, Vice Pres.

Application Procedures: Send resume and cover letter to contact.

▶ **Internships**

Contact: Harriet L. Wiggin, Vice Pres.

Type: Offers nonpaid interships that may be used for college credit. **Number Available Annually:** 12.

Duties: Varies according to position.

Application Procedure: Contact Ms. Wiggin.

Application Deadline: None.

Gardiner Advertising Agency
56 West 400, S.
PO Box 30
Salt Lake City, UT 84110
Phone: (801)364-5600

Employees: 21.

Average Entry-Level Hiring: Varies.

Opportunities: Advertising and public relations—college degree (B.A./B.S.) required; two to three years experience preferred.

Human Resources: Jim Brown, President.

Application Procedures: Send resume and cover letter to contact.

▶ **Internships**

Contact: Elese Adams, Dir. PR Services.

Type: Offers paid internships that can be used for college credit. **Number Available Annually:** 4.

Duties: Related public relations work.

Application Procedure: Send resume and cover letter along with P.R. writing samples to contact.

Application Deadline: None.

Garfield-Lynn and Co.
142 E. Ontario St.
Chicago, IL 60611
Phone: (312)943-1900

Employees: 42.

Average Entry-Level Hiring: 1.

Application Procedures: Send resume and cover letter to department heads.

Goldman & Associates
408 W. Bute St.
Norfolk, VA 23510
Phone: (804)625-2518

Employees: 13.

Average Entry-Level Hiring: 1.

Opportunities: Only hire experienced help with a college degree.

Application Procedures: Send resume and cover letter to the attention of Dean Goldman, President.

Goodwin, Dannebaum, Littman & Wingfield, Inc.
5847 San Felipe, Ste. 400
Houston, TX 77055
Phone: (713)266-7676

Employees: 85.

Average Entry-Level Hiring: 2, low turnover.

Opportunities: Traffic—college degree and secretarial skills. Mail service—college degree. Production artist—college degree and art instruction.

Human Resources: Kelly Dillmon.

Application Procedures: Send resume and cover letter to contact.

Grey Advertising Inc.
777 3rd Ave.
New York, NY 10017
Phone: (212)546-2000

Business Description: Engaged in the operation of advertising agencies.

JOB OPPORTUNITIES DATABANK

Advertising Career Directory

Officers: Barbara S. Feigin, Exec. VP of Mktg.; Steven G. Felsher, Exec. VP of Finance; Edward H. Meyer, Pres. & Chairman of the Board.

Employees: 6,000.

Application Procedures: Contact the company for more information.

Jeffrey A. Sonnenfeld, an Emory University management professor, divides U.S. corporations into 4 categories: the Baseball Team—advertising, entertainment, investment banking, software, biotech research, and other industries based on fad, fashion, new technologies, and novelty; the Club—utilities, government agencies, airlines, banks, and other organizations that tend to produce strong generalists; the Academy—manufacturers in electronics, pharmaceuticals, office products, autos, and consumer products; and the Fortress—companies in fields such as publishing, hotels, retailing, textiles, and natural resources.

Source: Fortune

Greykirk, Vansant
The World Trade Ctr.
Baltimore, MD 21202
Phone: (301)539-5400

Employees: 80.

Average Entry-Level Hiring: Unknown.

Opportunities: Service/traffic—college degree or high school graduate. The following positions require a college degree: media assistant, account executive, junior ad director, and junior writer.

Human Resources: John McClavghlin, Human Resources.

Application Procedures: Send resume and cover letter.

▶ **Internships**

Type: The company does not offer an internship program.

Harrison Marketing Counsel Ltd.
512 King St., E.
Toronto, ON, Canada M5A 1M1
Phone: (416)947-9167

Employees: 10.

Average Entry-Level Hiring: 0 in last few years.

Opportunities: Commercial artists—no requirements specified.

Human Resources: Erwin Ermel, Vice Pres.

Application Procedures: Send resume and cover letter, and a sample of the artist's work.

Henderson Advertising
PO Box 2247
Greenville, SC 29602
Phone: (803)271-6000

Employees: 100.

Average Entry-Level Hiring: Varies.

Opportunities: Opportunities available for media trainees, assistant planners, and assistant account executives. College degree required. No other requirements specified.

Human Resources: Jody Pfister, Personnel Dir.

Application Procedures: Send resume and cover letter to contact. The Personnel Department may be reached at (803)298-1442.

▶ **Internships**

Contact: Jody Pfister, Personnel Dir.

Type: Offers nonpaid internships that last six weeks. **Number Available Annually:** 8.

Duties: Hands-on experiences in the marketing, creative, media, and research departments.

Application Procedure: Send resume and cover letter to contact.

Application Deadline: April 1.

Ingalls, Quinn & Johnson
855 Boylston St.
Boston, MA 02116
Phone: (617)437-7000

Employees: 300.

Average Entry-Level Hiring: 15.

Opportunities: Coordinator—college or junior college degree; typing 55 wpm. Receptionist—high school graduate; "people" experience. Word processing operator—college, junior college, or high school graduate; word processing experience.

Human Resources: Susan Roche, VP of Employment.

▶ **Internships**

Contact: Ms. Mary Kelly, Asst. Dir.

Type: Offers nonpaid internships that can be used to earn college credit. **Number Available Annually:** Depends on company needs.

Duties: Depends on the department. Departments offering internships include creative and account services.

Application Procedure: Contact Ms. Mary Kelly by mail.

Application Deadline: None.

Jordan Associates
1000 W. Wilshire, Ste. 428
Oklahoma City, OK 73116
Phone: (405)840-3201

Employees: 52.

Average Entry-Level Hiring: 1.

Opportunities: Account executive—college degree (journalism preferred); good communication, writing, and personal presentation skills; one to two years experience preferred. Assistant media buyer—college degree (advertising preferred); good organizational and communication skills; one to two years experience preferred.

Human Resources: Barbara Murcen, Personnel Dept.

Application Procedures: Send resume and cover letter to contact.

▶ **Internships**

Contact: Helen Murcen, Personnel Dept.

Kaprielian O'Leary Advertising
99 Madison Ave.
New York, NY 10016
Phone: (212)696-1300

Employees: 20.

Average Entry-Level Hiring: 1.

Opportunities: Receptionist—college degree, interpersonal skills, articulate, and accurate. Paste-up artist—college degree, manual dexterity, and "pressure capable." Secretarial—college degree, interpersonal skilss, accurate, and "pressure capable."

Human Resources: Carolyn Aldrick, Office Mgr.

Application Procedures: Send resume and cover letter to the attention of Human Resources contact.

▶ **Internships**

Contact: Carolyn Aldrick, Office Mgr.

Type: Offers paid internships in the Media Department. **Number Available Annually:** 1.

Application Procedure: Send resume and cover letter to contact.

Application Deadline: April 30.

Some industry-watchers argue that the ad industry is heading in a very specific direction: "a 20-year-old concept called integrated marketing: getting a client to coordinate all its marketing efforts—TV ads, direct mail, special events, billboards, even public relations—preferably through one agency, which creates a single image for the product."

Source: *Fortune*

Kaufman, Goldman & Stral, Inc.
230 E. Ohio St.
Chicago, IL 60611
Phone: (312)944-0300

Employees: 15.

Average Entry-Level Hiring: 0, low turnover.

Opportunities: The company does not usually hire entry-level people.

Human Resources: Lee T. Stral, Vice Pres. Public Relations & Copy.

Keller-Crescent Co.
1100 E. Louisiana St.
Evansville, IN 47701
Phone: (812)464-2461
Fax: (812)426-7601

Average Entry-Level Hiring: The company has a low turnover rate.

Human Resources: Allen R. Mounts, VP of Human Resources.

Application Procedures: Send resume and cover letter to contact.

▶ **Internships**

Contact: Allen R. Mounts, VP of Human Resources.

JOB OPPORTUNITIES DATABANK

Type: Offers paid internships for college credit. **Number Available Annually:** 3-4.

Duties: Varies according to profession.

Application Procedure: Send resume and cover letter to Personnel Department.

Application Deadline: None.

Pay-for-performance plans start with reduced base wages and salaries but reward employees with sizeable bonuses for reaching production targets or meeting other goals. Workers under pay-for-performance plans typically earn from 10% less to 20% more than their jobs' average pay. About 4 million U.S. employees are currently paid under such plans.

Source: *Time*

Kelley Advertising Inc.
PO Box 2250
Hamilton, ON, Canada L8N 3E5
Phone: (416)525-3610

Average Entry-Level Hiring: 1-2.

Human Resources: John Parente', Corp. Controller.

Application Procedures: Send resume and cover letter.

▶ **Internships**

Contact: John Parente', Corp. Controller.

Type: Nonpaid with college credit. **Number Available Annually:** 2.

Duties: Report writing (clerical-typing). Miscellaneous duties; work is dependent on experience.

Application Procedure: Send resume and cover letter. Follow up application with a phone call.

Application Deadline: Open.

Kelly Advertising Inc.
20 Dundas St. W., Ste. 1030
Toronto, ON, Canada M5G 2C2
Phone: (416)977-2125

Employees: 25.

Average Entry-Level Hiring: 0-2.

Opportunities: Account secretary, account coordinator, media secretary, and receptionist—require computer or word processing experience.

Human Resources: Audrey Lanigan, Acctg. Supervisor.

Application Procedures: Send resume, cover letter, and sample.

Ketchum Public Relations
1133 Avenue of the Americas
New York, NY 10036
Phone: (212)536-8800
Fax: (212)944-0675

Business Description: Engaged in public relations and/or lobbying.

Officers: David Drobis, President.

Employees: 150.

Human Resources: Judy Algaze, Business Mgr.

▶ **Internships**

Contact: Susan Pagano, Personnel Mgr.

Type: Salaried and non-salaried (college credit may be arranged) internships available in the summer and fall. Departments include public relations, media, creative, and advertising. **Number Available Annually:** 2. **Applications Received:** 500.

Qualifications: College juniors or seniors; communications majors preferred.

Application Procedure: Send resume, cover letter, and writing samples to contact. An interview is required.

Application Deadline: March 31.

Koehler Marketplex
204 W. 8th St., Ste. 3
Cincinnati, OH 45202
Phone: (513)421-4411

Opportunities: Copywriter, advertising dept., assistant account executive—college degree; good writing, spelling and communication skills.

Human Resources: Karl Koehler, President.

Application Procedures: Send resume and cover letter to the attention of Karl Koehler, President.

Launey, Hachmann & Harris, Inc.
127 E. 59th St., Ste. 201
New York, NY 10022
Phone: (212)750-2001
Fax: (212)319-4692

Average Entry-Level Hiring: 1.

Human Resources: Robert E. Launey, President.

Application Procedures: Send resume and cover letter to the attention of Robert E. Launey, President.

▶ **Internships**

Contact: Robert E. Launey, President.

Type: Paid. **Number Available Annually:** Depends on company's needs.

Duties: Varies depending on project.

Application Procedure: Send resume and cover letter to contact.

Application Deadline: None.

Laven, Fuller & Perkins Advertising/Marketing Inc.
1233 E. Ontario
Chicago, IL 60611
Phone: (312)440-1818

Employees: 26.

Average Entry-Level Hiring: 1.

Opportunities: Account executives—college degree (advertising or marketing preferred); history of student employment; proof of grade average; ability to communicate both verbally and in writing. "Creative people must bring portfolio of work. Account executive candidates must provide pertinent information of part-time performance in workplace."

Human Resources: MaryAnne Miller, Exec. VP.

Application Procedures: Send resume and cover letter to contact.

Lawrence & Schiller
3932 S. Willow Ave.
Sioux Falls, SD 57105
Phone: (605)338-8000

Employees: 41.

Average Entry-Level Hiring: 3-4.

Opportunities: Opportunities available for account executives, writers/producers, and graphic designers. College degree (B.A./B.S.); one to two years experience preferred.

Human Resources: Craig Lawrence, Partner.

Application Procedures: Send resume and cover letter to contact.

▶ **Internships**

Contact: Karla Haugne, Hd. of Finance Admin.

Type: Offers paid and nonpaid internship(s). **Number Available Annually:** 2.

Duties: Varies according to project.

Application Procedure: Send resume and cover letter to contact.

Application Deadline: None specified.

By 1990 about 7500 movie screens across the country were showing commercial messages from more than 30 advertisers. But movie-goers began protesting the intrusion. Agencies responded by compiling 60-second mini-movies, without voice-overs and heavy on entertainment; the sponsor's product was absent until the final few seconds. Regardless of the switch to soft-sell, Disney was the first studio to prohibit theatres from screening commercials before its movies, as experts worried that in-theatre marketing would further alienate the dwindling movie-theatre audience.

Source: *Newsweek*

Al Paul Lefton Co.
Rohm/Haas Bldg.
Independence Mall, W.
Philadelphia, PA 19106
Phone: (215)923-9600

Employees: 155.

Average Entry-Level Hiring: 5.

Human Resources: Claire Russakoss, Admin. Asst.

Application Procedures: Send resume and cover letter to contact.

Levenson, Levenson & Hill
PO Box 619507
DFW Airport, TX 75261
Phone: (214)556-0944

Employees: 65.

JOB OPPORTUNITIES DATABANK

ADVERTISING CAREER DIRECTORY

Average Entry-Level Hiring: 2, low turnover.

Opportunities: Opportunities include promotions assistant, account services assistant, and public relations assistant. Candidates should be a college student or hold a college degree.

Human Resources: Cynthia Morrison, Human Resources.

Application Procedures: Send resume and cover letter to contact.

▶ **Internships**

Type: The company may offer an internship program. Contact the company for more information.

"Assessing one's own skills is one of the most difficult things in the world," says Kenneth Taylor, a partner at Egon Zehnder International Inc., one of the world's largest executive-search firms. "People usually have latent skills that are not obvious."

Source: *Business Week*

Levine, Huntley, Schmidt & Beaver Inc.
355 Park Ave., S.
New York, NY 10010-1799
Phone: (212)545-3500

Business Description: Engaged in the operation of advertising agencies

Officers: Jean L. Bergin, Sr. VP; Matthew R. Bud, Sr. VP & Finance Officer; Robert H. Schmidt, CEO & Pres.

Employees: 250.

Human Resources: Rose Marie Lyddan, Human Resources Dir.

Application Procedures: Send resume and cover letter.

▶ **Internships**

Contact: Harold Levine, CEO & Chairman of the Board.

Type: Salaried, summer internships available for 3-5 months. Departments include media, accounting, and production. **Number Available Annually:** 4.

Duties: According to the interests of the students and the needs of each department, interns will work directly with the department heads.

Qualifications: College students (any year) desiring a career in advertising.

Application Procedure: Send letter outlining interests with resume and letters of recommendation to the attention of Harold Levine, Chairman of the Executive Committee.

Lieberman Appalucci
4635 Crackersport Rd.
Allentown, PA 18104
Phone: (215)395-7111

Employees: 40.

Average Entry-Level Hiring: 1-2.

Opportunities: Opportunities include public relations assistant, research assistant, and account assistant. College degree and quality, summer experience required.

Human Resources: Judy Kweller, Personnel Coordinator.

Application Procedures: Send resume and cover letter to contact.

▶ **Internships**

Type: The company does not offer an internship program.

Lintas: Campbell Ewald
30400 Van Dyke
Warren, MI 48093
Phone: (313)574-3400

Average Entry-Level Hiring: The company has a low turnover rate.

Human Resources: Linda Zalewski, Human Resource Contact.

Application Procedures: Send resume and cover letter.

Lintas: New York
1 Dag Hammarskjold Plaza
New York, NY 10017
Phone: (212)605-8000

Human Resources: Patricia Ransom, Human Resources Mgr.

▶ **Internships**

Type: The company does not offer an internship program.

Lintas: New York Fahlgren & Swink
PO Box 1628
Parkersburg, WV 26101
Phone: (304)424-3591

Employees: 320.

Average Entry-Level Hiring: 4.

Opportunities: Account services and media assistant buyer—college degree preferred, usually in advertising, business, or marketing.

Human Resources: Michael Zagrodny, Personnel Dir.

Application Procedures: Send resume and cover letter to the attention of Human Resources contact.

▶ **Internships**

Contact: Mr. Tom Crooks.

Type: Offers internships. Contact the company for more information.

Long, Haymes & Carr Inc.
140 Charlois Blvd.
PO Box 5627
Winston-Salem, NC 27113
Phone: (919)765-3630

Employees: 141.

Average Entry-Level Hiring: 15.

Opportunities: Proofreader—college degree (B.A./B.S. English preferred); good grammar, punctuation & proofreading skills. Mechanical artist—college degree (B.F.A./B.S.); mechanical skills. Media assist.—college degree (B.A./B.S.); writing skills, math aptitude. Research analyst—college degree (B.A./B.S.); statistical skills. Print traffic coordinator—college degree (B.A./B.S.); detail oriented. Broadcast production coordinator—college degree (B.A./B.S.); some broadcast production experience. Account coordinator—college degree (B.A./B.S.). Asst. Account executive—M.B.A. Designer—B.F.A./B.A. Junior copywriter—college degree (B.A./B.S.); samples of published work.

▶ **Internships**

Type: Salaried and nonpaid, flexible internships available in all departments for a duration of two to three months. **Number Available Annually:** 3. **Applications Received:** 100.

Duties: Will be assistant to one professional staffer.

Application Procedure: Send resume and cover letter to Human Resources for interviewing consideration. "Portfolio needed for creative positions.".

Application Deadline: As early as possible (one year ahead is not too early).

Lowe Marschalk
1345 Avenue of the Americas
New York, NY 10105
Phone: (212)708-8800

Employees: 365.

Average Entry-Level Hiring: Hiring freeze at present time.

Opportunities: People with experience only.

Application Procedures: Send resume and cover letter to the attention of Personnel Manager.

▶ **Internships**

Type: The company may offer an internship program. Contact the company for more information.

Advertising flourished in the 1980s. In 1987, it reached 2.43% of gross national product, the highest (as a share of GNP) since World War II, reports Robert Coen of the ad agency McCann-Erickson, Inc. This was up 30% from the level of the 1970s (1.87% of GNP).

Source: *Newsweek*

Lunan Hoffman Advertising Ltd.
1440 St. Catherine W., Ste. 716
Montreal, PQ, Canada H3G 1R8
Phone: (514)874-1692

Employees: 4.

Average Entry-Level Hiring: 0 (since 1980).

Opportunities: Coordinator—no requirements specified.

Human Resources: Sally Davidson, Media Dir.

JOB OPPORTUNITIES DATABANK

ADVERTISING CAREER DIRECTORY

Application Procedures: Send resume, cover letter, and sample.

Maclaren Advertising
20 Dundas St. W.
Toronto, ON, Canada M5G 2H1
Phone: (416)977-2244

Employees: 318.

Average Entry-Level Hiring: 0-5.

Human Resources: Nancy Carroll, Personnel Officer.

Application Procedures: Send resume, cover letter, and sample.

Container Corp. of America ran a series of ads featuring contemporary art. Published from 1937 to 1983, the series was the longest-running corporate image campaign ever and, says advertising legend David Ogilvy, in its time "the best campaign of corporate advertising that ever appeared in print."

Source: *Fortune*

Marc and Company, Inc.
4 Station Sq., Ste. 500
Pittsburgh, PA 15219
Phone: (412)562-2000

Employees: 94.

Average Entry-Level Hiring: Unknown.

Human Resources: Aurelia Diggs, Receptions.

Application Procedures: Send resume and cover letter to contact; resumes are kept on file for one year.

▶ **Internships**

Type: Offers an internship(s) program through certain schools.

McCaffrey McCall
2 Carlton St., Ste. 801
Toronto, ON, Canada M5B 1J3
Phone: (416)977-2270

Employees: 6.

Average Entry-Level Hiring: 0.

Opportunities: Account executives—no requirements specified.

Human Resources: Robert Hobbs, VP & General Mgr. of Personnel.

Application Procedures: Send resume and cover letter.

▶ **Internships**

Contact: Robert Hobbs, VP & General Mgr. of Personnel.

Type: Paid. **Number Available Annually:** 1-2.

Duties: Whatever fits the needs of the department.

Application Procedure: Send resume and cover letter. Follow up with a phone call.

Application Deadline: Open.

McCann-Erickson Advertising of Canada Ltd.
Waterpark Place
10 Bay St., 13th Fl.
Toronto, ON, Canada M5J 2S3
Phone: (416)594-6000

Employees: 200.

Average Entry-Level Hiring: Varies.

Opportunities: Media estimator—post secondary degree/diploma (preferably in business or marketing) required. Must have strong organizational and communication skills, a commitment to advertising, high energy and enthusiasm, and the ability to work with numbers and people. On-the-job training will be provided, supplemented by in-house seminars. The company does not offer an internship program.

Human Resources: Cheryl Fry, Human Resources Dir.; Chris Hammond, Personnel Asst.

Application Procedures: Send resume and cover letter.

McCann-Erickson U.S.A.
750 3rd Ave.
New York, NY 10017
Phone: (212)697-6000

Business Description: Engaged in the operation of advertising agencies.

Officers: John J. Dooner, President; Robert James, CEO & Chairman of the Board.

Employees: 8,000.

Application Procedures: Contact the company for more information.

McKim Advertising Ltd.
2 Bloor St. W, 28th Fl.
Toronto, ON, Canada M4W 3R6
Phone: (416)960-1722

Average Entry-Level Hiring: Irregular in last few years.

Human Resources: Joanne Porter, Head of Personnel.

Application Procedures: Send resume and cover letter.

McKim Advertising Ltd.
600-237 Eighth Ave., SE
Calgary, AB, Canada T2G 5C3
Phone: (403)234-7400

Average Entry-Level Hiring: 0-2 (layed off 1 entry position in the last year).

Human Resources: Nadine Darcovich, Personnel Asst.

Application Procedures: Send resume and cover letter.

Mullen Advertising
PO Box 2700
Wenham, MA 01982
Phone: (508)468-1155

Employees: 90.

Average Entry-Level Hiring: 0.

Human Resources: Ray Belles.

▶ **Internships**

Contact: Ray Belles.

Type: Nonpaid. One semester or one year in all areas, including account services and media.
Number Available Annually: Varies.

Duties: Varies based upon placement.

Application Procedure: Call contact for more information.

Application Deadline: Ongoing.

Nationwide Advertising Service Inc.
280 Albert St., Ste. 703
Ottawa, ON, Canada K1P 5G8
Phone: (613)236-5839

Average Entry-Level Hiring: 0.

Human Resources: Natalie Payette, Customer Service Consultant.

Application Procedures: Send resume, cover letter, and samples of work.

Ogilvy & Mather
101 Sixth Ave. SW, Ste. 1600
Calgary, AB, Canada T2P 3P4

Average Entry-Level Hiring: 0, the company has not hired anyone in the last several years.

Human Resources: Jennifer Fletcher, Placement Mgr.

Application Procedures: Send resume, cover letter, and sample of work.

As a proponent of integrated marketing, Richard B. Fizdale of Leo Burnett agency recruited 80 specialists in direct mail, retail marketing, sales promotion, and public relations, who are responsible for teaching their disciplines to the rest of the staff. "There are over 50 forms of media in the U.S., and we want to choose the best ones to get maximum leverage for our clients' brands," Fizdale explains.

Source: *Fortune*

Parker Group, Inc.
Trinity Centre
6900 Delmar Blvd.
St. Louis, MO 63130
Phone: (314)727-4000

Employees: 47.

Average Entry-Level Hiring: Unknown.

Opportunities: Opportunities available for assistants in the media, marketing, account management, and data processing departments—college degree (B.A./B.S.) required. Two years of experience preferred.

Human Resources: Lori Jones, Copywriter.

Application Procedures: Accepts unsolicited resumes. Applications and/or resumes kept on file for six months.

▶ **Internships**

Type: Occasionally hires interns.

ADVERTISING CAREER DIRECTORY

Paul, John & Lee, Inc.
113 Twin Oaks Dr.
Syracuse, NY 13206
Phone: (315)463-1177

Employees: 9.

Average Entry-Level Hiring: Unknown.

Opportunities: Opportunitities available in creative services, accounting/finance, and marketing—college degree (B.A./B.S.) required. Two years experience preferred.

Human Resources: Sarah, Bookkeeping.

Application Procedures: Send resume and cover letter, and fill out an application. Applications and/or resumes kept on file for a short time.

▶ **Internships**

Type: The company does not offer an internship program.

The popular hype-busting ad genre of the 1990s may have been launched by the appealing Joe Isuzu parodies of the sleazy salesman. Some other hype-busting ads poke fun at how easily consumers jump on band-wagons, some no-frills campaigns sell fundamentals, and some rely on more believable role models.

Source: *New York*

Perri Debes Looney & Crane Inc.
46 Prince St.
Rochester, NY 14607
Phone: (716)442-9030

Employees: 22.

Average Entry-Level Hiring: Unknown.

Opportunities: Creative services, marketing, media, and broadcast production—college degree (B.A./B.S.) required; two years experience preferred. Accounting/Finance—M.B.A. and two years experience preferred.

Human Resources: Trish, Asst. Controller.

Application Procedures: Some hiring is done through an employment agency. Places newspaper advertisements for certain openings.

▶ **Internships**

Type: The company does not offer an internship program.

Pinne Garvin Herbers & Hock, Inc.
200 Vallejo St.
San Francisco, CA 94111
Phone: (415)956-4210

Employees: 25.

Average Entry-Level Hiring: 0-1.

Opportunities: Account coordinator—college degree and good communication and presentation skills. Junior copywriter—college degree; must demonstrate writing skills and an imagination. Junior art director—graduate art student (not necessarily college); must be able to draw/indicate and understand production techniques.

Human Resources: Linda Utterberg, Office Mgr.

Application Procedures: Send resume and cover letter. Applications and/or resumes kept on file for six months.

▶ **Internships**

Type: The company does not offer an internship program.

Publicite Leo Burnett Ltd.
175 Bloor St. E., N. Tower
Toronto, ON, Canada M4W 3R9
Phone: (416)925-5997

Employees: 165.

Average Entry-Level Hiring: 0-3.

Opportunities: Clerical, and Billing and Budget departments—no requirements specified.

Human Resources: Anne Andrichuck, Employment Admin.

Application Procedures: Send resume and cover letter.

Recruitment Enhancement Services
2 Lombard St., Ste. 300
Toronto, ON, Canada M5C 1M1
Phone: (416)362-7999

Employees: 18.

Average Entry-Level Hiring: 0-2.

Opportunities: New business director, account coordinator, account executive, and layout artists—college degree not required.

Human Resources: Sandra Higgins, Dir. Client Services.

Application Procedures: Send resume and cover letter.

Ian Roberts Inc.
One Brunswick Sq.
St. John, NF, Canada E2L 4V1
Phone: (506)634-7190

Employees: 7.

Average Entry-Level Hiring: 0-1.

Opportunities: Account services, account executive, media planners, and secretaries—college degree required. Art director and mechanical artist—formal training required.

Human Resources: Minnie McDonald, Secretary.

Application Procedures: Send resume and cover letter.

Romann & Tannenholz Advertising
100 5th Ave., 8th Fl.
New York, NY 10011
Phone: (212)661-8181

Employees: 25.

Average Entry-Level Hiring: Unknown.

Human Resources: Louise Hollinger.

Ross Roy, Inc.
100 Bloomfield Hills Pkwy.
Bloomfield Hills, MI 48013
Phone: (313)433-6000

Employees: 955.

Average Entry-Level Hiring: 25.

Opportunities: Management trainee—college degree with an advertising major and related activities. Account administrator—college degree and advertising-related experience. Assistant media buyer—college degree and media-related experience.

Application Procedures: Maintains a job hotline.

▶ **Internships**

Type: The company does not offer an internship program.

Ross Roy Ltd.
1737 Walker Rd.
Windsor, ON, Canada M8Y 4R8
Phone: (519)258-7584

Employees: 80.

Average Entry-Level Hiring: Unknown.

Human Resources: Claudette Munger, Human Resources Asst.

▶ **Internships**

Type: The company does not offer an internship program.

A new study by the outplacement firm Drake Beam Morin shows that job seekers who were willing to relocate saw a 6 percent increase in compensation during the 1990 and 1991, compared with a 1 percent decrease for those who stayed in place.

Source: *U.S. News & World Report*

Saatchi & Saatchi Advertising Worldwide
375 Hudson St.
New York, NY 10014
Phone: (212)463-2000
Fax: (212)463-3303

Business Description: Engaged in the operation of advertising agencies.

Employees: 7,267.

Average Entry-Level Hiring: Unknown.

Opportunities: Opportunities available for assistant planners and assistant account executives. Bachelor's degree, good analytical skills, and facility with numbers required.

Human Resources: Joseph Sansaverino; Linda Seale, Human Resources Dir.

Saatchi & Saatchi Compton Hayhurst Ltd.
145 King St. E.
Toronto, ON, Canada M5C 2Y8
Phone: (416)359-9595

Employees: 142.

Average Entry-Level Hiring: 5.

Opportunities: Advertising and Media departments.

JOB OPPORTUNITIES DATABANK

Advertising Career Directory

Human Resources: Cathy Dillon, Employment Representative.

Application Procedures: Send resume and cover letter.

Saffer Advertising Inc.
180 Lesmill Rd.
Don Mills, ON, Canada M3B 2T5
Phone: (416)449-7961

Employees: 165.

Average Entry-Level Hiring: 0-3.

Human Resources: Lynn Furley, Personnel Mgr.

Application Procedures: Send resume and cover letter.

From 1976 through 1988 total U.S. ad spending consistently grew faster than the economy as a whole. In 1981 and 1982, when the U.S. economy caught a nasty cold, the ad biz didn't even sneeze. Instead, it recorded eye-popping growth rates of 12.8% and 10.2%, respectively. By contrast total ad spending grew just 5% in 1989 and 3.8% in 1990. Network ad spending fell 7.1% in the first half of 1991 from the same period in 1990, while newspaper ad spending fell 7% in the first half of 1991.

Source: *Business Week*

Siano & Spitz Advertising
530 Oak St.
Syracuse, NY 13202
Phone: (315)479-5581

Employees: 10.

Average Entry-Level Hiring: Unknown.

Human Resources: Laura, Manager Operations.

Application Procedures: Applications and/or resumes kept on file.

▶ **Internships**

Type: Internship(s) program is offered.

Smith, Dorian & Burman, Inc.
110 New Britian Ave.
West Hartford, CT 06110
Phone: (203)522-3101

Employees: 15.

Average Entry-Level Hiring: Unknown.

Opportunities: Assistant account executive and assistant in the Advertising department—college degree (B.A./B.S.); no experience required.

Human Resources: John, Media Dir.

Application Procedures: Contact the company for more information.

Smith/Greenland Advertising, Inc.
555 W. 57th St.
New York, NY 10019
Phone: (212)757-3200

Employees: 110.

Human Resources: Gwen, Receptions.

Application Procedures: Places newspaper advertisements for certain openings.

J. Richard Smith Ltd.
225 Broadhollow Rd., Ste. 112W
Melville, NY 11747-4807
Phone: (516)293-8700

Employees: 50.

Average Entry-Level Hiring: Unknown.

Opportunities: Artists (freelancers)—portfolio required; experience preferred.

Application Procedures: Send resume and cover letter to the attention of Denise. Resumes are kept on file from six months to one year.

▶ **Internships**

Type: The company does not offer an internship program.

Spiro & Associates
100 S. Broad St.
Philadelphia, PA 19110
Phone: (215)851-9600

Employees: 150.

Average Entry-Level Hiring: 2-4.

Opportunities: Media assistant—some college (degree preferred), typing skills, familiar with word and data processing, good with numbers, and analytical. Research assistant—college degree in marketing and statistics preferred, typing skills, and familiar with word and data processing. Junior account executive—college degree, some work experience, communications skills, people and business oriented, and sales and writing ability.

Human Resources: Anne Kelley, VP of Human Resources.

Application Procedures: Send resume and cover letter for clerical positions.

▶ Internships

Contact: Bill Brunt, Human Resources.

Type: Non-salaried, summer internships available in account services, marketing research, production, traffic, and media. **Number Available Annually:** 14.

Duties: Duties will change with the positions depending on the current affairs of the department.

Application Procedure: Send resume and cover letter.

Application Deadline: None.

Taylor Brown, Smith & Perrault

4544 Post Oak Pl., Ste. 264
Houston, TX 77027
Phone: (713)877-1220

Employees: 52.

Average Entry-Level Hiring: Unknown.

Human Resources: Rochelle Yuga, Administrator.

Application Procedures: No hiring activity. When hiring, send resume and cover letter.

▶ Internships

Contact: Howard Bleren Program Dir.

Type: Paid internships available during the school year in all departments. **Number Available Annually:** Varies.

Duties: Analysis, filing, and research.

Application Procedure: Send resume and cover letter.

Application Deadline: April 1, Summer deadline.

Taylor-Tarpay Direct Advertising Ltd.

1039 McNicoll Ave.
Scarborough, ON, Canada M1W 3W6
Phone: (416)498-5550

Employees: 30.

Average Entry-Level Hiring: 1.

Opportunities: Junior account executive—college degree required, preferably in marketing.

Human Resources: Tim Pervin, Managing Dir.

Application Procedures: Send resume and cover letter.

J. Walter Thompson

466 Lexington Ave.
New York, NY 10017
Phone: (212)210-7000
Fax: (212)210-7066

Opportunities: Assistant account representatives must have strong analytical and organizational skills, excellent written and verbal communications skills, the ability to interact well with others, and enthusiasm. Responsibilities include tracking the status of projects; writing brand reviews that cover brand performance, competitive activity, and strategic direction; analyzing competitive copy and spending activities; coordinating day-to-day production; managing brand production and media budgets; and addressing network legal issues. Account representatives need the ability to work with numerical data, strong writing and presentation skills, and experience as an assistant representative on two diverse brand assignments. Assistant producers need technical ability, financial acumen, knowledge of union contracts and production costs, and must be able to work without supervision. Assistant copywriters must have good verbal and written communications skills. A portfolio of advertising samples is required. Assistant art directors must provide a portfolio of advertising samples that demonstrates talent and imagination. Broadcast negotiators must have the ability to work with numerical data. Liberal arts background is preferred. Marketing/advertising researchers must have coursework in the social sciences, experimental psychology, statistics, and possibly business or marketing. While the primary area of expertise of account managers is marketing, they must integrate consumer information, brand performance data, market trends,

ADVERTISING CAREER DIRECTORY

and competitive category activity to build and implement a cohesive advertising strategy for the brand. No particular educational background is required for media planners; "a strong liberal arts background is a fine base." Marketing knowledge is helpful, but not necessary. Successful candidates for media planning positions must solve problems efficiently; be willing to work hard and assume responsibility; interact well with other departments, with clients, and with others in the media industry; have the ability to work with numerical data; and have strong writing skills. Media planners assimilate product, research, and media data in order to determine how each medium can be used most effectively to meet the client's needs.

Human Resources: Melissa Statmore, Personnel Assoc.

▶ Internships

Contact: Melissa Statmore, Personnel.

Type: Summer internships are offered in Account Management. **Number Available Annually:** Unknown.

Americans beginning their careers in the 1990s will probably work in 10 or more jobs for five or more employers before retiring, according to Henry Conn and Joseph Boyett, authors of *Workplace 2000: The Revolution Reshaping American Business*. That means it's up to the individual to manage her or his own career.

Source: *Working Woman*

Duties: Interns are assigned to a specific piece of business and are viewed as a contributing member of the account team. Thus, interns can see how an ad concept is developed into effective and creative advertising. In addition, interns can work on a specific strategic/marketing project and present findings and recommendations to senior agency executives and clients; interact with all departments; and learn how the agency becomes an integral part of the client's business in terms of research, marketing, strategy, analysis and creativity.

Application Procedure: Send resume and cover letter to contact.

Travis/Walz & Associates, Inc.
8417 Sante Fe Dr.
Overland Pk., KS 66212
Phone: (913)341-5022

Employees: 18.

Average Entry-Level Hiring: 1-2.

Opportunities: Marketing, media, accounting/finance—college degree (B.A./B.S.); no experience, will train.

Human Resources: Marie Clark, Office Mgr.

Application Procedures: They have an application blank and one can send a resume which will be reviewed.

▶ Internships

Type: The company does not offer an internship program.

Tycer Fultz Bellack
3460 W. Bayshore Rd.
Palo Alto, CA 94303
Phone: (415)856-1600

Employees: 45.

Average Entry-Level Hiring: Unknown. No current hiring activity.

Human Resources: Dixie Pollace, Controller.

Application Procedures: Send resume and cover letter.

▶ Internships

Contact: Sherri Laveroni, Human Resources.

Type: Salaried, six week summer internships available in all departments. **Number Available Annually:** 2. **Applications Received:** Unknown.

Application Procedure: Send resume and cover letter.

Valentine-Radford, Inc.
911 Main St., Ste. 11
Kansas City, MO 64105
Phone: (816)842-5021

Employees: 150.

Average Entry-Level Hiring: Unknown.

Opportunities: Opportunities include account coordinators and media assistants. College degree in business, journalism, or advertising is required. Experience is helpful. New employees start in entry-level clerical positions, progress to trainees, and then qualify for other opportunities.

Human Resources: Cindy Kitchen, Office Mgr.

Application Procedures: Send resume and cover letter.

▶ **Internships**

Contact: Cindy Kitchen, Human Resources.

Type: Salaried and non-salaried Christmas break (two-three weeks) internships available. Students may request department placement.

Duties: Vary according to department placement.

Application Procedure: Send resume and cover letter.

Application Deadline: November. **Decision Date:** End of the fall semester.

Vriak Robinson Hayhurst Communications Ltd.
555 W. Hastings St., 8th Fl.
Vancouver, BC, Canada V6B 5G2
Phone: (604)684-1111

Employees: 35.

Average Entry-Level Hiring: 0-1.

Opportunities: Administrative—college degree preferred, and experience necessary.

Human Resources: Jane McQueen, Personnel Mgr.

Application Procedures: Send resume and cover letter.

Watson Ostby Direct
468 Queen St., E.
PO Box 24
Toronto, ON, Canada M5A 1T7
Phone: (416)369-1890

Employees: 6.

Average Entry-Level Hiring: 0-1 (0 in last year).

Opportunities: Secretarial, and Production and Account Services departments—experience preferred.

Human Resources: Gunner Ostby, President.

Application Procedures: Send resume and cover letter.

Wettstein, Bolchalk, Owens & Cooke Advertising & Public Relations
6200 E. 14th St., C-200
Tucson, AZ 85711
Phone: (602)745-8221

Opportunities: Opportunities include clerical and advertising positions.

Application Procedures: Send resume and cover letter.

▶ **Internships**

Contact: Earl Wettstern, Internship Coordinator.

Type: College credit internships available for all departments.

Application Procedure: Send resume and cover letter.

Americans watch television, listen to the radio, and read newspapers and magazines an average of 8 hours, 3 minutes per day. Youngstown, Ohio, spends the most hours per capita on all forms of media: 8 hours and 50 minutes, almost half of this time in front of the television. The ad agency Young & Rubicam found that Americans watch TV an average 3 hours, 48 minutes a day (up 22 minutes from 1975) and listen to the radio for 3 hours, 21 minutes (up 19 minutes). Newspapers get 34 minutes (a minute less) and magazines 20 minutes (5 more).

Source: *Fortune*

Roger White Advertising & Public Relations
206 State St.
Binghamton, NY 13901
Phone: (607)724-4356

Employees: 15.

Average Entry-Level Hiring: Unknown.

▶ **Internships**

Contact: Debbie Collett-O'Brien, Marketing Services Manager.

Type: Summer and semester, Non-salaried (college credit) internships available for the following departments: art and marketing. **Number**

Available Annually: 3-4. **Applications Received:** 10-15.

Duties: Art—writing ads, proofreading, design, drawing, and layout. Marketing—research. College credit should be arranged by the student.

Application Procedure: Send resume and cover letter and portfolio to contact. Interview required.

Wolf, Richards, Taylor Advertising
35 Prince Arthur Ave.
Toronto, ON, Canada M5R 1B2
Phone: (416)967-9000

Employees: 25.

Average Entry-Level Hiring: 1 (0 in last year).

Opportunities: Secretary/receptionist, account coordinator, traffic coordinator—no requirements specified.

Human Resources: Allan Kiddell, President.

Application Procedures: Send resume and cover letter.

Wunderman International Inc.
60 Bloor St. W., 15th Fl.
Toronto, ON, Canada M4W 3B8
Phone: (416)921-9050

Employees: 50.

Average Entry-Level Hiring: 0-2.

Human Resources: Deborah Benton, Office Mgr.

Application Procedures: Send resume and cover letter.

Young & Rubicam Inc.
285 Madison Ave.
New York, NY 10017
Phone: (212)210-3000

Business Description: Engaged in the operation of advertising agencies. Engaged in public relations and/or lobbying.

Officers: Roger Craton, Exec. VP of Finance; Susan Gianinno, Dir. of Mktg.; Alexander S. Kroll, CEO & Chairman of the Board.

Employees: 10,473.

Application Procedures: Send resume and cover letter to the attention of 285 Madison Ave., 19th Fl., New York, NY 10017.

▶ **Internships**

Contact: Cheryl Konopka, Media Internship Program.

Type: Internships include $50/week for travel and meals. Students should also receive course credit. Internships are available in the following areas: media planning, media research, network broadcast, print services, and Army group. Students must intern at least 15 hours per week for the duration of the fall or spring semester.

Duties: Media planning interns will recommend to clients how their advertising budget should be spent. The planning group recommends target audiences, maintains budgets, meets with salespeople, and keeps clients informed about new media opportunities that arise. Network broadcast interns assist clients in spending their television advertising budget in the best way possible. The group is also responsible for insuring that the advertising runs as ordered and that program environment is acceptable to the client. Media research interns provide information on media and demographic trends and test market design. Research also works with the planning and network departments on special projects. Print services interns assist clients in spending their magazine advertising budget in the best way possible. The department negotiates rates, ad positioning, and merchandising packages and is responsible for insuring that advertising runs as ordered. Army group interns will assist in the separate unit of Y&R that provides advertising, direct marketing, public relations, and sales promotion for the United States Army, which is the unit's client.

Qualifications: Open to juniors and seniors who are liberal arts or business majors, with a minimum Grade Point Average of 3.0.

Application Procedure: Send single-page, current resume and a short (500 words) essay on why your are interested in advertising. This is not a summer internship program. Any questions regarding summer internships should be directed to Virginia Hanchar, Human Resources, at the above address.

Application Deadline: Spring semester: November 25, 1992. Fall semester: May 10, 1993.

Additional Companies

Admarketing
1801 Century Park
Los Angeles, CA 90067
Phone: (213)203-8400

Ammirati and Puris
100 5th Ave.
New York, NY 10011
Phone: (212)206-0500

The Direct Marketing Group
477 Madison Ave.
New York, NY 10022
Phone: (212)355-2530

Doremus and Co.
120 Broadway
New York, NY 10005
Phone: (212)964-0700

Griffin Bacall
130 5th Ave.
New York, NY 10011
Phone: (212)645-4900

Hal Riney and Partners
735 Battery St.
San Francisco, CA 94111
Phone: (415)981-0850

HDM
810 7th Ave.
New York, NY 10019
Phone: (212)408-2100

Hill, Holliday, Connors, Cosmopoulos
200 Clarendon
Boston, MA 02116
Phone: (617)437-1600

Kallir, Philips, Ross
605 3rd Ave.
New York, NY 10022
Phone: (212)878-3700

Laurence, Charles, Free, and Lawson
261 Madison Ave.
New York, NY 10019
Phone: (212)661-0200

Lord, Geller, Federico, Einstein
655 Madison Ave.
New York, NY 10022
Phone: (212)421-6050

Scali, McCabe, Sloves
800 3rd Ave.
New York, NY 10022
Phone: (212)421-2050

Tatham-Laird and Kudner
980 N. Michigan Ave.
Chicago, IL 60611
Phone: (312)337-4400

TBWA Advertising
292 Madison Ave.
New York, NY 10011
Phone: (212)725-1150

Tracy-Locke
200 Crescent Ct.
Dallas, TX 75250
Phone: (214)969-9000

Warwick Advertising
875 3rd Ave.
New York, NY 10022
Phone: (212)751-4700

Wells, Rich, Greene
9 W. 57th St.
New York, NY 10019
Phone: (212)303-5000

JOB OPPORTUNITIES DATABANK

Career Resources

CHAPTER TWENTY-FIVE

Career Resources

The Career Resources chapter covers additional sources of job-related information that will aid you in your job search. It includes full, descriptive listings for sources of help wanted ads, professional associations, employment agencies and search firms, career guides, professional and trade periodicals, and basic reference guides and handbooks. Each of these sections is arranged alphabetically by organization, publication, or service name. For complete details on the information provided in this chapter, consult the introductory material at the front of this directory.

Sources of Help Wanted Ads

Adcrafter
The Adcraft Club of Detroit, Inc.
2630 Book Tower
Detroit, MI 48226
Phone: (313)962-7225
Fax: (313)962-3599

Weekly. Publication for the advertising and marketing communities of metropolitan Detroit, and the members of the Adcrafter Club of Detroit.

ADNET
National On-Line Classified, Inc.
1465 Andrews Ln.
East Meadow, NY 11554
Phone: (516)481-9222

Contains personnel and consulting firm listings and job seeker profiles. Enables the user to match employers seeking permanent and temporary personnel with entry-level and experienced job candidates, consultants, personnel recruiters, and technical consulting firms. Employer entries typically include company name, address, benefits, environment, and technical information. Job seeker listings generally contain candidate's name, skills, experience, and specific job criteria.

Advance Job Listings
PO Box 900
New York, NY 10020

Advertising/Communications Times
Advertising/Communication Times, Inc.
121 Chestnut St.
Philadelphia, PA 19106
Phone: (215)629-1666
Fax: (215)923-8358

Monthly. Magazine for advertising and marketing professionals in Pennsylvania, New Jersey, and Delaware. Covers such topics as personnel changes, meeting dates, outdoor advertising, and sports marketing.

Fortune writer Patricia Sellers calls *The Mirror Makers* by Stephen Fox "arguably the best book on advertising's history."

Adweek
49 E. 21st St.
New York, NY 10010
Phone: (212)995-7323

Weekly. $50.00/year.

Adweek/East
A/S/M Communications, Inc.
49 E. 21st St.
New York, NY 10010
Phone: (212)529-5500
Fax: (212)477-5365

Weekly. Publication covering advertising, communications, and marketing news in New York, Connecticut, New Jersey, Pennsylvania, Delaware, Maryland, the District of Columbia, and West Virginia.

Adweek/Midwest
A/S/M Communications, Inc.
435 N. Michigan Ave., Ste. 819
Chicago, IL 60611
Phone: (312)467-6500
Fax: (312)321-0039

Weekly. Publication covering advertising, communications, and marketing news in Kansas, Kentucky, Illinois, Indiana, Iowa, Michigan, Minnesota, Missouri, Nebraska, North Dakota, Ohio, South Dakota, and Wisconsin.

Adweek/New England
A/S/M Communications, Inc.
100 Boylston St., Ste. 210
Boston, MA 02116
Phone: (617)482-0876
Fax: (617)482-2921

Weekly. Publication covering advertising, communications, and marketing news in Connecticut, Maine, Massachusetts, New Hampshire, Rhode Island, and Vermont.

Adweek/Southeast
A/S/M Communications, Inc.
6 Piedmont Center
3525 Piedmont Rd., Ste. 300
Atlanta, GA 30305
Phone: (404)841-3333
Fax: (404)841-3332

Weekly. Publication covering advertising, communications, and marketing news in Alabama, Florida, Georgia, Mississippi, North Carolina, South Carolina, Tennessee, and Virginia.

Adweek/Southwest
A/S/M Communications, Inc.
2909 Cole Ave., Ste. 220
Dallas, TX 75204
Phone: (214)871-9550
Fax: (214)871-9557

Weekly. Publication covering advertising, communications, and marketing news in Arkansas, Louisiana, New Mexico, Oklahoma, and Texas.

Adweek/West
A/S/M Communications, Inc.
5757 Wilshire Blvd., Ste. M-110
Los Angeles, CA 90036
Phone: (213)937-4330
Fax: (213)938-4160

Weekly. Publication covering advertising, communications, and marketing news in Arizona, California, Colorado, Idaho, Montana, Nevada, Oregon, Utah, Washington, and Wyoming.

Adweek's Marketing Computers
A/S/M Communications, Inc.
49 E. 21st St.
New York, NY 10010
Phone: (212)529-5500
Fax: (212)254-5204

Monthly. Advertising/marketing magazine for the computer industry.

Affirmative Action Register
Affirmative Action, Inc.
8356 Olive Blvd.
St. Louis, MO 63132
Phone: (314)991-1335
Toll-free: 800-537-0655
Fax: (314)997-1788

Monthly. Publication containing listings of vacant administrative jobs in business, industry, government, and schools. Designed to aid advertising professionals in complying with equal employment guidelines.

Airbrush Action
Airbrush Action Inc.
400 Madison Ave.
Lakewood, NJ 08701
Phone: (908)364-2111
Fax: (908)367-5908

6x/year. Publication for airbrush artists.

Art Direction
Art Direction
10 E. 39th St.
New York, NY 10016
Phone: (212)889-6500
Fax: (212)889-6504

Monthly. Magazine covering advertising art and photography for visual professionals.

Black Careers
Project Magazine, Inc.
PO Box 8214
Philadelphia, PA 19101
Phone: (215)387-1600

Bimonthly. Magazine focusing on black men and women looking for job opportunities in government, industry, and commerce. Designed to serve mainly high school and college counselors, college graduates currently working in industry, and college seniors in black colleges.

The Black Collegian
1240 S. Broad St.
New Orleans, LA 70125-2091
Phone: (504)821-5694
Fax: (504)821-5713

Quarterly. $10.00/year; $5.00/year for students; $2.50/issue. Career and job-oriented publication for black college students.

Black Employment & Education Magazine
Hamdani Communications, Inc.
13428 Maxella Ave., Ste. 283
Marina Del Ray, CA 90292
Toll-free: 800-726-3907

7x/year. Magazine covering career opportunities for black people in the United States and abroad.

When you do your resume yourself, the process of sifting through your past helpfully forces you to zero in on the very things you will discuss at job interviews. Sam Marcus of Sibson & Company, a human-resources consulting firm in Princeton, NJ, suggests that you have a colleague or friend read your resume and ask them what message they get from it, to make sure you're highlighting your talents and the results of your labors. Use verbs like "improved," "planned," and "redesigned" followed by a briefly worded accomplishment.

Source: *U.S. News & World Report*

Career Opportunity Update
Career Research Systems, Inc.
PO Box 28799
Santa Ana, CA 92799-8799
Phone: (714)556-1200
Fax: (714)556-6548

Monthly, except December. $72.00/year; $24.00/three issues; $9.00/issue. Covers about 100 employers nationwide who anticipate having technical, professional or management employment opportunities in the coming six months. Consists of five regional editions for Pacific, Western, Midwestern, Southern, and Eastern states. Entries include: Company name, address, phone, name of contact, date established, num-

ADVERTISING CAREER DIRECTORY

ber of employees, description of the company and its products, and general description of openings expected. Arranged alphabetically and geographically.

Career Placement Registry (CPR)
Career Placement Registry, Inc.
302 Swann Ave.
Alexandria, VA 22301
Phone: (703)683-1085
Fax: (703)683-0246

Contains brief resumes of job candidates currently seeking employment. Comprises two files, covering college and university seniors and recent graduates, and alumni, executives, and others who have already acquired substantial work experience. Entries typically include applicant name, address, telephone number, degree level, function, language skills, name of school, major field of study, minor field of study, occupational preference, date available, city/area preference, special skills, citizenship status, employer name, employer address, description of duties, position/title, level of education, civil service register, security clearance type/availability, willingness to relocate, willingness to travel, salary expectation, and overall work experience. Available online through DIALOG Information Services, Inc.

In 1991 Campbell's Soup announced plans to increase its ad budget by 30% in 1992 to revive its fabled Campbell Kids campaign, joining a host of other advertisers bringing back echoes and images from past campaigns that elicit a response from nostalgic baby boomers.

Source: *Business Week*

Career Woman
Equal Opportunity Publications, Inc.
44 Broadway
Greenlawn, NY 11740
Phone: (516)261-8899
Fax: (516)261-8935

3x/year. Magazine addressing affirmative action issues for career-seeking college students. Covers such topics as career guidance, and opportunities in banking, communications, insurance, nursing, the government, and industry. Offers a free resume service.

Chicago Advertising & Media
KB Communications
1412 N. Halsted St.
Chicago, IL 60622
Phone: (312)944-0100
Fax: (312)915-5906

Semimonthly. Publication for Chicago's advertising community.

College Recruitment Database (CRD)
Executive Telecom System, Inc.
College Park N.
9585 Valparaiso Ct.
Indianapolis, IN 46268
Phone: (317)872-2045

Contains resume information for graduating undergraduate and graduate students in all disciplines at all colleges and universities for recruitment purposes. Enables the employer to create and maintain a private "skill" file meeting selection criteria. Typical entries include student identification number, home and campus addresses and telephone numbers, schools, degrees, dates of attendance, majors, grade point averages, date available, job objective, curricular statement, activities/honors, and employment history. Available online through the Human Resource Information Network.

Collegiate Career Woman
Equal Opportunity Publications, Inc.
44 Broadway
Greenlawn, NY 11740

Three times/year. $25.00/year. Recruitment magazine for women. Provides free resume service and assists women in identifying employers and applying for positions.

Communication World
International Assn. of Business Communicators
1 Hallidie Plaza, 6th Fl.
San Francisco, CA 94102
Phone: (415)433-3400
Fax: (415)362-8762

Monthly. Publication covering news and information of communications and public relations industries.

Community Jobs
Community Careers Resource Center
1601 Connecticut Ave., NW, 6th Fl.
Washington, DC 20009
Phone: (202)667-0661
Fax: (202)387-7915

Monthly. $30.00/year to institutions; $20.00/year to nonprofit organizations; $18.00/year to individuals; $3.50/issue. Covers: Jobs and internships available with nonprofit organizations active in issues such as the environment, foreign policy, consumer advocacy, housing, education, etc. Entries include: Position title, name, address, and phone of contact; description, responsibilities, requirements, salary. Arrangement: Geographical.

Confetti
Randall Publishing, Inc.
1401 Lunt Ave.
Elk Grove Village, IL 60007
Phone: (708)437-6604
Toll-free: 800-451-8166

Bimonthly. Communication arts magazine covering desktop design, illustration, photography, and production.

The Counselor
Advertising Specialty Institute
Bucks County Business Park
1120 Wheeler Way
Langhorne, PA 19047-1785
Phone: (215)752-4200
Fax: (215)752-9758

Monthly. $60.00/year.

Equal Opportunity Magazine
44 Broadway
Greenlawn, NY 11740

Three times/year. $13.00/year. Minority recruitment magazine. Includes a resume service.

Format
The Advertising Federation of Minnesota
275 Market St., No. C19
Minneapolis, MN 55405
Phone: (612)339-5470
Fax: (612)339-5818

12x/year. Publication for advertising professionals.

Hispanic Times Magazine
Hispanic Times Enterprises
PO Box 579
Winchester, CA 92396
Phone: (714)926-2119

Bimonthly. Magazine focusing on issues of interest to Hispanic and American Indian college students and professionals.

> Where jobs are rebounding, according to DRI/McGrawHill: the Pacific states, due to high-tech industries and trade with Asia; the southwest, due to free trade with Mexico and business diversification after the oil bust; the south Atlantic states, due to new investment lured by low labor and living costs.
>
> Source: *Newsweek*

How
F & W Publications, Inc.
1507 Dana Ave.
Cincinnati, OH 45207
Phone: (513)531-2222
Fax: (513)531-1843

Bimonthly. Publication for the graphic arts industry, including designers, illustrators, and art directors.

ID International Design
International Design Holdings LP
250 W. 57th St., Ste. 215
New York, NY 10107
Phone: (212)956-0535
Fax: (212)246-3925

6x/year. Publication focusing on business and consumer product, interior, environmental, and graphics design.

The Job Finder: A Checklist of Openings for Administrative and Governmental Research Employment in the West
Western Governmental Research Assn.
California State University, Long Beach
c/o Graduate Center for Public Policy and Administration
1250 Bellflower Blvd.
Long Beach, CA 90840

Monthly. $20.00/year. Listing of openings in city, county, and state government in 13 western states.

CAREER RESOURCES

ADVERTISING CAREER DIRECTORY

Job Ready
Quantum Publishing Inc.
1211 N. Westshore Blvd., Ste. 102
Tampa, FL 33607
Phone: (813)874-5550
Fax: (813)286-3649

Monthly. Magazine concerning disabled people in the workforce. Designed to help human resource professionals understand disabilities, and with interviewing techniques, and adaptive technology.

More and more companies are using computer software as an advertising and marketing medium. Mailed to selected computer enthusiasts, the software features not only games, but also animation, slick graphics, and other interactive features, along with the sales pitch. The software ad industry works on the principle that computer users are the most captive of captive audiences. And when you advertise on software, says Paula George, founder of The SoftAd Group of Sausalito, CA, "the computer becomes the salesman." Advertisers spent about $10 million on disk ads in 1990, up from almost nothing in 1987.

Source: *Newsweek*

Jobs Available
PO Box 1222
Newton, IA 50208-1222
Phone: (515)791-9019

Biweekly. $18.00/year. Lists a wide range of employment opportunities in the public sector. Published in Midwest/Eastern and Western editions.

Journal of Career Planning and Employment
College Placement Council, Inc.
62 Highland Ave.
Bethlehem, PA 18017
Phone: (215)868-1421
Fax: (215)868-0208

Quarterly. $65.00/year. Can be used to provide assistance to students in planning and implementing a job search.

Liberal Arts Jobs
Peterson's
PO Box 2123
Princeton, NJ 08543-2123
Phone: (609)243-9111

Nadler, Burton Jay. 1989. $9.95. 110 pages. Presents a list of the top 20 fields for liberal arts majors, covering more than 300 job opportunities. Discusses strategies for going after those jobs, including guidance on the language of a successful job search, informational interviews, and making networking work.

Medical Advertising News
Engel Communications, Inc.
Mountainview Corp. Pk.
820 Bear Tavern Rd.
West Trenton, NJ 08628
Phone: (609)530-0044

12x/year. Publication featuring pharmaceutical marketing news. Covers market trends, new product information, and regulations.

Minority Employment Journal
C.L. Lovick & Associates
1341 Ocean Ave., Ste. 228
Santa Monica, CA 90401
Phone: (213)338-8444
Fax: (213)338-0901

Bimonthly. Publication covering career opportunities in the aerospace, computer, financial, manufacturing, and retail industries for executives, community leaders, and minority professionals.

The National Ad Search
National Ad Search, Inc.
PO Box 2983
Milwaukee, WI 53201

Fifty issues/year. $215.00/year; $135.00/six months; $75.00/three months. Contains listings of "over 2,000 current career opportunities from over 72 employment markets."

National Employment Listing Service Bulletin
Sam Houston State University
College of Criminal Justice
Huntsville, TX 77341

Monthly. $30.00/year for individuals; $65.00/year for institutions/agencies.

National Job Market
Careers Information, Inc.
PO Box 1411
Alexandria, VA 22313-2011
Phone: (703)548-8500

Biweekly. $150.00/year; $6.50/issue. Career advancement magazine for professionals, containing articles and job listings.

Networking News
Networking Unlimited, Inc.
c/o Alina Novak
337 44th St., No. 6
Brooklyn, NY 11220-1105

Quarterly. $10.00/year. Newsletter concerned with career management, change, skills, problems, and prospects. Carries features about networking as a career strategy and practical articles on leadership and communication in business and professional spheres. Recurring features include reports of conferences, panel discussions, and speakers.

New England Advertising Week
100 Boylston St., No. 210
Boston, MA 02116
Phone: (617)482-0876

Weekly. $60.00/year; $30.00/year for members of associations affiliated with Adweek. News magazine serving the advertising, marketing, and media industries in New England.

New England Employment Week
PO Box 806
Rockport, ME 04856

New England Minority News
New England Minority News, Inc.
46 Battles St.
Hartford, CT 06120
Phone: (203)549-0809
Fax: (203)293-2402

Biweekly. Magazine aiming to help the minority community and business and government communicate. Highlights business and employment opportunities.

Occupational Outlook Quarterly
U.S. Government Printing Office
Superintendent of Documents
Washington, DC 20402-9322
Phone: (202)783-3238
Fax: (202)512-2250

Quarterly. Contains articles and information about career choices and job opportunities in a wide range of occupations.

In 1990 women's earnings as a percent of men's earnings for year-round, full-time workers in all occupations was 71%, up from 68% in 1989 and from 60% in 1980. Nonetheless, large pay differentials continue within job categories as well as across them. On average, women who are service workers or managers earn full-time pay closer to 60% of what men earn in the same occupations.

Source: *Business Week*

Opportunity Report
Job Bank, Inc.
PO Box 6028
Lafayette, IN 47903
Phone: (317)447-0549

Biweekly. $252.00/year. Lists 3,000-4,000 positions across the United States, from entry-level to upper management, in a variety of occupational fields. Ads are derived from newspapers, primarily in growth markets. Ads contain position description, employment requirements, and contact information.

Popai News
The Point-of-Purchase Advertising Institute
66 N. Van Brunt St.
Englewood, NJ 07631
Phone: (201)894-8899
Fax: (201)894-0529

6x/year. Publication covering marketing and retail industry news for the point-of-purchase industry. Includes such features as in-store and display case design, industry trends, and promotional campaigns.

CAREER RESOURCES

ADVERTISING CAREER DIRECTORY

Print
RC Publications, Inc.
104 5th Ave.
New York, NY 10011
Phone: (212)463-0600
Fax: (212)989-9891

Bimonthly. Magazine covering graphic design industry news. Features market trends and new technology.

Money can't always buy ad space. Even as the magazine environment grows more competitive, many publications are becoming more selective about the ads they take. *Architectural Digest* and *Bon Appetit* shun pet-food ads. The *New Yorker* has never run feminine-hygiene or condom ads. *Mirabella*, the highbrow fashion magazine, says no to "mass distributed" products such as Maybelline and Avon cosmetics and Jaclyn Smith clothes for Kmart. With consumer magazines competing ferociously for readers and ad dollars, many believe the key to success lies in appealing to an exclusive, upscale audience.

Source: *Newsweek*

The Professional Communicator
Women in Communications, Inc.
2101 Wilson Blvd., Ste. 417
Arlington, VA 22201
Phone: (703)528-4200
Fax: (703)528-4205

5x/year. Publication for members of Women in Communications, Inc. addressing such issues as legislative concerns, communications trends, and career development.

Signs of the Times
ST Publications
407 Gilbert Ave.
Cincinnati, OH 45202
Phone: (513)421-2050
Toll-free: 800-543-1925

13x/year. Magazine focusing on the sign and outdoor advertising industry.

Specialty Advertising Business
Specialty Advertising Assn. International
3125 Skyway Circle N.
Irving, TX 75038
Phone: (214)252-0404
Fax: (214)594-7224

Monthly. Magazine covering the specialty advertising industry. Features activities of the Specialty Advertising Association International.

WA&M Membership Directory
Women in Advertising and Marketing (WA&M)
4200 Wisconsin Ave., NW, Ste. 106-238
Washington, DC 20016
Phone: (202)833-4333

Quarterly.

Professional Associations

Academy for Health Services Marketing (AHSM)
c/o American Marketing Assn.
250 S. Wacker Dr., Ste. 200
Chicago, IL 60606
Phone: (312)648-0536

Membership: Marketing professionals in the health care field; vice presidents and directors of hospitals, health maintenance organizations, nursing homes, and other health care institutions. **Purpose:** Offers placement service. Promotes the marketing of health services; sponsors continuing education for and professional development of members to this end. Conducts seminars; bestows Philip Kotler and Academy Achievement and Contribution awards. A subsidiary of the American Marketing Association.

American Advertising Federation (AAF)
1400 K St., NW, Ste. 1000
Washington, DC 20005
Phone: (202)898-0089

Membership: Advertising clubs, agencies, trade associations, students, advertisers, and the media. **Purpose:** To promote a better understanding of advertising through government relations, public relations, and advertising education in order to further an effective program of advertising self-regulation. Sponsors National Student Advertising Competition and Best in the West and ADDY awards competitions. Bestows Silver Medal Award to outstanding advertising executives. Operates Advertising Hall of Fame and speakers' bureau; maintains western region office in San Francisco, CA. **Publication(s):** *American Advertising Federation—Annual Report to the Members.* • *American Advertising Federation—Washington Report*, monthly. • *American Advertising Magazine*, quarterly. • *Communicator*, monthly.

American Association of Advertising Agencies (AAAA)
666 3rd Ave., 13th Fl.
New York, NY 10017
Phone: (212)682-2500
Fax: (212)682-8391

Purpose: To foster, strengthen, and improve the advertising agency business; to advance the cause of advertising as a whole; to aid its member agencies to operate more efficiently and profitably. Sponsors member information and international services. Maintains 28 committees. Bestows awards; compiles statistics. **Publication(s):** *Bulletin*, periodic. • *401(K) News*, monthly. • *Media Newsletter*, quarterly. • *New York and Washington, DC Newsletter*, monthly. • *Roster*, annual. • Also publishes booklets.

Bank Marketing Association (BMA)
309 W. Washington St.
Chicago, IL 60606
Phone: (312)782-1442

Membership: Public relations and marketing executives for commercial and savings banks, credit unions, and savings and loan associations, and related groups such as advertising agencies and research firms. **Purpose:** Offers placement service. Provides marketing education, information, and services to the financial services industry; conducts research, educational workshops, and seminars; cosponsors summer sessions of fundamentals and advanced courses in marketing at the University of Colorado at Boulder and the University of Georgia. Maintains information center, housing a 4000 volume collection on public relations, marketing, advertising, business development, and special promotions. Sponsors competitions; compiles statistics. Maintains biographical archives and speakers' bureau. Bestows Golden Coin awards in marketing and communication and awards for the best advertisements in print, on radio, and on television. Affiliated with: American Bankers Association.

Some companies are using "behavioral interviewing" to gain greater insight into job candidates. By asking the interviewee to address hypothetical situations relating to the job, interviewers go behind the resume to assess likely performance. "What you get on a resume are education and experience," explains Jim Kennedy, president of Management Team. "You want to find out how a person is going to do a job, not only whether he has the credentials to do it."

Source: *Business Week*

Broadcast Designers Association (BDA)
251 Kearny St., Ste. 611
San Francisco, CA 94108
Phone: (415)788-2324
Fax: (415)982-5140

Membership: Designers, artists, art directors, illustrators, photographers, animators, and other professionals in the television industry; educators and students; commercial and industrial companies that manufacture products related to design. **Purpose:** Maintains placement service. Informs members of new design trends, graphic/technical information, and state-of-the-art equipment and materials. Presents awards in various catagories of television art. Maintains library and compiles statistics.

Council of Sales Promotion Agencies (CSPA)
750 Summer St.
Stamford, CT 06901
Phone: (203)325-3911
Fax: (203)969-1499

Membership: Agencies with a primary interest in sales promotion. **Purpose:** Seeks to increase understanding, by management, of sales promotion as a special component of the total market-

Advertising Career Directory

ing management and corporate communication function; will stimulate methods of scientific research and evaluation of sales promotion. Sponsors intern program; maintains speakers' bureau.

Council of Writers Organizations (CWO)
1501 Broadway, Ste. 1907
New York, NY 10036
Phone: (212)302-4006

Membership: Twenty-four organizations representing 25,000 writers. **Purpose:** Maintains referral service. Serves as an umbrella agency for organizations representing writers. Provides a means of sharing information among organizations and their members as well as a voice for professional writers.

According to Dave Pelliccioni, Toyota's national merchandising manager, "Today's 23- to 30-year-olds aren't so much interested in figuring out how to get a cheaper Europass as they are in just getting their feet on the ground. In focus group after focus group, what we heard is that after seven years of riding high on the hog, the recession, the war, and slumping sales have changed our consumers' sensibilities. They're telling us that the frivolity of the 80s is irrelevant and not to bother them with that."

Source: *New York*

Direct Marketing Association (DMA)
11 W. 42nd St.
New York, NY 10036-8096
Phone: (212)768-7277
Fax: (212)768-4546

Membership: Manufacturers, wholesalers, public utilities, retailers, mail order firms, publishers, schools, clubs, insurance companies, financial organizations, business equipment manufacturers, paper and envelope manufacturers, list brokers, compilers, managers, owners, computer service bureaus, advertising agencies, lettershops, research organizations, printers, lithographers, creators, and producers of direct mail and direct response advertising. **Purpose:** Offers placement service. Studies consumer and business attitudes toward direct mail and related direct marketing statistics. Offers Mail Preference Service for consumers who wish to receive less mail advertising, Mail Order Action Line to help resolve difficulties with mail order purchases, and Telephone Preference Service for people who wish to receive fewer telephone sales calls. Maintains hall of fame; compiles statistics. Sponsors several three-day Basic Direct Marketing Institutes, Advanced Direct Marketing Institutes, and special interest seminars and workshops. Sponsors annual Direct Marketing Echo Awards competitions and maintains library of portfolios of contest entries. Maintains Government Affairs office in Washington, D.C. Operates Direct Marketing Educational Foundation. Maintains 2500 volume library containing ECHO Award winning direct marketing campaigns, 500 reference books, and 1200 topical files.

Fastbreak Syndicate, Inc. (FSI)
PO Box 1626
Orem, UT 84059
Phone: (801)785-1300

Membership: Freelancers including writers, graphic artists, and photographers. **Purpose:** Operates placement service. Seeks to enhance the profitability of freelance work and to facilitate the exchange of information and the marketing of finished works, using a computer network. Sponsors competitions for beginning freelancers; bestows awards. Maintains library and archive. Plans to conduct regional workshops and seminars.

National Association of Media Brokers (NAMB)
c/o James A. Gammon
Gammon Media Brokers, Inc.
1925 K St., NW, Ste. 304
Washington, DC 20006
Phone: (202)862-2020
Fax: (202)862-2023

Membership: Media brokerage firms. **Purpose:** Media brokers deal in newspaper, radio, and television properties. To share information on activities of mutual interest. Compiles statistics. **Publication(s):** *Membership Directory and Organization Brochure*, annual.

National Network for Artist Placement
935 W. Ave. 37
Los Angeles, CA 90065
Phone: (213)222-4035

A resource center for providing information about opportunities in dance; music; theatre; literature; fine and visual arts; and film and video.

Promotion Marketing Association of America (PMAA)
322 8th Ave., Ste. 1201
New York, NY 10001
Phone: (212)206-1100
Fax: (212)929-1408

Membership: Promotion service companies, sales incentive organizations, and companies using promotion programs; associate members are manufacturers of premium merchandise, consultants, and advertising agencies. **Purpose:** Conducts surveys and studies of industry groups and premium usage. Sponsors area seminars. Bestows awards. **Publication(s):** *Outlook*, 5/year. • *PMAA Membership Directory*, annual.

Publishers' Ad Club (PAC)
c/o Jerry Younger
New York Times
229 W. 43rd St.
New York, NY 10036
Phone: (212)556-1375

Membership: Book publishing companies, book ad agencies, and media representatives. **Purpose:** Maintains placement service. Provides scholarships.

Self-Help Clearinghouse
St. Clares-Riverside Medical Center
Pocono Rd.
Denville, NJ 07834
Phone: (201)625-9565

Edward Madara, Director. A central source of information on self-help groups across the U.S. and in Canada. Can direct interested persons to clearinghouses in their own states which in turn can provide help in finding local self-help groups for job hunters. (A variety of self-help groups exist for job hunters: 40-plus; disabled; those in certain professions such as social work; etc.)

University and College Designers Association (UCDA)
2811 Mishawaka Ave.
South Bend, IN 46615
Phone: (219)288-8232

Membership: Colleges, universities, junior colleges, or technical institutions that have an interest in visual communication design; individuals who are involved in the active production of such communication design or as teachers or students of these related disciplines. **Purpose:** Maintains placement service. Purposes are to: aid, assist, and educate members through various programs of education; improve members' skills and techniques in communication and design areas such as graphics, photography, signage, films, and other related fields of communication design; be concerned with the individual members' relationships within their own institutions as well as the larger communities in which they serve; aid and assist members in their efforts to be professionals in their respective fields through programs of education and information. Sponsors competitions; bestows awards.

Senior job seekers need to stress that your experience is worth something, that you have actually learned some lessons during all those years in harness that make you still a valuable commodity, a problem solver. Gerald M. Sturman, chairman of a Greenwich, CT, management-consulting firm called the Career Development Team, notes that when seeking a career move in the later years of your career you should make sure you focus on performance, the actual business challenges and responsibilities you face.

Source: *Fortune*

Women in Advertising and Marketing (WA&M)
4200 Wisconsin Ave., NW, Ste. 106-238
Washington, DC 20016
Phone: (202)833-4333

Membership: Women professionals in advertising, marketing, and related fields. **Purpose:** Organized to function as a network for women in the advertising and marketing fields. Keeps members abreast of new developments. Facilitates the exchange of ideas and the devel-

CAREER RESOURCES

opment of professional contacts among members.

Women in Communications, Inc. (WICI)
2101 Wilson Blvd., Ste. 417
Arlington, VA 22201
Phone: (703)528-4200

Purpose: Offers placement service. Sponsors National Clarion Awards Competition; presents Vanguard Award for positive recognition of women. Compiles statistics.

Employment Agencies and Search Firms

ABC Employment Service
25 S. Bemiston
St. Louis, MO 63105
Phone: (314)725-3140

Employment agency.

A.C. Personnel Consultants
262 Havana St., Ste. 1018
Aurora, CO 80010
Phone: (303)341-5477

Sibson & Company, a human-resource firm based in Princeton, NJ, reports that 53% of the 630 companies it surveyed in 1990 provided variable incentives to workers below the executive level, up from 46% in 1989.

Source: U.S. News & World Report

Adworld Personnel Agency
15 E. 40th St.
New York, NY 10016
Phone: (212)889-6532

Employment agency.

Alpha Resource Group, Inc.
10300 N. Central Expy.
Bldg. V, Ste. 190
Dallas, TX 75231

Executive search firm.

Alpine Consultants
10300 SW Greenburg Rd., Ste. 290
Portland, OR 97223
Phone: (503)244-3393

Employment agency.

Amherst Personnel Group Inc.
550 Old Country Rd., Ste. 203
Hicksville, NY 11801
Phone: (516)433-7610

Employment agency. Executive search firm. Other offices in Milltown, NJ, and Rochelle Park, NJ.

Arancio Associates
542 High Rock St.
Needham, MA 02192
Phone: (617)449-4436

Employment agency. Executive search firm.

Austin Employment Agency
71-09 Austin St.
Forest Hills, NY 11325
Phone: (718)268-2700

Employment agency.

Best Personnel Services
9229 Ward Pkwy., Ste. 335
Kansas City, MO 64114
Phone: (816)361-3100

Employment agency. Fills openings on a regular or temporary basis.

Calvert Associates, Inc.
202 E. Washington St., Ste. 304
Ann Arbor, MI 48104
Phone: (313)769-5413

Employment agency.

Capitol Search Employment Services
915 Clifton Ave.
Clifton, NJ 07013
Phone: (201)779-8700

Employment agency. Second location in Ridgewood, NJ.

Career Specialties
210 G St., NE, 1st Fl.
Washington, DC 20002

Executive search firm. Recruits for a variety of fields.

Chaloner Associates
Box 1097
Back Bay Sta.
Boston, MA 02117

Executive search firm.

Claremont-Branan, Inc.
2295 Parklake Dr., Ste. 520
Atlanta, GA 30345

Employment agency. Executive search firm.

Consultants and Designers Inc.
3601 W. 31st St.
New York, NY 10001
Phone: (212)563-8400

Places staff in temporary positions.

Dartmouth Consultants
275 Madison Ave.
New York, NY 10016
Phone: (212)889-9600

Employment agency. Handles placements in variety of fields.

Dunhill Personnel Systems, Inc.
1 Old Country Rd.
Carle Place, NY 11514

Executive search firm. Over 300 affiliated locations coast-to-coast.

Helen Edwards and Staff Agency
2500 Wilshire Blvd., Ste. 1018
Los Angeles, CA 90057
Phone: (213)388-0493

Employment agency.

Esquire Personnel Services, Inc.
222 S. Riverside Plaza, Ste. 320
Chicago, IL 60606
Phone: (312)648-4600

Employment agency. Places individuals in variety of fields. Handles temporary assignments as well.

Fox-Morris
1617 JFK Blvd., Ste. 210
Philadelphia, PA 19103

Executive search firm. Branch locations in many states throughout the U.S.

Fuller Williams Placement
406 W. 34th
Kansas City, MO 64111
Phone: (816)931-8236

Employment agency.

CAREER RESOURCES

> Citizens of Greenwood-Greenville, Mississippi, watch the most television per capita in the U.S.: an average of 4 hours, 39 minutes per day. In Miami-Fort Lauderdale the per capita average for listening to the radio is 3 hours, 43 minutes, tops in the nation. Other national highs: people living in Charlottesville, Virginia, average 53 minutes per day reading newspapers, and Boston leads the nation in magazine reading, with an average of 29 minutes per day.
>
> Source: *Fortune*

Howard-Sloan Associates, Inc.
545 5th Ave.
New York, NY 10017

Executive search firm.

I.D.E.A. of Charleston, Inc.
PO Box 11100
Charleston, SC 29411
Phone: (803)723-6944

Employment agency. Places individuals on a temporary or regular basis.

JR Professional Search
7477 E. Broadway
Tucson, AZ 85710
Phone: (602)721-1855

Employment agency.

Advertising Career Directory

Mell D. Leonard and Associates Inc.
Florida Federal Bldg., Ste. 260
919 West Hwy., No. 436
Altamonte Springs, FL 32714
Phone: (407)869-6355

Employment agency. Executive search firm. Places individuals in variety of fields.

> A narrow focus on a single specialty doesn't do much for your employability quotient. The more tasks you've performed and the more problems you've solved, the greater your chances of getting another job. A diverse resume should also help you ride out the twists of the economy and the whims of financial fashion. Since no one knows exactly which skills will be in demand in the future, you'd better have several to offer.
>
> Source: *Business Week*

MBC Systems Ltd.
7444 Dulaney Valley Ct., Ste. 11
Towson, MD 21204
Phone: (301)583-8600

Employment agency.

The Pathfinder Group
295 Danbury Rd.
Wilton, CT 06897
Phone: (203)762-9418

Employment agency. Executive search firm. Recruits staff in a variety of fields.

Printers Placement
1609 Gessner
Houston, TX 77080
Phone: (713)973-8687

Employment agency. Provides regular or temporary placement of staff.

Pro-Files
379 The Mall Office Center
Louisville, KY 40207

Employment agency.

Randolph Associates, Inc.
PO Box 1586
Boston, MA 02104-1586
Phone: (617)227-2554

Employment agency. Provides regular or temporary placement of staff.

Remer-Ribolow and Associates
275 Madison Ave., Ste. 1605
New York, NY 10016
Phone: (212)808-0580

Employment agency.

Sanford Rose Associates
265 S. Main St.
Akron, OH 44308
Phone: (216)762-6211

Executive search firm. Over 80 office locations nationwide.

Selected Executives Inc.
959 Park Sq. Bldg.
Boston, MA 02116
Phone: (617)426-3100

Employment agency.

RitaSue Siegel Agency, Inc.
60 W. 55th St.
New York, NY 10019

Executive search firm. Affiliate office located in London.

Snelling and Snelling
4000 S. Tamiami Tr.
Sarasota, FL 33581
Phone: (813)922-9616

Employment agency. Over 50 offices across the country.

The Stanford Gilbert Agency
1377 Westwood Blvd.
Los Angeles, CA 90024
Phone: (213)473-3097

Employment agency. Also located in Hollywood, CA.

The Wright Group
6846 Spring Valley Rd., Ste. A
Dallas, TX 75240

Executive search firm.

Career Guides

Advertising Account Executive
Vocational Biographies, Inc.
PO Box 31
Sauk Centre, MN 56378-0031
Phone: (612)352-6516

1986. Four-page pamphlet containing a personal narrative about a worker's job, work likes and dislikes, career path from high school to the present, education and training, the rewards and frustrations, and the effects of the job on the rest of the worker's life. The data file portion of this pamphlet gives a concise occupational summary, including work description, working conditions, places of employment, personal characteristics, education and training, job outlook, and salary range.

Advertising Agencies: What They Are, What They Do, How They Do It
American Assn. of Advertising Agencies-Publisher
666 3rd Ave., 13th Fl.
New York, NY 10017-4565
Phone: (212)682-2500

Revised edition, 1987. This 15-page booklet includes information on advertising agency service standards and agency compensation and organization.

Advertising Careers: How Advertising Works and the People Who Make It Happen
Henry Holt and Co.
115 W. 18th St.
New York, NY 10011
Phone: (212)886-9200
Toll-free: 800-247-3912

Jan W. Greenberg. First edition, 1987. Includes an index.

After College: The Business of Getting Jobs
The Career Press
62 Beverly Rd.
PO Box 34
Hawthorne, NJ 07507
Phone: 800-227-3371

Falvey, Jack. $9.95. 192 pages. Provides students with the perspective and tools to meet career and job-hunting challenges.

The Berkeley Guide to Employment for New College Graduates
Ten Speed Press
PO Box 7123
Berkeley, CA 94707
Phone: (415)845-8414

Briggs, James I. $7.95. 256 pages. Basic job-hunting advice for the college student.

> Jobs are increasingly determined by skills, and titles are meaningless. A resume that reads "Executive Vice President for Marketing" won't guarantee employment. Companies want people who can solve problems and complete projects. Security derives from the salability of a "can-do" reputation in a job market that spans all industries.
>
> Source: *Business Week*

The Big Book of Free Career Services and Programs
Ready Reference Press
PO Box 5249
Santa Monica, CA 90405
Phone: (213)474-5175

$95.00. Two-volume set. Presents thousands of free or low-cost career and job-hunting resources. Includes such things as job referral services, vocational testing programs, and job training. Entries include organization name, type of service offered, background, description, audience served, hours, address, and telephone number. Subject and geographic indexes.

California Connections
CALCON
PO Box 90396
Long Beach, CA 90809-0396
Phone: (213)434-7843
Fax: (213)434-4202

Includes job opportunities in California listed by city, county, federal, school district, community college, and university personnel offices. Typical entries contain employer name, address, telephone number, job title, salary, benefits offered,

Career Choices for the 90's for Students of Communications and Journalism
Walker and Co.
720 5th Ave.
New York, NY 10019
Phone: (212)265-3632
Toll-free: 800-289-2553
Fax: (212)307-1764

Compiled by Career Associates Staff. Revised edition, 1990. This book offers alternatives for students of communications and journalism, and includes information on advertising. Gives information about the job outlook and competition for entry-level candidates. Provides job hunting tips.

> No automobile company today would risk ignoring female buyers—who make or influence 80% of all car purchases—with a line such as Packard's 1930's pitch, "Ask the man who owns one."
>
> Source: *Every Bite a Delight and Other Slogans*

Career Choices for the 90's for Students of English
Walker and Co.
720 5th Ave.
New York, NY 10019
Phone: (212)265-3632
Toll-free: 800-289-2553
Fax: (212)307-1764

Compiled by Career Associates Staff. Revised edition, 1990. The goal of this book is to offer career alternatives for students of English. It includes information on advertising careers. Gives the outlook and competition for entry-level candidates. Provides job hunting tips.

Career Choices for the 90's for Students of Psychology
Walker and Co.
720 5th Ave.
New York, NY 10019
Phone: (212)265-3632
Toll-free: 800-289-2553
Fax: (212)307-1764

Compiled by Career Associates Staff. 1990. This book offers alternatives for students of psychology, including careers within the advertising field. Gives information about the outlook and competition for entry-level candidates. Provides job hunting tips.

The Career Fitness Program: Exercising Your Options
Gorsuch Scarisbrick Publishers
8233 Via Paseo del Norte, Ste. F-400
Scottsdale, AZ 85258

Sukiennik et al. 1989. $15.00. 227 pages. Textbook, with second half devoted to the job search process.

Career Information System (CIS)
National Career Information System
1787 Agate St.
Eugene, OR 97403
Phone: (503)686-3872

Includes information on job search techniques and self-employment options. Also provides extensive career planning information.

Career Opportunities in Advertising and Public Relations
Facts on File, Inc.
460 Carl Ave., S.
New York, NY 10016
Phone: (212)683-2244

Shelly Field. 1990. Describes 85 jobs and includes salary information, employment prospects, and education and skills needed for the jobs.

Career Opportunities News
Garrett Park Press
PO Box 190 C
Garrett Park, MD 20986-0190
Phone: (301)946-2553

Calvert, Robert, Jr., and French, Mary Blake, editors. Bimonthly. $30.00/year; $4.00 sample issue. Each issue covers such things as resources to job seekers, special opportunities for minorities, women's career notes, and the current outlook in various occupations. Cites free and inexpensive job-hunting materials and new reports and books.

Careering and Re-Careering for the 1990's
Consultants Bookstore
Templeton Rd.
Fitzwilliam, NH 03447
Phone: (603)585-6544
Fax: (603)585-9221

Krannich, Ronald. 1989. $13.95. 314 pages. Details trends in the marketplace, how to identify opportunities, how to retrain for them, and how to land jobs. Includes a chapter on starting a business. Contains index, bibliography, and illustrations.

Careers in Advertising
National Textbook Co.
4255 W. Touhy Ave.
Lincoln, IL 60646
Phone: (312)679-5500
Toll-free: 800-323-4900

S. William Pattis. 1990. Describes employment in creative and media services, research, account management, production and traffic, agency management, and sales.

Careers and the College Grad
Bob Adams, Inc.
260 Center St.
Holbrook, MA 02343
Phone: (617)767-8100
Fax: (617)767-0994

Ranno, Gigi. 1990. $12.95. Approximately 150 pages. An annual resource guide addressing the career and job-hunting interests of undergraduates. Provides company profiles and leads.

Careers in Communications
National Textbook Co.
4255 W. Touhy Ave.
Lincolnwood, IL 60646-1975
Phone: (708)679-5500
Toll-free: 800-323-4900

Shonan F. Noronha. 1987.

Chronicle Career Index
Chronicle Guidance Publications
PO Box 1190
Moravia, NY 13118-1190
Phone: (315)497-0330

Annual. $14.25. Provides bibliographic listings of career and vocational guidance publications and other resources. Arrangement: Alphabetical by source. Indexes: Occupation; vocational and professional information.

Coming Alive from Nine to Five
Mayfield Publishing
1240 Villa St.
Mountain View, CA 94041

Micheolzzi, Betty N. 1988. $12.95. In addition to general job-hunting advice, provides special information for women, young adults, minorities, older workers, and persons with handicaps.

Large companies can be great schools: Think of them as learn-while-you-earn programs. Hands-on management, for example, is an absolute requirement in today's job market. So people in staff jobs should seek line responsibilities. Seasoned operating managers, on the other hand, should pick up planning or development experience to round out their portfolios.

Source: *Business Week*

The Complete Job Search Book
John Wiley and Sons
General Books Div.
605 3rd Ave.
New York, NY 10158
Phone: (212)850-6000
Fax: (212)850-6088

Beatty, Richard H. 1988. $12.95. 256 pages.

The Complete Job-Search Handbook
Consultants Bookstore
Templeton Rd.
Fitzwilliam, NH 03447
Phone: (603)585-6544
Fax: (603)585-9221

Figler, Howard. 1988. $11.95. 366 pages. Contains information on how to look for career opportunities every day. Focuses on twenty life skills in self-assessment, detective work, communication skills, and selling oneself. Includes skill-building exercises.

CAREER RESOURCES

ADVERTISING CAREER DIRECTORY

Exploring Careers in Advertising
Rosen Publishing Group, Inc.
29 E. 21st St.
New York, NY 10010
Phone: (212)777-3017
Toll-free: 800-237-9932

E. L. Deckinger. 1985. Describes jobs in advertising, educational requirements, college selection, and job hunting. Provides sources of career information in advertising, a list of periodicals, and an annotated bibliography.

> As corporate America struggles through its own identity crisis during the next decade, the burden will be on employees to be both adaptable and opportunistic. From learning to cope with paychecks that are increasingly tied to a company's or department's overall performance to designing flexible work schedules that make raising a family and pursuing a career compatible goals, being successful in the 1990s will more than ever be synonymous with achieving personal satisfaction.
>
> Source: *U.S. News & World Report*

Federal Career Opportunities
Federal Research Service, Inc.
370 W. Maple Ave.
Vienna, VA 22180
Phone: (703)281-0200

Biweekly. $147.00/year; $71.00/six months; $37.00/three months; $7.50/copy. Provides information on more than 4,200 current federal job vacancies in the United States and overseas; includes permanent, part-time, and temporary positions. Entries include: Position title, location, series and grade, job requirements, special forms, announcement number, closing date, application address. Arrangement: Classified by federal agency and occupation.

Federal Jobs Digest
Federal Jobs Digest
325 Pennsylvania Ave., SE
Washington, DC 20003
Phone: (914)762-5111

Biweekly. $110.00/year; $29.00/three months; $4.50/issue. Covers over 20,000 specific job openings in the federal government in each issue. Entries include: Position name, title, General Schedule grade and Wage Grade, closing date for applications, announcement number, application address, phone, and name of contact. Arrangement: By federal department or agency, then geographical.

Freelance Jobs for Writers
Writer's Digest Books
1507 Dana Ave.
Cincinnati, OH 45207
Phone: (513)531-2222

Polking, Kirk. 1984. $8.95. 281 pages. Suggests opportunities for writers in many fields, including advertising and public relations, political campaigns, radio and television, education, business and industry, and others.

Freelance Writing Start-Up Manual
American Entrepreneurs Assn.
2311 Pontius Ave.
Los Angeles, CA 90064

$59.50 ($54.40 for AEA members). A step-by-step guide to starting a freelance writing business, as well as information on market potential, profits, advertising and promotion, and related topics.

Get a Better Job!
Peterson's
PO Box 2123
Princeton, NJ 08543-2123
Phone: (609)243-9111

Ed Rushlow. 1990. $11.95. 225 pages. Counsels the reader on job search techniques. Discusses how to win the job by bypassing the Personnel Department and how to understand the employer's system for screening and selecting candidates. Written in an irreverent and humorous style.

Getting Hired: How to Sell Yourself
Carolina Pacific Publishing
7808 SE 28th Ave.
PO Box 02399
Portland, OR 97202

Costanzo, W. Kenneth. 1987. $8.95. 103 pages.

Getting Into Advertising
Ballantine Books
201 E. 50th St.
New York, NY 10022
Phone: (212)751-2600
Toll-free: 800-630-6460

David Laskin. 1986. Profiles advertising professionals; provides tips on how to obtain employment in the field of advertising. Includes educational preparation and income information.

Getting a Job in the Computer Age
Peterson's
PO Box 2123
Princeton, NJ 08543-2123
Phone: (609)243-9111

Compiled by the staff of the National Institute for Work and Learning. $7.95. 101 pages. Describes more than 75 of the most popular occupational categories and the computer requirements for each.

Getting to the Right Job
Workman Publishing
708 Broadway
New York, NY 10003
Phone: (212)254-5900

Cohen, Steve, and de Oliveira, Paulo. 1987. $6.95. 288 pages.

Go Hire Yourself an Employer
Doubleday and Co., Inc.
666 5th Ave.
New York, NY 10103
Phone: (212)984-7561

Irish, Richard K. 1987. $9.95. 312 pages.

Guerilla Tactics in the Job Market
Bantam Books
666 5th Ave.
New York, NY 10103
Phone: (212)765-6500

Jackson, Tom. 1987. $4.50. 384 pages. Provides 79 action-oriented tips for getting the job or changing jobs.

Have You Considered Advertising? Focus: Account Management
Catalyst
250 Park Ave., S.
New York, NY 10003
Phone: (212)777-8900

1987. This 12-page pamphlet profiles women in account management and describes where the jobs are, the nature of the work, salary, educational preparation, and employment outlook.

Cynical consumers are wearying of the constant barrage of marketing messages. They're becoming less receptive to the blandishments of Madison Avenue. And their loyalty to brands has eroded as they see more products as commodities distinguished only by price. At the same time that consumers have changed, technology and the proliferation of media are transforming the science of marketing to them. Now, companies increasingly can aim their messages to carefully pinpointed consumers through direct mail. Or they can advertise on one of the new and sharply targeted media.

Source: *Business Week*

How to Apply for a Job
Acoma Books
PO Box 4
Ramona, CA 92065

Post, L.H. $2.50. 32 pages. Also available in Spanish.

How to Be a Freelance Writer: A Guide to Building a Full-Time Career
Bantam Books
666 5th Ave.
New York, NY 10103
Phone: (212)765-6500

Martindale, David. 1984. 225 pages. Includes index and illustrations.

ADVERTISING CAREER DIRECTORY

How to Create Your Ideal Job or Next Career
Ten Speed Press
PO Box 7123
Berkeley, CA 94707
Phone: (415)845-8414

Bolles, Richard N. 1990. $4.95. 64 pages. Trade edition of the new job-hunting guide from *What Color Is Your Parachute?*

How to Find and Get the Job You Want
Johnson/Rudolph Educational Resources, Inc.
1004 State St.
Bowling Green, KY 42101

1989. $20.50. 160 pages. Aimed at the college student.

Job-search scams are springing up all over the country, charging advance fees ranging from $2,000 to $30,000, with 25 to 30 percent paid up front; complaints against such scams rose 75% between 1990 and 1991. Ask your state attorney general's office whether any complaints have been filed against a placement agency before you contact it; be wary if a fee is required before services are rendered or if a job is guaranteed within 6 to 12 weeks.

Source: *Working Woman*

How to Get a Better Job Quicker
Taplinger Publishing Co., Inc.
132 W. 22nd St.
New York, NY 10011
Phone: (212)877-1040

Payne, Richard A. 1987. $16.95. 217 pages.

How to Get a Better Job in This Crazy World
Crown Publishers, Inc.
225 Park Ave., S.
New York, NY 10003
Phone: (212)254-1600

Half, Robert. $17.95.

How to Get and Get Ahead on Your First Job
VGM Career Horizons
4255 W. Touhy Ave.
Lincolnwood, IL 60646-1975
Phone: (708)679-5500

Bloch, Deborah Perlmutter. 1988. $6.95. 160 pages. Details in step-by-step ways how to go about finding that first job, apply for it, write the winning resume, and manage the successful interview.

How to Get Interviews from Job Ads
Elderkin Associates
PO Box 1293
Dedham, MA 02026

Elderkin, Kenton W. 1989. $19.50. 256 pages. Outlines how to select and follow up ads to get the job. Includes unique ways to get interview offers and how to incorporate the use of a computer and a fax machine in arranging interviews. Illustrated.

How to Land a Better Job
VGM Career Horizons
4255 W. Touhy Ave.
Lincolnwood, IL 60646-1975
Phone: (708)679-5500

Lott, Catherine S., and Lott, Oscar C. 1989. $7.95. 160 pages. Tells the job seeker how to enhance his or her credentials, overcome past weaknesses, uncover job leads, get appointments, organize an appealing resume, and score points in interviews. A special section devoted to getting a better job without changing companies covers the process of transferring departments and gives pointers on moving up to the boss's job.

How to Seek a New and Better Job
Consultants Bookstore
Templeton Rd.
Fitzwilliam, NH 03447
Phone: (603)585-6544
Fax: (603)585-9221

Gerraughty, William. 1987. $5.95. 64 pages. Presents information on cover letters, resumes, and mailings. Includes a self-analysis, fifty-six questions asked by interviewers, and a variety of forms and lists.

How to Use Job Ads to Land the Job You Really Want
Jeffrey Lant Associates
50 Follen St., No. 507
Cambridge, MA 02138
Phone: (617)547-6372

$4.00. A summary of an interview with Kenton Elderkin, author of *How to Get Interviews from Job Ads: Where to Look, What To Select, Who to Write, What to Say, When to Follow-up, How to Save Time.*

How to Win the Job You Really Want
Henry Holt and Co.
115 W. 18th St.
New York, NY 10011

Weinberg, Janice. 1988. $10.95. 290 pages.

How You Can Make $25,000 a Year Writing (No Matter Where You Live)
Writer's Digest Books
1507 Dana Ave.
Cincinnati, OH 45207
Phone: (513)531-2222

Hanson, Nancy Edmonds. 1987. $15.95. 224 pages. Discussion of the freelance market for writing.

I Got the Job!
Crisp Publications, Inc.
95 1st St.
Los Altos, CA 94022

Chapman, Elwood N. 1988. $7.95. 80 pages. Provides case studies and demonstrates how to plan a targeted job search.

International Employment Hotline
International Employment Hotline
PO Box 3030
Oakton, VA 22124
Phone: (703)620-1972
Fax: (703)620-1973

Monthly. $29.00/year. Covers temporary and career job openings overseas and advice for international job hunters. Entries include: Company name, job title, description of job, requirements, geographic location of job. Arranged geographically.

Job and Career Building
Ten Speed Press
PO Box 7123
Berkeley, CA 94707
Phone: (415)845-8414

Germann, Richard, and Arnold, Peter. $7.95. 256 pages.

> "Most job seekers are not successful because they don't have support during the search," reveals Debbie Featherston of JIST Works, Inc., a career-planning and job-search company in Indianapolis. Featherston says the group approach to realizing career goals really works, and "success teams" inspired by the 1980 book *Wishcraft* are springing up all over the country. Team members encourage each other to act: to develop career plans, find jobs, or build independent businesses. To find a success team near you, send a self-addressed, stamped envelope to: Wishcraft and Success Teams, Box 20052 Park West Station, New York, NY 10025.
>
> Source: *Working Woman*

The Job Hunt
Ten Speed Press
PO Box 7123
Berkeley, CA 94707
Phone: (415)845-8414

Nelson, Robert. $2.95. 64 pages. A compact guide with a direct, question-and-answer format with space for notations.

The Job HUNTER
University of Missouri-Columbia
Career Planning and Placement Center
100 Noyes Bldg.
Columbia, MO 65211

Biweekly. $50.00/6 months; $75.00/year. Lists opportunities for college graduates with 0-3 years experience in many fields. Includes information on internships and summer jobs.

The Job Hunter's Final Exam
Surrey Books, Inc.
500 N. Michigan, No. 1940
Chicago, IL 60611
Phone: (312)661-0050

Camden, Thomas. 1990. $8.95. 140 pages. Helps

CAREER RESOURCES

ADVERTISING CAREER DIRECTORY

job seeker quiz self about resumes, interviews, and general job-hunting strategies.

The Job Hunter's Workbook
Peterson's
PO Box 2123
Princeton, NJ 08543-2123
Phone: (609)243-9111

Taggart, Judith; Moore, Lynn; and Naylor, Mary. $12.95. 140 pages. Deals with such job-seeking topics as assessing personal strengths, networking, interviewing and answering interview questions, dealing with salaries and benefits, and preparing resumes, cover letters, and portfolios. A combination of self-assessment exercises, work sheets, checklists, and advice.

> Even with declining audience share, each network still commands 20% of the viewing audience every night. Cable networks, by contrast, rarely reach more than 2% a piece.
>
> Source: *Business Week*

Job Search: Career Planning Guidebook, Book II
Brooks/Cole Publishing Co.
Marketing Dept.
511 Forest Lodge Rd.
Pacific Grove, CA 93950

Lock. 1988. $9.00. 248 pages. Assists the reader in a production job search.

The Job Search Companion: The Organizer for Job Seekers
The Harvard Common Press
535 Albany St.
Boston, MA 02118
Phone: (617)423-5803

Wallach and Arnold. 1987. $7.95. 160 pages. An organizer with resources and forms to assist in and direct the job search process.

The Job Search Handbook
Bob Adams, Inc.
260 Center St.
Holbrook, MA 02343
Phone: (617)767-8100
Fax: (617)767-0994

Noble, John. $6.95. 144 pages. Identifies and provides advice on the essential elements of the job search, including networking, cover letters, interviewing, and salary negotiation. Aimed at first-time entrants to the job market, those looking for a job in a new field, and middle-level professionals looking to take their next step up.

Job Search: The Total System
Consultants Bookstore
Templeton Rd.
Fitzwilliam, NH 03447
Phone: (603)585-6544
Fax: (603)585-9221

Dawson, Kenneth, and Dawson, Sheryl. 1988. $12.95. 244 pages. A guide that shows how to link networking, resume writing, interviewing, references, and follow-up letters to land the job. Thirty resumes are included.

Job Seeking Guide
Delmar Publishers, Inc.
2 Computer Dr., W.
PO Box 15015
Albany, NY 12212-5015
Phone: (518)459-1150
Fax: (518)459-3552

Pautler, Albert J., Jr. 80 pages. Covers the job search, from preparation to interviewing to results.

Jobs '92
Prentice Hall Press
15 Columbus Circle
New York, NY 10023

Kathryn and Ross Petras. 1992, annual. Provides career outlook information for 15 career fields, as well as special reports on disabled workers, minorities, and women. Also includes industry forecasts for 29 industry segments and a look at regional conditions in the United States.

JOBS! What They Are, Where They Are, What They Pay
The New Careers Center
1515 23rd St.
Box 297-CT
Boulder, CO 80306

Snelling, Robert, and Snelling, Anne. 1989. $12.95. Covers jobs available in today's job market, their duties and responsiblities, what they pay, and how to pursue them. Focuses on the seven top entry-level job areas.

Journeying Outward: A Guide to Career Development
Delmar Publishers, Inc.
2 Computer Dr., W.
PO Box 15015
Albany, NY 12212-5015
Phone: (518)459-1150
Fax: (518)459-3552

Lynton, Jonathan. 1989. 224 pages. Examines the correct way to present oneself in the job search, covering appearance, interviewing, writing a resume, and completing a job application. Resume writing section illustrates models of various resume formats. Includes sections on planning the job search and working the plan.

Joyce Lain Kennedy's Career Book
VGM Career Horizons
4255 W. Touhy Ave.
Lincolnwood, IL 60646-1975
Phone: (708)679-5500

Kennedy, Joyce Lain. Co-authored by Dr. Darryl Laramore. 1988. $14.95 paperback. $29.95 hardcover. 448 pages. Guides the reader through the entire career-planning and job-hunting process. Addresses how to find the kinds of jobs available and what to do once the job is secured. Provides a number of case histories to give examples.

Kennedy's Career Strategist
Marilyn Moats Kennedy Career Strategies
1153 Wilmette Ave.
Wilmette, IL 60091

Twelve issues/year. $75.00/year. Offers job search guidance.

Liberal Education and Careers Today
The Career Press, Inc.
PO Box 34
Hawthorne, NJ 07507
Phone: 800-227-3371

Figler, Howard. 1989. $10.95 108 pages. Shows job seekers with liberal arts education how to link their majors to the specific needs of employers.

Managing Your Career
Dow Jones and Co.
420 Lexington Ave.
New York, NY 10170

College version of the *National Business Employment Weekly*. Excludes job openings, but provides job-hunting advice.

Martin's Magic Formula for Getting the Right Job
St. Martin's Press
Special Sales Dept.
175 5th Ave.
New York, NY 10010
Phone: (212)674-5151

Martin, Phyllis. 1987. $7.95. 192 pages. A comprehensive approach to the job campaign.

Career paths in the future will more closely resemble a series of loosely connected dots than a neat line headed upward. To advance, professionals will have to resist pigeon-holing themselves in one industry, location, company or even career. Instead, they will need to be prepared to move backward and sideways from large companies to small ones, from one city to another, from the corporate womb to their own small enterprises. Those with portable skills may discover opportunity even in struggling industries.

Source: *U.S. News & World Report*

Merchandising Your Job Talents
U.S. Government Printing Office
Superintendent of Documents
Washington, DC 20402

Booklet. 1986. 21 pages. General advice for job seekers. Illustrated.

Network Your Way to Job and Career Success
The Career Press Inc.
PO Box 34
Hawthorne, NJ 07507
Phone: 800-227-3371

Krannich, Ron, and Krannich, Caryl. 1989. $11.95. 180 pages. Based on a comprehensive career planning framework, each chapter outlines the best strategies for identifying, finding, and transforming networks to gather information and obtain advice and referrals that lead to job interviews and offers. Includes exercises, sample interviewing dialogues, and a directory of organizations for initiating and sustaining networking activities.

ADVERTISING CAREER DIRECTORY

The New Quick Job-Hunting Map
Ten Speed Press
PO Box 7123
Berkeley, CA 94707
Phone: (415)845-8414

Bolles, Richard N. $2.95. 64 pages. Trade version of *The Quick Job-Hunting Map* in *What Color Is Your Parachute?* Provides a personal blueprint for the job search.

> **S**elf-assessment in the job-search process can pay off. Some candidates find it helpful to articulate what type of organization they want to work with in terms of its culture and how it values its people.
>
> Source: *Fortune*

Occupational Outlook Handbook
Bureau of Labor Statistics
441 G St., NW
Washington, DC 20212
Phone: (202)523-1327

Biennial, May of even years. $24.00 hardcover. $22.00 paperback. Contains profiles of various occupations, which include description of occupation, educational requirements, market demand, and expected earnings. Also lists over 100 state employment agencies and State Occupational Information Coordinating Committees that provide state and local job market and career information; various occupational organizations that provide career information. Arranged by occupation; agencies and committees are geographical. Send orders to: Superintendent of Documents, U.S. Government Printing Office, Washington, D.C. 20402 (202-783-3238).

The One Day Plan for Jobhunters
Prakken Publications, Inc.
416 Longshore Dr.
PO Box 8623
Ann Arbor, MI 48107

Segalini and Kurtz. 1988. $9.95. 100 pages.

Online Hotline News Service
Information Intelligence, Inc.
PO Box 31098
Phoenix, AZ 85046
Phone: (602)996-2283

Contains five files, one of which is Joblines, featuring listings of employment and resume services available in voice, print, and online throughout North America.

The Only Job Hunting Guide You'll Ever Need
Poseidon Press
Simon and Schuster Bldg.
1230 Ave. of the Americas
New York, NY 10020
Phone: (212)698-7290

Petras, Kathryn, and Petras, Ross. 1989. $8.95. 318 pages. Covers the full range of the job search process.

Opportunities in Advertising
National Textbook Co.
4255 W. Touhy Ave.
Lincolnwood, IL 60646-1975
Phone: (708)679-5500
Toll-free: 800-323-4900

S. William Pattis. 1990. Illustrated. Includes a bibliography.

Opportunities in Non-Profit Organizations
ACCESS/Networking in the Public Interest
96 Mt. Auburn St.
Cambridge, MA 02138

Monthly. Lists opportunities in many fields, including public interest law.

Opportunities in Writing Careers
National Textbook Co.
4255 W. Touhy Ave.
Lincolnwood, IL 60646-1975
Phone: (708)679-5500
Toll-free: 800-323-4900

Elizabeth Foote-Smith. 1988. Describes writing career opportunities. Covers articles, novels, short stories, nonfiction books, reviews, and interviews. Also includes information on playwrights, poets, journalists, and broadcasters. Discusses educational preparation. Includes a bibliography.

Out of Work but Not Alone
Self-Help Clearinghouse
Publications Dept.
St. Clares-Riverside Medical Center
Pocono Rd.
Denville, NJ 07834
Phone: (201)625-9565

1984. $9.00.

Peterson's Job Opportunities for Business and Liberal Arts Graduates 1991
Peterson's
PO Box 2123
Princeton, NJ 08543-2123
Phone: (609)243-9111

Compiled by the Peterson's staff. 1991. $19.95 paperback. $35.95 hardcover. 300 pages. Lists hundreds of organizations that are hiring new business, humanities, and social science graduates in the areas of business and management. Explores how to match academic backgrounds to specific job openings. Provides information about opportunities for experienced personnel as well. Includes data on starting locations by city and state, summer jobs, co-op jobs, internships, and international assignments.

Professional Job Finder
Planning/Communications
7215 Oak Ave.
River Forest, IL 60305-1935
Phone: (708)366-5200

Daniel Lauber. 1992. Provides information on approximately 2,000 specialized sources of help wanted ads, including periodicals, job hotlines, and computerized databases. Arranged by subject and also by state.

A Rewarding and Stimulating Life Awaits You With a Career in Specialty Advertising
Speciality Advertising Assn. International
3125 Skyway Circle, N.
Irving, TX 75038
Phone: (214)580-0404

This booklet describes what specialty advertising is, career opportunities available, compensation and benefits, and training needed.

The Right Place at the Right Time
Ten Speed Press
PO Box 7123
Berkeley, CA 94707
Phone: (415)845-8414

Wegmann, Robert G. $9.95. 192 pages. A comprehensive approach to career planning and job seeking developed to find the right job in the new economy.

Media entrepreneur Chris Whittle says marketers can get more bang for their buck by using his targeted media for advertising. His products include Special Reports Family Network, a group of publications and a TV channel distributed to doctors' waiting rooms, and Channel One, a satellite service that beams 12 minutes of programming and commercials each day into school classrooms. "There are still people who believe in a core buy: three networks and a dose of women's magazines," remarks Whittle. "But a lot of people understand that's not the way things work anymore."

Source: *Business Week*

Secrets of the Hidden Job Market
Betterway Publications, Inc.
White Hall, VA 22987
Phone: (804)823-5661

Rodgers, Bob; Johnson, Steve; and Alexander, Bill. 1986.

Skills in Action: A Job-Finding Workbook
Univ. of Akron
Adult Resource Center
Akron, OH 44325

Selden, J.H. $12.50. 75 pages. Workbook format; aimed at job seekers looking for initial or transitional employment.

So You Want to Be in Advertising: A Guide to Success in a Fast-Paced Business
Arco Publishing Co.
15 Columbus Circle
New York, NY 10023
Phone: (212)373-8931

Ed Caffrey, editor. 1988. Describes the day-to-day activities in an advertising agency.

The Source Passport to Advertising/Public Relations/Marketing and Job Opportunities in the West
Rachel P.R. Services
513 Wilshire Blvd., Ste. 238
Santa Monica, CA 90401
Phone: (213)395-7678

Annual, December. $40.00. Covers over 300 job banks, referral services, recruiters, employment agencies, schools/colleges, internships/mentors, trade groups, telephone hotlines, directories, trade journals, and other organizations offering information on employment opportunities in advertising, public relations, and marketing. Entries include company name, address, phone, name and title of contact, products or services. Classified by product or service. Indexes: Product/service, organization name, subject, geographical.

Some typical questions for the job candidate: "Give me an example of a problem in which you and your manager disagreed over how to accomplish a goal." "Do your talents lean more toward strategy or tactics, being creative or analytical?" "How would you compare, say, the marketing of consumer goods vs. financial services?" "A year from now, what might your boss say about your work for the company during a performance review?"

Source: *Business Week*

Student Guide to Mass Media Internships
Southwestern Texas State University
Dept. of Journalism
Intern Research Group
San Marcos, TX 78666
Phone: (512)245-3408

Annual, December. $25.00 per volume, payment with order; $30.00 billed; $45.00 per set, payment with order; $50.00 billed. Covers: In two volumes - About 10,000 internships offered by 2,700 newspapers, radio and television stations, cable television companies, magazines, advertising agencies, and other firms. Volume 1 covers print media, volume 2 covers broadcast media. Entries include: Organization name, address, type and number of internships offered, eligibility requirements, application deadline, salary or other stipend offered, name and title of contact; many listings also include description of intern's duties. Arrangement: Classified by type of medium, then geographical.

The Student's Guide to Finding a Superior Job
Slawson Communications
165 Vallecitos de Oro
San Marcos, CA 92069

Cohen, William A. 1987. $9.95. Aimed at the new college graduate.

The Successful Job Hunter's Handbook
Johnson/Rudolph Educational Resources, Inc.
1004 State St.
Bowling Green, KY 42101

1987. $12.95. 150 pages.

Suggestions for Career Exploration and Jobseeking
New York State Dept. of Labor
Div. of Research and Statistics
NY-SOICC
State Office Bldg. Campus, Bldg. 12, Rm. 488
Albany, NY 12240
Phone: (518)457-6182

Brochure. 1989. Free. Prepared for New York State labor market. Includes roster of state Job Service offices.

Super Job Search: The Complete Manual for Job-Seekers and Career-Changers
Jeffrey Lant Associates
50 Follen St., No. 507
Cambridge, MA 02138
Phone: (617)547-6372

Studner, Peter. $25.95. 325 pages. A step-by-step guidebook for getting a job, with sections on getting started, how to present accomplishments, networking strategies, telemarketing tips, and negotiating tactics.

Taking Charge of Your Career Direction: Career Planning Guidebook, Book I
Brooks/Cole Publishing Co.
Marketing Dept.
511 Forest Lodge Rd.
Pacific Grove, CA 93950

Lock. 1988. $13.50. 377 pages. Provides guidance for the job search process.

U.S. Employment Opportunities: A Career News Service
Washington Research Associates
7500 E. Arapaho Plaza, Ste. 250
Englewood, CO 80112
Phone: (303)694-1259
Fax: (303)770-1945

Annual; quarterly updates. $166.00 per year to libraries; $184.00 per year to others. List of over 1,000 employment contacts in companies and agencies in the banking, arts, telecommunications, education, and 14 other industries and professions, including the federal government. Entries include: Company name, name of representative, address, description of products or services, hiring and recruiting practices, training programs, and year established. Classified by industry. Indexes: Occupation.

U.S. Employment Opportunities - Advertising/Public Relations
Washington Research Associates
2103 N. Lincoln St.
Arlington, VA 22207
Phone: (703)276-8260

Online database. Includes company listings of current openings in advertising and public relations and company recruiting programs. Provides discussion and forecasts of trends and developments affecting professional employment opportunities in advertising and public relations.

What Color Is Your Parachute?
Ten Speed Press
PO Box 7123
Berkeley, CA 94707
Phone: (415)845-8414

Bolles, Richard N. 1992. $12.95 paperback. Subtitled: *A Practical Manual for Job-Hunters and Career-Changers*. One of the best-known works on job hunting, this book provides detailed and strategic advice on all aspects of the job search.

Where Can I Find Help With. . .
Ready Reference Press
PO Box 5249
Santa Monica, CA 90405
Phone: (213)474-5175

$95.00. Two-volume set. Subtitled: *The Sourcebook of Career Services and Programs*. Lists extensive resources aimed at the young job seeker, including job banks, resume preparation services, testing programs, job referral sources, career training programs, and others. Entries provide organization name, type of service, description, audience served, costs (if any), hours, address, and telephone number. Subject and geographic indexes.

Most people's careers divide into three stages, each with pitfalls and possibilities. The first stage, running from your 20s into your middle to late 30s, is the time to expose yourself to as many varied job situations as possible, assembling a repertory of basic skills. By your late 30s or early 40s, you must be a key player, attuned to your company's strategic goals and fully conversant with customer needs, new-product possibilities, and all the vagaries of your particular marketplace; or else you should switch jobs. Most people reach their career peak in their late 40s or early 50s.

Source: *Fortune*

Where Do I Go from Here with My Life?
Ten Speed Press
PO Box 7123
Berkeley, CA 94707
Phone: (415)845-8414

Crystal, John C., and Bolles, Richard N. $9.95. 272 pages. A planning manual for students of all ages, instructors, counselors, career seekers, and career changers.

ADVERTISING CAREER DIRECTORY

Where the Jobs Are: A Comprehensive Directory of 1200 Journals Listing Career Opportunities
Garrett Park Press
PO Box 190
Garrett Park, MD 20896
Phone: (301)946-2553

1989. $15.00; $14.00, prepaid. Contains list of approximately 1,200 journals that publish advertisements announcing job opportunities. Arranged alphabetically. Indexes: Occupational field.

> Today's wave of nostalgia advertising, bringing back favorite campaigns from the 1950s, 1960s, and 1970s, proves that the slogans don't have to change to be effective; in fact, if they resonate with phrases you've already learned, they'll probably gain in power.
>
> Source: *Every Bite a Delight and Other Slogans*

Where to Start Career Planning
Peterson's
PO Box 2123
Princeton, NJ 08543-2123
Phone: (609)243-9111

Lindquist, Carolyn Lloyd, and Feodoroff, Pamela L. 1989. $15.95. 315 pages. Lists and describes the career-planning publications used by Cornell University's Career Center, one of the largest career libraries in the country. Covers more than 2,000 books, periodicals, and audiovisual resources on topics such as financial aid, minority and foreign students, overseas employment and travel, resources for the disabled, second careers, study-and-work options, summer and short-term jobs, women's issues, and careers for those without a bachelor's degree. Includes a bibliographic title index.

Which Niche?
Bob Adams, Inc.
260 Center St.
Holbrook, MA 02343
Phone: (617)767-8100
Fax: (617)767-0994

Shingleton, Jack. $4.95. 164 pages. Subtitled: *Answers to the Most Common Questions about Careers and Job Hunting.* Designed to convey essential job-hunting information without adding unnecessary jargon. Each section is accompanied by a humorous cartoon illustrating the lighter side of job prospecting.

Who's Hiring Who
Ten Speed Press
PO Box 7123
Berkeley, CA 94707
Phone: (415)845-8414

Lathrop, Richard. $9.95. 268 pages. Provides advice on finding a better job faster and at a higher rate of pay.

Work in the New Economy: Careers and Job Seeking into the 21st Century
The New Careers Center
1515 23rd St.
Box 297-CT
Boulder, CO 80306

1989. $15.95.

Professional and Trade Periodicals

Advertising Age
Crain Communications, Inc.
220 E. 42nd St.
New York, NY 10017
Phone: (212)210-0725
Fax: (212)210-0111

Fred Danzig, editor. Weekly. Advertising trade publication covering agency, media, and advertiser news and trends.

Adweek's Marketing Week
A/S/M Communications, Inc.
49 E. 21st St.
New York, NY 10010
Phone: (212)529-5500

Tony DiCamillo, publisher. Weekly. Advertising and marketing magazine.

Journal of Advertising Research
Advertising Research Foundation, Inc.
3 E. 54th St.
New York, NY 10022-3180
Phone: (212)751-5656
Fax: (212)319-5265

Kathryn Kucharski Grubb, managing editor. Six issues/year. Journal of advertising and marketing research.

Marketing & Media Decisions
ACT III Publishing, Media Group
401 Park Ave., S.
New York, NY 10036
Phone: (212)695-4215

Sandra Rifkin, editor-in-chief. Monthly. Advertising magazine.

Basic Reference Guides

AAAA Roster
666 3rd Ave., 13th Fl.
New York, NY 10017
Phone: (212)682-2500
Fax: (212)682-8391

Annual.

Advertisers and their Agencies
Engel Communications, Inc.
820 Bear Tavern Rd., Ste. 302
West Trenton, NJ 08628
Phone: (609)530-0044
Fax: (609)530-0207

Annual, spring. $125.00. Covers: More than 500 manufacturers of health care products and the advertising agencies that represent them. Entries include: Company name, address, phone, names and titles of key personnel; advertising agency name, names and titles of key personnel. Arrangement: Alphabetical. Indexes: Product/service, therapeutic category, industry personnel.

Advertising Age Advertising Agency Income Report Issue
Crain Communications, Inc.
740 Rush St.
Chicago, IL 60611
Phone: (312)649-5200
Fax: (312)649-5331

Annual, March. $4.00. Publication includes: About 550 U.S. advertising agencies and 1,000 foreign agencies which reported billings and gross income, or whose billings and gross incomes were ascertained through research. Entries include: Agency name, ranking by gross income, number of employees. Arrangement: Ranked by income.

Personality tests to assess job applicants are too expensive for many companies to administer, but they still want to base hiring decisions on some diagnostic tool. Lately more companies seem to be turning to handwriting analysis in screening job seekers. It's a popular technique in Europe, but not universally accepted or openly used in the United States. In Rhode Island a legislator tried unsuccessfully in 1991 to ban the use of handwriting analysis in job selection. Critics and skeptics abound, but the practice is gaining ground and some companies swear by it.

Source: *Newsweek*

Advertising Age - U.S. Advertising Agency Profiles Issue
Crain Communications, Inc.
740 Rush St.
Chicago, IL 60611
Phone: (312)649-5200

Annual, March. $3.00. Publication includes: About 700 advertising agencies which reported billings and gross income, or whose billings and gross incomes were ascertained through research. Entries include: agency name, ranking by gross income, number of employees. Arrangement: Ranked by income.

Advertising - Agencies Directory
American Business Information, Inc.
American Business Directories, Inc.
5711 S. 86th Circle
Omaha, NE 68127
Phone: (402)593-4600
Fax: (402)331-1505

Annual. $765.00, payment with order. Covers: Approximately 25,815 advertising agencies. Entries include: Name, address, phone (including area code), year first in "Yellow Pages." Arrangement: Geographical.

ADVERTISING CAREER DIRECTORY

Advertising Manager's Handbook
Dartnell Corp.
4660 Ravenswood Ave.
Chicago, IL 60640
Phone: (312)561-4000

Richard H. Stansfield. Third edition, 1982.

Lester Minsuk and Phyllis Macklin, outplacement specialists in Princeton, NJ, advise clients to dress like the boss of the person you're hoping to work for. They also stress that compromises with your natural inclinations may be necessary, like touching up a greying beard with Grecian Formula, toning down makeup, or buying a serious watch. "You've got to remember that you are a product, and you need to be packaged."

Source: *Fortune*

Advertising: What It Is and How to Do It
McGraw-Hill, Inc.
1221 Ave. of the Americas
New York, NY 10020
Phone: (212)512-2000
Toll-free: 800-722-4726

Roderick White. Second edition, 1988. Introductory text that discusses media ad agencies, ad design, economics, and legal issues.

ADWEEK Portfolio
A/S/M Communications, Inc.
49 E. 21st St.
New York, NY 10010
Phone: (212)529-5500
Fax: (212)254-5204

Annual, spring. Covers: Artists, companies, suppliers, agencies, and others whose products or services are used in advertising. Entries include: Company name, address, phone.

Creative Black Book
Macmillan Creative Services Group
115 5th Ave.
New York, NY 10003
Phone: (212)254-1330
Fax: (212)598-4497

Annual. $100.00, plus $7.00 shipping. Covers: 20,000 model and advertising agencies, art suppliers, photographers, printers, illustrators, designers, television directors and producers, color labs, and others whose products or services are used in advertising. Entries include: Company name, address, phone.

Dictionary of Advertising and Direct Mail Terms
Barron's Educational Series, Inc.
250 Wireless Blvd.
Hauppauge, NY 11788
Phone: (516)434-3311

Jane Imber and Betsy Toffler. 1987. Contains illustrations.

Dictionary of Marketing and Advertising
Nichols Publishing
11 Harts Ln., Ste. I
East Brunswick, NJ 08816
Phone: (908)238-4880

Michael J. Baker. Second edition, 1990. Illustrated.

Directory of Minority Public Relations Professionals
Public Relations Society of America
33 Irving Pl., 3rd Fl.
15th and 16th Sts.
New York, NY 10003
Phone: (212)995-2230

Irregular; latest edition 1990. $10.00. Covers: About 190 minority individuals in the field of public relations. Entries include: Individual name, title, company name, address, phone. Arrangement: Geographical.

ENR Directory of Design Firms
McGraw Hill, Inc.
1221 Avenue of the Americas
New York, NY 10020
Phone: (212)512-2111
Fax: (212)312-2007

Biennial, Fall of even years. $34.50. Covers: About 145 architects, architectural engineers, consultants, and other design firms; limited to advertisers. Also includes lists of top 500 design firms in the United States, top 200 international design firms, top 50 United States design-construction firms, and top 50 international design-construction firms, based on total amount of billings. Entries include: For advertisers - Company name, address, branch locations, subsidiaries, list of key personnel, territory served, capabilities. In ranked lists - Company name, address, phone; international firms include telex. Arrangement: Alphabetical.

ENR Top 500 Design Firms Issue
McGraw Hill, Inc.
1221 Avenue of the Americas
New York, NY 10020
Phone: (212)512-2111
Fax: (212)312-2007

Annual, August. $10.00, payment with order. Publication includes: List of 500 leading architectural, engineering, and specialty design firms selected on basis of annual billings. Entries include: Company name, location, code for type of firm, current and prior year rank in billings, types of services, number of *Engineering News-Record* subscribers. Arrangement: Ranked by billings.

ENR Top International Design Firms Issue
McGraw Hill, Inc.
1221 Avenue of the Americas
New York, NY 10020
Phone: (212)512-2111
Fax: (212)312-2007

Annual, August. $10.00. Publication includes: List of 200 design firms (including United States firms) competing outside their own national borders who received largest dollar volume of foreign contracts in preceding calendar year. Entries include: Company name, headquarters location, total value of contracts received in preceding year, design specialties, rank and countries in which they are operating in current year. Arrangement: Geographical by country.

Hawaii Advertising Agency Directory
East West Research Institute
735 Bishop St., Ste. 235
Honolulu, HI 96813
Phone: (808)531-7244

Biennial, spring of odd years. $19.50 postpaid; payment must accompany order. Covers: Over 70 advertising agencies, public relations agencies, associations, commercial artists, photographers, graphic designers, radio and television broadcasting stations, newspapers, magazines, and advertising services in Hawaii. Entries include: For agencies - Name, address; names of principals, account executives, creative directors, media contacts; and accounts handled. Other listings contain similar information. Arrangement: Alphabetical. Indexes: Client name, personal name.

International Advertising Association Membership Directory
International Advertising Assn.
342 Madison Ave.
New York, NY 10017
Phone: (212)557-1133
Fax: (212)983-0455

Annual, January/February. $300.00. Covers: Approximately 2,600 advertisers, advertising agencies, media and other firms involved in advertising. Entries include: Company name, address, phone, name of principal executive. Arrangement: Geographical.

"As the founding president of Santa Monica-based Williams Television Time, the largest independent agency purchasing airtime for infomercials, Kathleen Williams was one of the first to see that 30-minute hard sells of everything from mixers to makeup were going to mean big money. Her five-year-old business had billings of $40 million in 1991, and she predicts that most of the Fortune 1000 will soon be pitching products to insomniacs."

Source: *Working Woman*

Macmillan Dictionary of Marketing and Advertising
Macmillan Publishing Co.
866 3rd Ave.
New York, NY 10022
Phone: (212)702-2000
Toll-free: 800-257-5755

Michael J. Baker. 1984. Contains illustrations.

Macmillan Directory of Leading Private Companies
National Register Publishing Co.,
Macmillan, Inc.
3004 Glenview Rd.
Wilmette, IL 60091
Phone: (708)441-2202

Annual, March. $427.00, plus $6.45 shipping.

ADVERTISING CAREER DIRECTORY

Covers: Over 6,400 privately owned companies. Entries include: Company name, address, phone, telex, year founded, financial assets and liabilities, net worth, approximate sales, names and titles of key personnel, number of employees, number of U.S. and foreign offices, and other information. Arrangement: Alphabetical. Indexes: Geographical, parent company, Standard Industrial Classification number.

> The Bureau of Labor Statistics predicts that 18 million new jobs will be created in the U.S. in the 1990s.

Michigan Business - A Guide to Michigan Advertising Agencies Issue
Detroit Business
26111 Evergreen, Ste. 303
Southfield, MI 48076
Phone: (313)357-8300

Annual, July. $2.00. Publication includes: List of about 180 advertising agencies in Michigan. Entries include: Name of firm, address, phone, name of principal officer, year established, annual billings (where reported), number of employees, description of service or specialization, affiliates, major clients or industries served. Arrangement: By sales volume.

New Jersey Business - Ad Agency Directory Issue
New Jersey Business and Industry Assn.
102 W. State
Trenton, NJ 08608
Phone: (609)393-7707

Annual, November. $1.75. Publication includes: List of New Jersey advertising agencies. Entries include: Name of firm, city or town. Arrangement: Geographical.

O'Dwyer's Directory of Corporate Communications
J.R. O'Dwyer Co., Inc.
271 Madison Ave.
New York, NY 10016
Phone: (212)679-2471

Annual, January. $110.00. Covers: Public relations departments of approximately 4,450 major United States companies; also includes similar information on over 900 large trade associations and foreign embassies in the United States. Entries include: Company name, address, phone, sales, type of business; names and duties of principal public relations personnel at headquarters and other major offices, plus name and title of person to whom PR head reports; name and address of outside PR counsel, if any; PR budget. Arrangement: Alphabetical. Indexes: Geographical, product.

Standard Directory of Advertising Agencies
National Register Publishing Co.
Macmillan, Inc.
3004 Glenview Rd.
Wilmette, IL 60091
Phone: (708)256-6067

February, June, and October; supplements in other months. $457.00 per year, including supplements; single copy, without supplements, $247.00. Covers: Over 5,000 advertising agencies. Entries include: Agency name, address, phone, year founded, number of employees, association memberships, annual billing, breakdown of gross billings by media, clients, executives, special markets, and new agencies. Arrangement: Alphabetical. Indexes: Geographical (includes address and phone).

Standard and Poor's Register of Corporations, Directors and Executives
Standard and Poor's Corp.
25 Broadway
New York, NY 10004
Phone: (212)208-8283

Annual, January; supplements in April, July, and October. $498.00, lease basis. Covers: Over 50,000 corporations in the United States, including names and titles of over 400,000 officials (Volume I); 70,000 biographies of directors and executives (Volume 2). Entries include: For companies - Name, address, phone, names of principal executives and accountants; number of employees, estimated annual sales, outside directors. For directors and executives - Name, home and principal business addresses, date and place of birth, fraternal organization memberships, business affiliations. Arranged alphabetically. Indexes: Volume 3 indexes companies geographically, by Standard Industrial

Classification number, and by corporate family groups.

Ward's Business Directory of U.S. Private and Public Companies

Gale Research Inc.
835 Penobscot Bldg.
Detroit, MI 48226
Phone: (313)961-2242
Toll-free: 800-877-GALE
Fax: (313)961-6083

1992, annual. Five-volume directory that provides information on more than 133,000 businesses in the United States, over 90 percent of which are privately held. Includes all major companies, as well as companies with an annual sales volume of less than $50,000. Entries include: company name, address, telephone, and fax; financial information and employee figures; four-digit SIC codes; fiscal year end; year founded; import/export information; immediate parent; and up to five company officers. Arrangement: Volumes 1, 2, and 3 list the companies in alphabetical order. Volume 4 lists companies in ZIP Code order by state and includes a number of other indexes. Volume 5 ranks companies by sales volume withing four-digit SIC classifications.

WICI National Directory of Professional Members

Women in Communications, Inc.
2101 Wilson Blvd., Ste. 417
Arlington, VA 22201
Phone: (703)528-4200

Biennial.

Master Index

Master Index

The Master Index provides comprehensive access to all four sections of the Directory by citing all subjects, organizations, publications, and services listed throughout in a single alphabetic sequence. The index also includes inversions on significant words appearing in cited organization, publication, and service names. For example, "Ward's Business Directory of U.S. Private and Public Companies" could also be listed in the index under "Companies; Ward's Business Directory of U.S. Private and Public."

AAAA Roster - American Association of
   Advertising Agencies (AAAA) 239
ABC Employment Service 222
A.C. Personnel Consultants 222
Academy for Health Services Marketing
   (AHSM) 218
Account manager
   client expectations 41
   employer expectations 42
   job requirements 41, 43, 44
   personal qualifications 42, 43
Ackerman Advertising 177
Ackerman, Hood & McQueen, Inc. 178, 179
*Ad Agency Directory Issue; New Jersey
   Business* - 242
Adcrafter 211
Admarketing 207

ADNET 211
Advance Job Listings 212
Advanswers 179
Advertisers and their Agencies 239
*Advertising: A Guide to Success in a Fast-Paced
   Business; So You Want to Be in* 235
Advertising Account Executive 225
Advertising Age 238
*Advertising Age Advertising Agency Income
   Report Issue* 239
*Advertising Age - U.S. Advertising Agency
   Profiles Issue* 239
Advertising agencies
   positive characteristics of 9
Advertising Agencies; American Association
   of 219
Advertising - Agencies Directory 239

ADVERTISING CAREER DIRECTORY

Advertising Agencies Issue; Michigan Business - A Guide to Michigan 242
Advertising Agencies; Standard Directory of 242
Advertising Agencies: What They Are, What They Do, How They Do It 225
Advertising Agency Directory; Hawaii 241
Advertising and Direct Mail Terms; Dictionary of 240
Advertising and Marketing (WA&M); Women in 221
Advertising & Media; Chicago 214
Advertising and Public Relations; Career Opportunities in 226
Advertising Association Membership Directory; International 241
Advertising Business; Specialty 218
Advertising Careers: How Advertising Works and the People Who Make It Happen 225
Advertising; Careers in 227
Advertising/Communications Times 212
Advertising design portfolio 38
    what to exclude 16
    what to include 16, 38
Advertising Development Specialists 179
Advertising; Dictionary of Marketing and 240
Advertising; Exploring Careers in 228
Advertising Federation; American 218
Advertising? Focus: Account Management; Have You Considered... 229
Advertising; Getting Into 229
Advertising history
    in the 1950s 16
    in the 1960s 16
    in the 1970s 16
    in the 1980s 16
Advertising; Macmillan Dictionary of Marketing and 241
Advertising Manager's Handbook 240
Advertising; Opportunities in 234
Advertising/Public Relations/Marketing and Job Opportunities in the West; The Source Passport to 236
Advertising/Public Relations; U.S. Employment Opportunities - 237
Advertising Research; Journal of 239
Advertising; A Rewarding and Stimulating Life Awaits You...With a Career in Specialty 235
Advertising strategy 16
Advertising Week; New England 217

Advertising: What It Is and How to Do It 240
AdWeek 212
Adweek/East 212
Adweek/Midwest 212
Adweek/New England 212
ADWEEK Portfolio 240
Adweek/Southeast 212
Adweek/Southwest 212
Adweek/West 212
Adweek's Marketing Computers 213
Adweek's Marketing Week 238
Adworld Personnel Agency 222
Affirmative Action Register 213
After College: The Business of Getting Jobs 225
Airbrush Action 213
Ally & Gargano, Inc. 179
Aloysius, Butler & Clark, Inc. 179
Alpha Resource Group, Inc. 222
Alpine Consultants 222
American Advertising Federation 218
American Association of Advertising Agencies 219
Amherst Personnel Group Inc. 222
Ammirati and Puris 207
Andrew/Mautner, Inc. 179
Arancio Associates 222
Art Direction 213
Art director 25
Artist Placement; National Network for 221
Associations
    importance of 102
Auger, Babuex, McKim Advertising Ltd. 180
Austin Employment Agency 222
N.W. Ayer Inc. 180
Backer Spielvogel Bates Worldwide Inc. [New York, NY] 180
Bader Rutter & Assoc. 180
Bank Marketing Association (BMA) 219
Barnhart & Co. 180
Base Brown & Partners Ltd. 181
BBDO Worldwide [New York, NY] 181
BCP Advertising 181
Beckman Associates Advertising Agency, Inc. 181
Benefits 108
The Berkeley Guide to Employment for New College Graduates 225
Best Personnel Services 222
The Big Book of Free Career Services and Programs 225

William R. Biggs-Gilmore Associates Inc.
    [Kalamazoo, MI] 182
Billboards
    definition of 56
    history of 56
Black Careers 213
The Black Collegian 213
Black Employment & Education
    Magazine 213
The Bloom Cos. 182
Bolt Advertising, Inc. 182
Boston, MA
    advertising agency size in 85
    advertising characteristics of 84
    advertising scene in 84
    cultural climate in 83, 84
    economic climate in 84, 85
Broadcast Designers Association (BDA) 219
Broadcast negotiator 49
Bronson Communications, Inc. 182
T. Stewart Brown & Company, Ltd. 183
Broyles, Allebaugh & Davis Inc. 183
Leo Burnett Company Inc. [Chicago, IL] 183
Business and Liberal Arts Graduates 1991;
    Peterson's Job Opportunities for 235
Cabot Communications 183
California Connections 225
Calvert Associates, Inc. 222
Campbell-Mithun-Esty Advertising
    Minneapolis Branch 184
    New York Branch 184
Capitol Search Employment Services 222
*Career Choices for the 90's for Students of
    Communications and Journalism* 226
*Career Choices for the 90's for Students of
    English* 226
*Career Choices for the 90's for Students of
    Psychology* 226
*The Career Fitness Program: Exercising Your
    Options* 226
Career Information System (CIS) 226
Career objective
    establishing a 102
*Career Opportunities in Advertising and Public
    Relations* 226
Career Opportunities News 226
Career Opportunity Update 213
Career Placement Registry (CPR) 214
*Career Planning and Employment; Journal
    of* 216
Career Specialties 223

Career Woman 214
*Careering and Re-Careering for the
    1990's* 227
Careers and the College Grad 227
Careers in Advertising 227
Careers in Communications 227
Chaloner Associates 223
Changing jobs 28
Chiat/Day/Mojo Inc. [Venice, CA] 184
Chicago
    advertising employer expectations in 80
    advertising in 79
    advertising jobs in 80
    commuting to 81
    former style of advertising 79
    location of advertising agencies in 80
    major national advertising accounts in 80
    major transportation 80
    world rank in advertising 79
    year-round climate 80
Chicago Advertising & Media 214
Chronicle Career Index 227
Claremont-Branan, Inc. 223
Colle & McVoy Inc. 184
College degree, importance of 96
College Recruitment Database (CRD) 214
Collegiate Career Woman 214
Coming Alive from Nine to Five 227
Commercial art and design 35
    career options 35
Communication World 214
*Communications and Journalism; Career
    Choices for the 90's for Students of* 226
Communications, Inc. (WICI); Women
    in 222
Community Jobs 215
The Complete Job Search Book 227
The Complete Job-Search Handbook 227
Confetti 215
Consultants; Alpine 222
Consultants and Designers Inc. 223
Consumer promotion
    definition of 66
Coons Corker & Associates 185
Copy trainee 13
Copywriter
    getting started as a 15
Frank J. Corbett Inc. 185
*Corporate Communications; O'Dwyer's
    Directory of* 242

ADVERTISING CAREER DIRECTORY

Corporate promotion
    employer expectations 68
    employment benefits 68
    salaries 68
Council of Sales Promotion Agencies 219
Council of Writers Organizations (CWO) 220
The Counselor 215
Cramer Krasselt 185
Creative assistant 18
Creative Black Book 240
Creative process 21
CTS Advertising 185
CV Advertising 186
Dailey & Associates 186
D'Arcy Masius Benton & Bowles Inc. [New York, NY] 186
Dartmouth Consultants 223
DCA Advertising 186
DDB Needham Worldwide Inc. [New York, NY] 186
Deacon Day Advertising 187
Della Femina, McNamee WCRS 187
Design Firms; ENR Directory of 240
Design Firms Issue; ENR Top 500 241
Design Firms Issue; ENR Top International 241
Design; ID International 215
Design portfolio
    how to prepare 38, 39
    types of 38
Designers Association (UCDA); University and College 281
Detroit
    advertising internships in 78
    advertising philosophy in 76
    educational requirements for advertising career in 77
    job preparation for advertising career in 77, 78
    retail advertising in 76
Detrow & Underwood 187
Dictionary of Advertising and Direct Mail Terms 240
Dictionary of Marketing and Advertising 240
Direct Mail Terms; Dictionary of Advertising and 240
Direct Marketing Association (DMA) 220
The Direct Marketing Group 207
Directory of Minority Public Relations Professionals 240
Discovery Music 188

Dodson, Craddock & Born 188
W.B. Doner & Company Advertising 188
Doremus and Co. 207
Dudreck, Depaul, Ficco and Morgan 188
Dugan Farley Communications 189
Dunhill Personnel Systems, Inc. 223
Earle Palmer Brown 189
Edelmann Scott Inc. 189
Editorial design portfolio 38
    what to include 38
Education 27
Helen Edwards and Staff Agency 223
Employer expectations 90
Employment agencies 17
Employment criteria 105, 107
Employment Listing Service Bulletin; National 216
Employment networking 17
English; Career Choices for the 90's for Students of 226
ENR Directory of Design Firms 240
ENR Top 500 Design Firms Issue 241
ENR Top International Design Firms Issue 241
Equal Opportunity Magazine 215
Esquire Personnel Services, Inc. 223
Evans Communications 189
Evans-San Francisco 189
Exploring Careers in Advertising 228
Export advertising 3
Fastbreak Syndicate, Inc. (FSI) 220
FCB/Ronalds-Reynolds 189
Federal Career Opportunities 228
Federal Jobs Digest 228
First job
    responsibilities of 27
Focus groups
    function of 9
Foote, Cone & Belding 190
Format 215
Fox-Morris 223
Francis, Williams & Johnson Ltd. 190
Franklin Advertising Associates Inc. 191
Freelance copywriting 19
    advertising your services 22
    importance of networking 22
    importance of professional organizations 22
    job requirements 20
    portfolio 19
    role of technology in 20

salaries 19, 22, 23
tip clubs 22
where to find clients 21
Freelance Jobs for Writers 228
Freelance Writing Start-Up Manual 228
Fuller Williams Placement 223
Gardiner Advertising Agency 191
Garfield-Lynn and Co. 191
Get a Better Job! 228
Getting a Job in the Computer Age 229
Getting Hired: How to Sell Yourself 228
Getting Into Advertising 229
Getting to the Right Job 229
Globalization 2, 3
Go Hire Yourself an Employer 229
Goldman & Associates 191
Goodwin, Dannebaum, Littman & Wingfield, Inc. 191
Graphics design
    internships in 32, 33
Graphics designer
    educational requirements 32
    personal qualifications 32
Grey Advertising Inc. [New York, NY] 191
Greykirk, Vansant 192
Griffin Bacall 207
Guerilla Tactics in the Job Market 229
Hal Riney and Partners 207
Harrison Marketing Counsel Ltd. 192
Have You Considered...Advertising? Focus: Account Management 229
Hawaii Advertising Agency Directory 241
HDM 207
Health Services Marketing (AHSM); Academy for 218
Henderson Advertising 192
Hill, Holliday, Connors, Cosmopoulos 207
Hispanic Times Magazine 215
How 215
How to Apply for a Job 229
How to Be a Freelance Writer: A Guide to Building a Full-Time Career 229
How to Create Your Ideal Job or Next Career 230
How to Find and Get the Job You Want 230
How to Get a Better Job in This Crazy World 230
How to Get a Better Job Quicker 230
How to Get and Get Ahead on Your First Job 230
How to Get Interviews from Job Ads 230
How to Land a Better Job 230
How to Seek a New and Better Job 230
How to Use Job Ads to Land the Job You Really Want 231
How to Win the Job You Really Want 231
How You Can Make $25,000 a Year Writing (No Matter Where You Live) 231
Howard-Sloan Associates, Inc. 223
I Got the Job! 231
ID International Design 215
I.D.E.A. of Charleston, Inc. 223
Ideal company profile 105
Illustration portfolio 36
    appearance of 36
    what to include 36
Industrial sales 62, 63
Information gathering
    through publications 102
Informational interview 108
    definition of 110
    example of an 111
    letters to send when seeking an 149
    vs. a job interview 110
Ingalls, Quinn & Johnson 192
International advertising 1
    beginning of 2
    career opportunities in 4
    career preparation 4, 5
    growth of 2, 3
    in the 1950s 3
    in the 1960s 3
    in the 1970s 3
    in the 1980s 3
    in the 1990s 4
    reasons for growth of 4
International Advertising Association Membership Directory 241
International Employment Hotline 231
Interviewing 17, 26
    preparation for 32, 33, 77, 85, 97
Job and Career Building 231
Job applications 173, 174
The Job Finder: A Checklist of Openings for Administrative and Governmental Research Employment in the West 215
The Job Hunt 231
The Job HUNTER 231
The Job Hunter's Final Exam 231
The Job Hunter's Workbook 231
Job interviews 108
    answering questions at 168, 169, 170, 171

definition of 110
following up on 167
format of 167, 168
how to behave at 165, 166
how to dress for 165
how to prepare for 162
illegal questions at 173
importance of 161
importance of doing research before 163
questions commonly asked at 169, 170, 171
questions for you to ask at 172
selection vs. screening 164
vs. an informational interview 110
what to avoid at 167
what to take with you 165
Job Opportunities for Business and Liberal Arts Graduates 1991; Peterson's 235
Job Ready 216
Job Search: Career Planning Guidebook, Book II 232
The Job Search Companion: The Organizer for Job Seekers 232
The Job Search Handbook 232
Job Search Process 95
steps in the 96
when to start the 97
Job Search: The Total System 232
Job security 28
Job Seeking Guide 232
Jobs '92 232
Jobs Available 216
JOBS! What They Are, Where They Are, What They Pay 232
Jordan Associates 193
Journal of Advertising Research 239
Journal of Career Planning and Employment 216
Journalism; Career Choices for the 90's for Students of Communications and 226
Journeying Outward: A Guide to Career Development 233
Joyce Lain Kennedy's Career Book 233
JR Professional Search 223
Junior art director 13
Junior copywriter 17
Kallir, Philips, Ross 207
Kaprielian O'Leary Advertising 193
Kaufman, Goldman & Stral, Inc. 193
Keller-Crescent Co. 193
Kelley Advertising Inc. 194

Kelly Advertising Inc. 194
Kennedy's Career Strategist 233
Ketchum Public Relations [New York, NY] 194
Koehler Marketplex 194
Labor unions 108
Launey, Hachmann & Harris, Inc. 195
Laurence, Charles, Free, and Lawson 207
Laven, Fuller & Perkins Advertising/Marketing Inc. 195
Lawrence & Schiller 195
Left-brain thinker
fear of...in advertising 8
in advertising 7
Al Paul Lefton Co. 195
Mell D. Leonard and Associates Inc. 224
Letters
examples of 150
for an informational interview 149
for blanket prospecting 148
for networking 149
of thanks 149
questions to answer before preparing 145
rules to follow when sending 147
types of 145
when answering an ad 148
when inquiring about job openings 148
when to send 147
Levenson, Levenson & Hill 195
Levine, Huntley, Schmidt & Beaver Inc. [New York, NY] 196
Liberal Arts Jobs 216
Liberal Education and Careers Today 233
Lieberman Appalucci 196
Lintas: Campbell Ewald 196
Lintas: New York 196
Fahlgren & Swink 197
Long, Haymes & Carr Inc. 197
Lord, Geller, Federico, Einstein 207
Lowe Marschalk 197
Lunan Hoffman Advertising Ltd. 197
Maclaren Advertising 198
Macmillan Dictionary of Marketing and Advertising 241
Macmillan Directory of Leading Private Companies 241
Managing Your Career 233
Manual skills 26
Marc and Company, Inc. 198
Marketing and Advertising; Dictionary of 240

Marketing and Advertising; Macmillan Dictionary of 241
Marketing and Job Opportunities in the West; The Source Passport to Advertising/ Public Relations/ 236
Marketing & Media Decisions 239
Marketing Computers; Adweek's 213
Marketing services agencies
  account coordinator 68
  college preparation for 68
  employer expectations 68
  employment benefits 68
  salaries 68
Marketing (WA&M); Women in Advertising and 221
Marketing Week; Adweek's 238
Martin's Magic Formula for Getting the Right Job 233
Mass Media Internships; Student Guide to 236
MBC Systems Ltd. 224
McCaffrey McCall 198
McCann-Erickson Advertising of Canada Ltd. 198
McCann-Erickson U.S.A. [New York, NY] 198
McKim Advertising Ltd. 199
Media Brokers; National Association of 220
Media department 47
  buying 48
  misconceptions about 47
  planning 48
  qualifications needed to work in 48
  relationship with Account Management department 52
  relationship with Creative department 51, 52
  relationship with Research department 51
  research tools used by 50, 51
  responsibilities of 48, 50
  training programs 54
Media negotiator 49
  responsibilities of 49
Media planners 48
  responsibilities of 48, 49
Media specialist 47
  career paths 54
  college preparation for 52
  interviewing for a job as a 53
  job requirements 52, 53
  responsibilities of 53
Media synergy 48

Medical Advertising News 216
Merchandising Your Job Talents 233
Michigan Business - A Guide to Michigan Advertising Agencies Issue 242
Minority Employment Journal 216
Minority News; New England 217
Mullen Advertising 199
Multinational advertising 3
The National Ad Search 216
National Association of Media Brokers 220
National Employment Listing Service Bulletin 216
National Job Market 217
National Network for Artist Placement 221
Nationwide Advertising Service Inc. 199
Network Your Way to Job and Career Success 233
Networking 22, 86, 108
  definition of 108
  history of 109
  how to do it 109
  letters to send when 149
  reasons for 115
  rules to follow when 114
  who to include 109
Networking News 217
New England Advertising Week 217
New England Employment Week 217
New England Minority News 217
New Jersey Business - Ad Agency Directory Issue 242
The New Quick Job-Hunting Map 234
Non-Profit Organizations; Opportunities in 234
Occupational Outlook Handbook 234
Occupational Outlook Quarterly 217
O'Dwyer's Directory of Corporate Communications 242
Ogilvy & Mather 199
The One Day Plan for Jobhunters 234
Online Hotline News Service 234
The Only Job Hunting Guide You'll Ever Need 234
Opportunities in Advertising 234
Opportunities in Non-Profit Organizations 234
Opportunities in Writing Careers 234
Opportunity Report 217
Out of Work but Not Alone 235
Outdoor advertising
  categories of 56

growth of 56
history of 55, 56
job requirements 56
knowledge needed to sell 58
personal qualifications 57
salaries 58
sales 56
special skills needed for 56
vs. other media 56
Parker Group, Inc. 199
The Pathfinder Group 224
Paul, John & Lee, Inc. 200
Perri Debes Looney & Crane Inc. 200
Peterson's Job Opportunities for Business and Liberal Arts Graduates 1991 235
Photographic portfolio 36, 37
appearance of 37
what to include 37
Photography
freelance 37
getting started in 37
Pinne Garvin Herbers & Hock, Inc. 200
Popai News 217
Portfolio 15, 19, 26
importance of 15, 35
preparation of 32
types of 36
Poster panels
definition of 56
Price off promotion methods
cash rebate programs 66
couponing 66
modified sales price 66
sales price 66
Print 218
Printers Placement 224
Private Companies; Macmillan Directory of Leading 241
Pro bono advertising 13, 14
Pro-Files 224
Product manager 41, 42
college preparation for 42
The Professional Communicator 218
Professional Job Finder 235
Promotion 107
Promotion Marketing Association of America 221
Reggie Awards 67
Promotional products sales representative
salaries 64

Promotional products supplier sales representative
employer expectations 63
Promotional products customer service representative
career paths 63
Promotional products distributor
career paths 61
college preparation for 61
definition of 62
personal qualifications 61
sales representative 62
Promotional products distributor sales representative
career paths 62
commissions 62
job training 63
salaries 62
Promotional products industry 61
customer service representative 63
distributors 61
supplier 61
Promotional products supplier
career paths 61
college preparation for 61
definition of 63
personal qualifications 61
Promotional products supplier sales representative
career paths 62, 63
college preparation for 63
job training 63
personal qualifications 64
Psychology; Career Choices for the 90's for Students of 226
Public Relations; Career Opportunities in Advertising and 226
Public Relations/Marketing and Job Opportunities in the West; The Source Passport to Advertising/ 236
Public Relations Professionals; Directory of Minority 240
Publications
importance of 102
Publicite Leo Burnett Ltd. 200
Publishers' Ad Club (PAC) 221
Randolph Associates, Inc. 224
Record-keeping
example of 113
importance of 113
Recruitment Enhancement Services 200

Referrals 108
Regional advertising 84
Remer-Ribolow and Associates 224
Resume
    chronological format 118, 125
    examples of a 126
    for business and finance positions 117
    functional format 118, 125
    how to prepare a 118
    importance of 74, 117
    organizing your data before
        preparing a 118, 119
    preparing your first 123
    rules to follow when preparing a 117
    targeted format 118, 125
    using power words in a 124, 125
    what to include in a 119, 123
    what to not include in a 124
Resume Data Input Sheets 120, 121
    how to fill out 121
A Rewarding and Stimulating Life Awaits You...With a Career in Specialty Advertising 235
Right-brain thinker
    fear of...in advertising 8
    in advertising 7
The Right Place at the Right Time 235
Ian Roberts Inc. 201
Romann & Tannenholz Advertising 201
Ross Roy, Inc. 201
Ross Roy Ltd. 201
Saatchi & Saatchi Advertising Worldwide [New York, NY] 201
Saatchi & Saatchi Compton Hayhurst Ltd. 201
Saffer Advertising Inc. 202
Salary 107
Sales promotion
    agency positions v. client positions 73
    college preparation for 72
    definition of 71
    elements of 71
    employer expectations 73
    entry-level positions 72
    function of 65
    internships in 74
    job mobility 73
    job opportunities 66
    job requirements 73
    methods of 66
    personal qualifications 73, 74
    portion of marketing budget 65
    price-off promotions 66
    primary objectives 72
    salaries 73
    third party employment sources 73
    value added promotions 67
    working conditions 73
Sales Promotion Agencies; Council of 219
Sales promotion agency
    function of 72
    strategic function of 72
    typical services 72
Sanford Rose Associates 224
Scali, McCabe, Sloves 207
Second opinion
    importance of 99
Secretary 18
Secrets of the Hidden Job Market 235
Selected Executives Inc. 224
Self-evaluation form 98
    creating a 98
    example of a 99
Self-evaluation process 98
Self-Help Clearinghouse 221
Siano & Spitz Advertising 202
RitaSue Siegel Agency, Inc. 224
Signs of the Times 218
Skills in Action: A Job-Finding Workbook 235
Small graphics design agency
    advantages of
Smith, Dorian & Burman, Inc. 202
Smith/Greenland Advertising, Inc. 202
J. Richard Smith Ltd. 202
Snelling and Snelling 224
So You Want to Be in Advertising: A Guide to Success in a Fast-Paced Business 235
The Source Passport to Advertising/Public Relations/Marketing and Job Opportunities in the West 236
Specialty Advertising Business 218
Spiro & Associates 202
Standard and Poor's Register of Corporations, Directors and Executives 242
Standard Directory of Advertising Agencies 242
The Stanford Gilbert Agency 224
Student Guide to Mass Media Internships 236
The Student's Guide to Finding a Superior Job 236
The Successful Job Hunter's Handbook 236

ADVERTISING CAREER DIRECTORY

Suggestions for Career Exploration and Jobseeking 236
Super Job Search: The Complete Manual for Job-Seekers and Career-Changers 236
Tag line 16
Taking Charge of Your Career Direction: Career Planning Guidebook, Book I 237
Tatham-Laird and Kudner 207
Taylor Brown, Smith & Perrault 203
Taylor-Tarpay Direct Advertising Ltd. 203
TBWA Advertising 207
J. Walter Thompson 203
Tracy-Locke 207
Travis/Walz & Associates, Inc. 204
Tycer Fultz Bellack 204
U.S. Employment Opportunities: A Career News Service 237
U.S. Employment Opportunities - Advertising/Public Relations 237
University and College Designers Association (UCDA) 221
Valentine-Radford, Inc. 204
Value added promotion methods
   contests 67
   free with proof-of-purchase offers 67
   self liquidators 67
   sweepstakes 67
Vriak Robinson Hayhurst Communications Ltd. 205
W.B. Doner & Company Advertising 188
WA&M Membership Directory 218
Ward's Business Directory of U.S. Private and Public Companies 243
Warwick Advertising 207
Watson Ostby Direct 205
Wells, Rich, Greene 207
West Coast
   advertising career disadvantages 90
   advertising market sizes 89
   major advertising clients 90
   reasons for creative excellence in advertising 88
   salaries 89, 90
Wettstein, Bolchalk, Owens & Cooke Advertising & Public Relations 205
What Color Is Your Parachute? 237
Where Can I Find Help With... 237
Where Do I Go from Here with My Life? 237
Where the Jobs Are: A Comprehensive Directory of 1200 Journals Listing Career Opportunities 237
Where to Start Career Planning 238
Which Niche? 238
Roger White Advertising & Public Relations 205
Who's Hiring Who 238
WICI National Directory of Professional Members 243
Wolf, Richards, Taylor Advertising 206
Woman; Collegiate Career 214
Women in Advertising and Marketing (WA&M) 221
Women in Communications, Inc. (WICI) 222
Work in the New Economy: Careers and Job Seeking into the 21st Century 238
The Wright Group 224
Writer: A Guide to Building a Full-Time Career, How to Be a Freelance 229
Writers; Freelance Jobs for 228
Writers Organizations (CWO); Council of 220
Writing (No Matter Where You Live); How You Can Make $25,000 a Year 231
Writing Start-Up Manual; Freelance 228
Wunderman International Inc. 206
Young & Rubicam Inc. [New York, NY] 206